D1164125

JUSTIFICATION AND THE TRUTH-CONNECTION

The internalism–externalism debate is one of the oldest debates in epistemology. Internalists assert that the justification of our beliefs can only depend on facts internal to us, while externalists insist that justification can depend on additional, for example environmental, factors. In this book Clayton Littlejohn proposes and defends a new strategy for resolving this debate. Focusing on the connections between practical and theoretical reason, he explores the question of whether the priority of the good to the right (in ethics) might be used to defend an epistemological version of consequentialism, and proceeds to formulate a new "deontological externalist" view. His discussion is rich with insights and will be valuable for a wide range of readers in epistemology, ethics, and practical reason.

CLAYTON LITTLEJOHN is Lecturer in Philosophy at King's College London. He has published a number of articles in epistemology and ethical theory in journals including *Journal of Philosophy* and *American Philosophical Quarterly*.

JUSTIFICATION AND THE TRUTH-CONNECTION

CLAYTON LITTLEJOHN

King's College London

CAMBRIDGE
UNIVERSITY PRESS

CAMBRIDGE UNIVERSITY PRESS
Cambridge, New York, Melbourne, Madrid, Cape Town,
Singapore, São Paulo, Delhi, Mexico City

Cambridge University Press
The Edinburgh Building, Cambridge CB2 8RU, UK

Published in the United States of America by Cambridge University Press, New York

www.cambridge.org
Information on this title: www.cambridge.org/9781107016125

© Clayton Littlejohn 2012

This publication is in copyright. Subject to statutory exception
and to the provisions of relevant collective licensing agreements,
no reproduction of any part may take place without the written
permission of Cambridge University Press.

First published 2012

Printed in the United Kingdom at the University Press, Cambridge

A catalogue record for this publication is available from the British Library

Library of Congress Cataloguing in Publication data
Littlejohn, Clayton.
Justification and the truth-connection / Clayton Littlejohn.
p. cm.
Includes bibliographical references (p.) and index.
ISBN 978-1-107-01612-5 (hardback)
1. Justification (Theory of knowledge) 2. Knowledge, Theory of. 3. Truthfulness
and falsehood. 4. Epistemics. 5. Belief and doubt. I. Title.
BD212.L58 2012
121'.6—dc23
2012007359

ISBN 978-1-107-01612-5 Hardback

Cambridge University Press has no responsibility for the persistence or
accuracy of URLs for external or third-party internet websites referred to in
this publication, and does not guarantee that any content on such websites is,
or will remain, accurate or appropriate.

Contents

Acknowledgments

There are a great number of friends and colleagues that I would like to thank for helpful discussion and comments: Mike Almeida, Robert Audi, Eric Barnes, Bryan Belknap, Selim Berker, Tim Black, Brent Braga, John Brunero, Ray Buchanan, Matthew Burstein, Al Casullo, Richard Yetter Chappell, Nate Charlow, Matthew Chrisman, Philippe Chuard, Chris Cloos, E. J. Coffman, Stewart Cohen, Juan Comesaña, Michael Conboy, Earl Conee, Andrew Cullison, Rodney Cupp, Ken Daley, Jonathan Dancy, Mark Decker, Keith DeRose, Kimberly Dill, Dylan Dodd, Sinan Dogramaci, Dale Dorsey, Trent Dougherty, Janice Dowell, Dough Ehring, Meylan Engel Jr., David Enoch, Jeremy Fantl, Richard Feldman, Steve Finlay, Branden Fitelson, Dorit Ganson, Mikkel Gerken, John Gibbons, Emily Given, Sandy Goldberg, Soraya Gollop, Peter Graham, Stephen Grimm, Danielle Hampton, John Harris, Ali Hasan, John Hawthorne, Allan Hazlett, David Henderson, Jill Hernandez, Pamela Hieronymi, Steve Hiltz, Leo Iacono, Jonathan Ichikawa, Harry Ide, Chris Kelp, Justin Klocksiem, Danny Z. Korman, Tim Kraft, Jonathan Kvanvig, Larry Lacy, Brian Leiter, Lauren Leydon-Hardy, S. Matthew Liao, Dustin Locke, Errol Lord, Jack Lyons, Kevin McCain, Christopher McCammon, Aidan McGlynn, Matt McGrath, Anna-Sara Malmgren, Jon Matheson, Neil Mehta, Joe Mendola, Anne Meylan, Giovanni Mion, Andrew Moon, Matthew Mullins, Mark Murphy, Peter Murphy, Eric Nelson, Ram Neta, Nathan Nobis, Alastair Norcross, Nicolette Ocheltree, Steve Odmark, David Pitt, Albert Popovic, Doug Portmore, Lewis Powell, Duncan Pritchard, Andrew Reiser, Luke Robinson, Guy Rohrbaugh, Sruthi Rothenfluch, Dylan Sabo, Sarah Sawyer, Mark Schroeder, David Sosa, Jason Stanley, Daniel Star, Asbjorn Steglich-Petersen, Matthias Steup, Jussi Suikkanen, Jonathan Sutton, Steve Sverdlik, Steven Swartzer, Bradley Thomas, Brad Thomson, Chris Tucker, John Turri, Candice Upton, Charles Wallis, Brian Weatherson,

Ralph Wedgwood, Alistair Welchman, Matt Weiner, Dennis Whitcomb, Daniel Whiting, Eric Wiland, Sarah Wright, and Becky Zavada. Two anonymous referees offered generous amounts of wonderful feedback. Thanks to Larry Lacy and Pat Shade for introducing me to philosophy and encouraging me to pursue graduate work. I am especially grateful to Howard Hewitt, Robert Howell, and Mark van Roojen for philosophical discussion and for their friendship. I would like to thank my editor Hilary Gaskin for her encouragement and guidance. I have (I believe) benefitted tremendously from the work of Jonathan Dancy, John Gardner, Judith Thomson, and Timothy Williamson, and it seems appropriate to express my appreciation here.

I would like to thank audiences at Boston University, King's College London, Southern Methodist University, the University of Edinburgh, and the University of Texas at San Antonio, as well as those who attended my talks at the 2010 *Episteme* Conference at the University of Edinburgh, the 2010 Royal Ethics Conference at the University of Texas at Austin, the 2010 Pacific Division Meetings of the American Philosophical Association, the 2010 Central Division Meetings of the American Philosophical Association, the 2009 Eastern Division Meetings of the American Philosophical Association, the 2009 Rocky Mountain Ethics Congress at the University of Colorado, the 2008 Eastern Division Meetings of the American Philosophical Association, the 2007 Northwest Philosophy Conference, and the 2006 Conference for the Central States Philosophical Association for helpful feedback.

Sigurdur Gudmundsson has generously agreed to let me use his *Study for Horizon* for the cover. I cannot think of a more fitting image for a book on epistemic normativity.

I would like to take this opportunity to thank my family (Brianna, Jaimie, Taylor, Roger, Lorraine, and now Sherri, John, Melissa, and Scott) for their love and unflagging support. To Amy, I dedicate this work to you. You are a wonderful mother to our beloved dog Agnes and the best friend I could ever hope to have. Every day I am reminded how incredibly fortunate I am to spend my time with you.

CHAPTER I

Introduction

I.I INTRODUCTION

Justified beliefs are justified because they have been sprayed with some sort of justificatory fluid.[1] Epistemologists want to know what this fluid is made of. Is it made entirely from conditions internal to you and your perspective on the world or might it include some external conditions (e.g., truth, knowledge, causal relations between you and your surroundings, etc.)? The internalists insist that justification depends exclusively upon conditions internal to you. Externalists deny this. When you survey the vast literature dedicated to the debate between the internalists and externalists, you might start to sympathize with the pessimists who think this dispute will never be resolved. Both sides offer plausible arguments, but neither side makes a compelling case. I think recent work on epistemic value, the ontology of reasons, and epistemic norms gives us good reason to think we can bring this dispute to a close.

I defend an unorthodox externalist view. To justifiably believe something, it is not enough to fit your belief to your evidence, put your trust in reliable methods, or keep your virtue intact. You can only justifiably believe something when your reasons show you are right. In justifying an action, you have to show that the agent acted rightly. If she committed any wrongs, she did so with sufficient reason. In justifying a belief, you have to show that the subject did not violate any epistemic norms without sufficient reason. If the norms governing belief enjoin you to believe only what is true, only true beliefs can be justified. If justification required anything less than this, justification ascriptions could not identify those beliefs that are fit for deliberation and so it would be obscure what exactly justification ascriptions are for.

---

[1] Field 1998, p. 7.

This clashes with the orthodox view, which has long been that justification differs from knowledge in two significant respects. The first is that you can justifiably believe falsehoods if you have solid evidence for your beliefs, but you can never know what is not true.[2] Knowledge is factive, but justification is not. The second is that the accidental connections between belief and truth that are the grist for Gettier's mill undermine knowledge without undermining justification. Naturally, if justified beliefs do not have to be true, they do not have to be non-accidentally true.

Suppose the orthodox view is right and justification requires neither truth nor a non-accidental connection to truth. If you could factor justification from these other conditions, what would the point of justification be? One possibility might be that justified belief is something you can aim at when you know that knowledge on some matter is unattainable. If so, this might tell us how we ought to engage in doxastic deliberation. Rather than aim for knowledge, we can aim lower. This appears to be Wright's view:

[K]nowledge is not really the proper central concern of epistemologico-sceptical enquiry. There is not necessarily any lasting discomfort in the claim that, contrary to our preconceptions, we have no genuine knowledge in some broad area of our thought – say in the area of theoretical science. We can live with the concession that we do not, strictly, know some of the things we believed ourselves to know, provided we can retain the thought that we are fully justified in accepting them. That concession is what we might call the Russellian Retreat. For Russell … proposed that such is exactly the message which philosophical epistemology generally has for us: we must content ourselves with probability, defeasibility and inconclusive justifications where standardly we had wanted to claim more. What, however, is not tolerable is the thesis that, among propositions about, for instance, the material world, other minds, or the past, we never actually attain to genuinely justified opinion; that no real distinction corresponds to that which we are accustomed to draw between grounded and ungrounded beliefs, earned information and mere prejudice or dogma.[3]

I think this is a mistake. If you could beat out a Russellian Retreat, you could justifiably believe what you knew you were in no position to know. I think this is impossible.[4] Consider: Custer died at Little Big Horn, but I do not know that he did. Even if I could believe such a thing (which I

[2] Alston declares that "by common consent, justification is distinct from truth … false beliefs can be justified" (1993, p. 535).
[3] Wright 1991, p. 88.
[4] For a dissenting view, see McGlynn in press.

doubt), I doubt that I could *rationally* believe such a thing. Since the difference between knowledge and justified belief is counterprivate, you can never see yourself as being in a position to justifiably believe what you know you do not know.[5] It is impossible to retreat without abandoning belief, so the point of justification cannot be to steer us towards a more easily attainable goal than knowledge.

The orthodox view is not committed to the idea that it is possible to tell in any particular case that you could justifiably believe what you cannot know, so it is not committed to the possibility of a Russellian Retreat. It simply says that it is possible to have justification without knowledge. There is a difference between believing and believing correctly even if this difference is counterprivate. If the difference between knowledge and justification is counterprivate it can play no role in doxastic deliberation. We know what the point of justification is not, but not what it is.

Let's try a different tack. Even if you cannot tell with respect to anything you currently believe that you do not know you are right, you can look back on beliefs you no longer hold and ask whether they were justified. If you discovered that the reason you mistakenly thought that there was an owl outside your window was that you were hallucinating, you might think to yourself:

[G]iven the vivid hallucination, I am in no way at fault for believing what I do, nor do I deserve criticism. Far from it. I am like a surgeon who skillfully does all that can be expected but loses the patient. There I should feel regret, but not guilt; I should explain, but need not apologize; and when we know what my evidence was, we approve of what I did; *we consider it reasonable.*[6]

You can say that when you discover that you did not know what you thought you knew that you do not deserve criticism, that you cannot be faulted, and perhaps that you can be praised for the way you formed your beliefs. Can this really be all there is to justification, that you can take some consolation in having had it when you discover you were wrong? Certainly not. That is what excuses do. They show you in a positive light without giving you a justification.[7] You look for justifications to determine what to believe and believe with justification when you properly respond

---

[5] See Adler 2002a; Huemer 2007b; Sorensen 1988; and Williamson 2000a.
[6] Audi 2001, p. 23.
[7] Following Austin 1956, many writers would say that excuses exculpate without showing the agent or the agent's conduct in a positive light. For reasons discussed below, we should think that some excuses exculpate only by showing that the agent did what could be reasonably expected of them.

to the reasons that apply to you. You do not reach for a justification only after you discover that mistakes were made.

The point of a justification is not to distinguish knowledge from ignorance, it is not to lift you up when you are feeling blue, and it is not a consolation prize awarded to the virtuous for their mistakes. Justifications show that you were in the right. You have a justification when you meet your obligations, but not if you do not. In the passage quoted above, Audi's suggestion might have been that the proper way to show that you met your responsibilities is by showing that you believed what any reasonable and responsible person would if they were in your situation. If so, we disagree about the marks of permissibility and justification, but we still might agree that the point of a justification is to distinguish what would be right or permissible from what would not be.

Suppose this is right and that justification is a deontological notion, not in the sense that your justified beliefs are blamelessly held or in the sense that your justified beliefs are beliefs you should be praised for holding, but in the sense that your justified beliefs are the beliefs you can have while meeting your epistemic obligations.[8] I fear that the orthodox view cannot do justice to this point about the point of justification, because the orthodox view insists that the truth-condition and the anti-luck conditions required for knowledge have nothing to do with justification. This implies that your epistemic obligation has nothing to do with seeing to it that your beliefs satisfy these conditions. This is a mistake. As such, the orthodox view either undermines the idea that the point of a justification is to show what it takes to meet your obligations and respond rightly to the reasons that apply to you, or reflects a mistaken view as to what epistemic duty requires. Obviously, this is something that I have to defend, but I shall argue that you can only meet your epistemic obligations when you believe the truth. Knowledge and justification are distinct statuses, but both require cognitive success.

---

[8] Zimmerman distinguishes hypological judgments from deontological judgments. The former have to do with laudability and culpability whereas the latter have to do with right, wrong, and obligation. I very much doubt that the hypological can be reduced to the deontological or the deontological to the hypological. As such, those who say that justification is a deontological notion should not say that justified beliefs are beliefs we are either not culpable for holding or which we can be lauded for holding until they can show that these reductions are possible. See Zimmerman 2002 for discussion.

1.2 KNOWLEDGE AND JUSTIFICATION

This discussion focuses primarily on justification and whether it is an externalist notion, not on knowledge. The term 'Externalism' first found its way into the epistemological literature in a discussion of an externalist account of knowledge, an account on which knowledge can involve natural relations between you and your surroundings (e.g., causal relations between your perceptual beliefs and the states of affairs that determine whether your beliefs are true).[9] Assuming that it is possible to justifiably believe something without knowing that it is true, Externalism about knowledge is compatible with Internalism about justification.[10] Externalists about knowledge who think justification is an internalist notion can either say that justification is a component of knowledge that depends wholly upon what is internal to us or deny that knowledge requires justification. Since my views concerning knowledge and justification are somewhat unorthodox, I should take a moment to explain how I take these notions to be related.

Consider two questions:

Q1:   Is it possible to have knowledge without justification?
Q2:   Is it possible to have justification without knowledge?

To answer these questions properly, we need to distinguish between three kinds of justification ascription:

Personal justification: S is justified in believing *p*.
Doxastic justification: S's belief that *p* is justified/S justifiably believes *p*.
Propositional justification: S has a justification for believing *p*/There is a justification for S to believe *p*.

Ascriptions of personal justification tell us something about a believer – whether *she* is justified in believing. An ascription of doxastic justification tells us something about a belief – whether *the belief* is justifiably held. An ascription of propositional justification tells us something about a proposition – whether *the proposition* is such that there is sufficient justification for someone to believe it. There is not to my knowledge a standard view about how these ascriptions are related, but there is a common practice of treating personal and doxastic justification as interchangeable. It is a

---

[9] Kornblith 2001 notes that Armstrong 1973 was the first to describe his views as 'externalist'.
[10] See Audi 1993.

mistake to treat these notions as interchangeable even if, as seems to be the case, the mistake is usually quite harmless.

I think Lowy was the first to recognize the importance of the distinction between personal and doxastic justification. Some of Gettier's critics thought that his cases were not counterexamples to the traditional analysis of knowledge because they thought beliefs inferred from false beliefs were not justified.[11] These concerns were irrelevant, she said, because the notion Gettier was interested in was that of a person being justified in believing a proposition, not the notion of a belief that is justified:

> To get at Gettier's notion of justification, we might then ask, when is a person justified in believing something in such a way that Gettier's points about justification apply? A person is justified in believing a proposition when no more can reasonably be expected of him with respect to finding out whether that proposition is true. Clearly, Gettier's points about justification hold here: there can be cases where no more can reasonably be expected of a person as a truth-seeker with respect to some proposition, and yet the proposition be false.[12]

If this is what personal justification comes to, there must be more to doxastic justification than just personal justification. It is possible for a truth-seeker to do all that could be reasonably expected of him and still fail to meet his epistemic obligations. This is a point on which internalists and externalists should agree. As Conee and Feldman observe, you might do all that can be reasonably expected of you and still form beliefs that do not fit your evidence. So long as you are clear that evaluating the subject's beliefs is not simply a matter of evaluating the person that holds them, there is no reason to think that doxastic justification reduces to evaluations of the believer.[13] This distinction between personal and doxastic justification matters for our purposes for two reasons. First, while I think some of Gettier's critics were right that his cases were not cases of doxastic justification without knowledge, Gettier and Lowy were right that his cases were cases of personal justification without knowledge. As such, Gettier was right that a person could be justified in believing some true proposition without knowing that the proposition is true.[14] Second, externalists can accommodate internalist intuitions by conceding that

---

[11] See Dreher 1974 and Thalberg 1969, for example.
[12] Lowy 1978, p. 106.
[13] Conee and Feldman 2004, p. 85.
[14] Fogelin 1994 seems to think that if a person is justified in believing *p* and justifiably believes *p*, this person will know *p*. I do not think that there is any JTB account of knowledge that can accommodate our intuitions.

personal justification is an internalist notion while insisting that doxastic justification is not.[15]

The personal/doxastic justification distinction is analogous to the act/agent distinction in ethics. You can be fully excused for wrongdoing when you are non-culpably ignorant of some fact or acting on a mistaken belief, so knowing that you are morally upstanding and your actions reflect well on you does not show that your actions conformed to morality's demands. Moreover, your actions can conform to morality's demand even if you act from selfish motives and your actions are not a credit to you or a sign of good character.[16] In general, I think it is helpful to think of justifications as defenses. To understand personal, doxastic, and propositional justification, we need to understand what is involved in defending persons, particular beliefs, and prospective beliefs. To defend a person who believes *p* is to show that the way she forms her beliefs shows her in a positive light. When we see how she forms her beliefs, we can see that she is epistemically responsible. To defend her beliefs, however, is to show that her beliefs conform to the norms governing belief.

How are these different kinds of justification ascription related? It seems plausible that you can justifiably believe *p* only if you have a justification for believing *p* and that justification plays some role in explaining why you believe what you do. It certainly seems that Cooper contradicts himself if he says that Harry's belief in Leo's guilt is perfectly justified while insisting that there is no justification whatever for Harry to believe that Leo is guilty. The standard view is that doxastic justification involves propositional justification and proper basing. To justifiably believe *p*, you have to have a justification to believe *p* and it has to be the reason for which you believe what you do. While doxastic justification suffices for personal justification, the converse is not true. There can be sufficient justification for you to believe things you do not believe, but you cannot justifiably believe what you do not believe.

Some maintain that personal and doxastic justification ascriptions are logically equivalent.[17] I think this is a mistake. While Harry's beliefs cannot be justified if Harry is not justified in holding them, it is possible for

---

[15] Bach 1985; Engel 1992a; and Fogelin 1994 try to accommodate intuitions about cases of systematic deception by saying that you can be personally justified in believing something even if your belief is not justified.

[16] For a helpful discussion of the relation between act and agent evaluations, see Bennett 1995; M. Moore 1997; Stocker 1973; Thomson 1991; and Zimmerman 1996.

[17] Kvanvig and Menzel 1990. Alston 1989 also denies that there is any important distinction between a person being justified in a belief and a belief being justified for a person.

Harry to be justified in believing something even if Harry's beliefs are not justified. A person is justified in her beliefs if she can be held responsible for her beliefs and cannot be blamed for any breach of epistemic duty. That is to say, a person is justified in her beliefs if she pursues her epistemic ends responsibly and can rationally take it that she has met her epistemic obligations. A belief, however, is justified iff it is permissibly held. You can be excused if you do not meet your epistemic obligations, but you cannot justifiably fail to meet your obligations. Whereas personal justification requires nothing more than an excuse, doxastic justification requires permissibility.

If Q1 has to do with personal justification, the question is whether you can be blamed for believing what you know. If you know that your beliefs are true, you cannot rightly be blamed for a breach of epistemic duty. It would be unreasonable for me to say that you were irresponsible or unreasonable in believing *p* having conceded that you knew you were right. If Q1 is a question about doxastic justification, the question is whether your obligation can be to refrain from believing what you know is true. If Cooper concedes that Harry knows *p*, he cannot then say that Harry was in no position to rightly judge whether *p* was true. Knowledge suffices for doxastic justification if your justified beliefs are permissibly held beliefs. Since doxastic justification requires propositional justification, knowledge suffices for propositional justification.

It is controversial whether doxastic justification should be thought of as a deontological notion because it is controversial whether there are any epistemological obligations.[18] We can show that knowledge requires doxastic justification without arguing from the assumption that justified beliefs are permissibly held beliefs.[19] Suppose it is possible to know something without justifiably believing it and that it is possible to justifiably believe something without knowing it. Suppose Coop justifiably believes that *p* without knowing this is so and that he knows *p* entails *q* without justifiably believing that this is so. If Coop competently deduces *q*, what is the status of Coop's belief? Coop does not have knowledge of both premises, so it seems Coop does not know *q*. Since Coop does justifiably believe both premises, Coop does not justifiably believe *q*. Surely there is *something* epistemically good going for a belief that is competently deduced from a set of premises either known or justifiably believed. If not justification, what would it be? Since there seems to be no good answer to this

---

[18] Alston 1989 rejects the deontological theory of justification.
[19] Williamson 2007, p. 112.

question, perhaps we should say that Coop justifiably believed each of the premises in his deduction after all.

Turning now to Q2, it is obvious that propositional justification does not suffice for knowledge. You can have sufficient propositional justification for propositions you have never entertained, but you cannot know *p* without having ever had *p* in mind. It is also clear that personal justification does not require knowledge. Gettier's cases show that you can be personally justified in believing true propositions without knowing that they are true:

Coins: Suppose that Smith and Jones have applied for a certain job. And suppose that Smith has strong evidence for the following conjunctive proposition:

> d. Jones is the man who will get the job, and Jones has ten coins in his pocket.

Smith's evidence for (d) might be that the president of the company assured him that Jones would in the end be selected, and that he, Smith, had counted the coins in Jones's pocket ten minutes ago. Proposition (d) entails:

> e. The man who will get the job has ten coins in his pocket.

Let us suppose that Smith sees the entailment from (d) to (e), and accepts (e) on the grounds of (d), for which he has strong evidence. In this case, Smith is clearly justified in believing that (e) is true.

But imagine, further, that unknown to Smith, he himself, not Jones, will get the job. And, also, unknown to Smith, he himself has ten coins in his pocket. Proposition (e) is then true, though proposition (d), from which Smith inferred (e), is false ... [I]t is equally clear that Smith does not know that (e) is true; for (e) is true in virtue of the number of coins in Smith's pocket, while Smith does not know how many coins are in Smith's pocket, and bases his belief in (e) on a count of the coins in Jones's pocket, whom he falsely believes to be the man who will get the job.[20]

For reasons discussed below, I think Smith is justified in believing (e), but he does not justifiably believe (e).

Even if Coins is not a case of doxastic justification without knowledge, we have good reason to think that there is more to knowledge than doxastic justification:

Fake Barns: Henry is driving in the countryside with his son. For the boy's edification Henry identifies various objects on the landscape as they come into view. "That's a cow," says Henry, "That's a tractor," "That's a silo," "That's a barn," etc. Henry has no doubt about the identity of these objects; in particular, he has no

---

[20] Gettier 1963, p. 122.

doubt that the last-mentioned object is a barn, which indeed it is. Each of the identified objects has features characteristic of its type. Moreover, each object is fully in view, Henry has excellent eyesight, and he has enough time to look at them reasonably carefully, since there is little traffic to distract him … Suppose we are told that, unknown to Henry, the district he has just entered is full of papier-mâché facsimiles of barns. These facsimiles look from the road exactly like barns, but are really just facades, without back walls or interiors … having just entered the district, Henry has not encountered any facsimiles; the object he sees is a genuine barn. But if the object on that site were a facsimile, Henry would mistake it for a barn. Given this new information, we would be strongly inclined to withdraw the claim that Henry knows the object is a barn.[21]

Newspaper: A political leader is assassinated. His associates, fearing a coup, decide to pretend that the bullet hit someone else. On nationwide television they announce that an assassination attempt has failed to kill the leader but has killed a secret service man by mistake. However, before the announcement is made, an enterprising reporter on the scene telephones the real story to his newspaper, which has included the story in its final edition. Jill buys a copy of that paper and reads the story of the assassination. What she reads is true and so are her assumptions about how the story came to be in the paper. The reporter, whose byline appears, saw the assassination and dictated his report, which is now printed just as he dictated it. Jill has justified true belief and, it would seem, all her intermediate conclusions are true. But she does not know that the political leader has been assassinated. For everyone else has heard about the televised announcement. They may also have seen the story in the paper and, perhaps, do not know what to believe; and it is highly implausible that Jill should know simply because she lacks evidence everyone else has. Jill does not know. Her knowledge is undermined by evidence she does not possess.[22]

I think Goldman and Harman are right that you can justifiably believe what you do not know if, say, you form your beliefs in an environment rife with evidence that easily could have led you astray.[23] While I shall argue that justification requires a kind of non-accidental connection to truth, I do not intend to defend any kind of JTB (the 'justified in holding a true belief') account of knowledge.[24] There is no sense in which justification requires knowledge and no sense in which knowledge does not require justification.

In what follows, my primary focus will be on the notion of doxastic justification. This is not because the notion of personal justification is uninteresting, but because doxastic justification is the notion most

[21] Goldman 1976, p. 772. He credits the case to Carl Ginet.
[22] Harman 1973, p. 144.
[23] For a dissenting view, see Sosa 2007.
[24] An increasing number of epistemologists now think that justification is knowledge. I believe Sutton 2007 was the first to defend this view. Also see Haddock 2010 and Rödl 2007.

intimately connected with issues having to do with epistemic duty and the right to believe. I am happy to concede that personal justification is an internalist notion in that whether you pursue your epistemic ends responsibly turns entirely upon conditions common to you and those internally just like you (e.g., how things seem to you and how you reason given the considerations you have in mind). The interesting question, to my mind, is whether the right to believe what you do could depend upon anything external to you. If not, perhaps whether you believe with justification does not depend upon whether you are fortunate or lucky to have things turn out well for you.

1.3 THE STANDARD OPTIONS

Internalists about doxastic justification say that the only factors that determine whether your beliefs are justified are internal to you in some epistemically significant sense. (We can refer to this view as 'Generic Internalism'.) Internalists draw the line between the internal and the external in different ways, but however the line is drawn, internalists typically believe that it is possible for someone internally just like you (i.e., your epistemic counterpart) to get things reliably wrong even if your beliefs typically constitute knowledge. Knowledge is an externalist notion because it requires a proper fit between your beliefs and the facts. The facts and the fit do not supervene upon conditions internal to you.[25] If justification is an internalist notion, the justification of belief does not depend upon any of the external factors that distinguish you from your systematically deceived epistemic counterpart. When you think about the various external factors that prevent their beliefs from constituting knowledge (e.g., interference from Cartesian demons, fake barns, etc.), you might think that it would be better for you to worry about the internal factors that determine whether your beliefs are reasonably held. If justification depends upon external factors that distinguish you from your counterparts, it would seem to be partially a matter of good fortune that your beliefs turned out to be justified. Intuitively, you might think, it should be up to you whether you believe with justification.

---

[25] If McDowell's 1995 view is classified as internalist, this does not hold true for all internalist views. If you think there are factive mental states, you might think that some facts having to do with the external world supervene upon facts about your mental life (e.g., if we suppose that seeing is a mental state and you see that the cat is in the corner, the fact that the cat is in the corner supervenes upon facts about your mental states). Since most internalists believe that the conditions that matter to justification supervene upon your non-factive mental states, I shall ignore this complication until we discuss McDowell's views in Chapter 4.

Intuitively, you might also think, you cannot benefit because of factors beyond your ken. As such, you might think, there should not be justificatory differences between you and your counterparts since any such difference would be beyond your ken.

For their part, externalists (i.e., those that reject Generic Internalism) might say that that which supervenes wholly upon the internal will have little by way of epistemic value. Belief aims at the truth. Justification as the internalists conceive of it might not be a reliable guide to truth and it would play little role in eliminating the kinds of accidental connections between you and the facts that undermine knowledge. If justification were something you could have even if you are systematically deceived, would you really count yourself as fortunate for having had it if you discovered later that you were systematically deceived? If the reason you were led astray was that you responded rationally to the reasons given to you, you might think these reasons turned out to be worthless. The same would hold true for any allegedly positive status you have by virtue of responding to what you were given in the way that you did. To play the regulative role justification must play, justification has to connect you to the truth in such a way that it would be surprising to discover that you were wrong, not a happy coincidence if it turned out you were right.

Before turning to consider the arguments for Internalism and Externalism, I should say something less impressionistic about what these views are. Let's look at two standard ways of understanding the epistemically internal. First, mentalists say that the internal consists of features of your mental life, typically your non-factive mental states (e.g., beliefs, apparent memories, and experiences).[26] On this view, there cannot be any justificatory differences between two subjects' beliefs without some further mental difference between these subjects. If two subjects are mentally the same down to the last qualia, the same beliefs will be justified for them by the same things and to the same degree even if these subjects are in radically different environments.

Accessibilists characterize the internal in terms of what is accessible to you.[27] Let me flag two potential differences between the mentalist and

---

[26] Conee and Feldman 2004. They refer to doxastically justified beliefs as 'well-founded' beliefs. Huemer's 2007a Phenomenal Conservatism is in many respects similar to Mentalism in that he takes states in which it seems to you that *p* is true to be *pro tanto* reason to believe that *p* is true.

[27] Audi 1993; BonJour 1985; Chisholm 1989; Foley 1987; Fumerton 1995; Ginet 1975; Pollock 1974; Smithies in press; and Steup 1999. Because he is critical of various access internalist views, Fumerton's view is not happily brought under this label. His view is that in cases of non-inferential justification, you are acquainted with that which justifies your belief and that the objects of acquaintance are mental (1995, p. 79). Although they are the standard-bearers for

accessibilist account of the internal. First, some accessibilists might say that non-factive mental duplicates differ in terms of what they have access to. It might be, for example, that you have access to facts about the external world even if your non-factive mental duplicates do not (e.g., I might have a kind of access to facts about the position of my own limbs that my limbless epistemic counterparts do not). Second, some accessibilists might say that you do not have the right kind of access to some of your non-factive mental states for those states to be accessible to you (e.g., I might not have access to all of my beliefs, in which case my beliefs might provide inaccessible defeaters for me if these beliefs are inconsistent).[28] For various reasons (e.g., arguments from error, causal considerations, intuitions about cases of systematic deception), most access internalists prefer to say that we do not have access to the external world. If so, the main difference between the mentalists and accessibilists seems to be that the mentalists might say that some inaccessible features of your mental life might make a difference to the justification of your beliefs.

A number of diverse views have been lumped together under the general heading of Accessibilism. Accessibilists need to tell us (i) what we have access to, (ii) what it is to have access to something, and (iii) whether we have to access our reasons for belief or whether accessibility is enough. Speaking to this first issue, Chisholm thought that you have access to the justificatory status of your beliefs:

The internalist assumes that, merely by reflecting upon his own conscious state, he can formulate a set of epistemic principles that will enable him to find out, with respect to any possible belief he has, whether he is justified in having that belief. The epistemic principles that he formulates are principles that one may come upon and apply merely by sitting in one's armchair, so to speak, and without calling for any outside assistance. In a word, one need only consider one's own state of mind.[29]

Mentalism, Conee and Feldman say in various places that justifying reasons have to be available to you. See Conee and Feldman 2004, pp. 35 and 49. Some authors say that we can have reflective access to facts that do not supervene upon our non-factive mental states. See McDowell 1995, for example. If you work with a very liberal conception of access (e.g., what is accessible to you includes all and only what you know), your view might be hard to square with intuitions about arguments from error. That depends upon whether you think facts that do not supervene upon your non-factive mental states are idle. If you work with this very liberal conception of access and defend Access Internalism, you do avoid some of the problems that beset more restrictive accounts of access. Even this view is open to objections, as we will see in Chapter 4.

[28] Conee and Feldman 2004, p. 81. While they suggest that defeaters might be inaccessible, they insist that any evidence that justifies your beliefs is accessible upon reflection. See Conee and Feldman 2004, p. 50. For helpful discussion of the relation between Mentalism and Accessibilism, see Bergmann 2006, Ch. 3.

[29] Chisholm 1988, p. 286. See also Chisholm 1989, p. 7.

Most accessibilists prefer a more modest approach according to which you have access to the reasons that support your belief.[30] It is hard to see how you could have access to justificatory status unless you also had access to the reasons that determine justificatory standing. Since externalists will often argue that even this more modest claim is indefensible, I see no reason to pin on the internalists the less modest claim that Chisholm defends.

One caveat is in order. Alston and Swain defended externalist views on which you have access to the justifying reasons or grounds that justify your beliefs.[31] How should we distinguish their views from Accessibilism? The key difference is that accessibilists hold that the *adequacy* of your justifying reasons does not depend upon external factors that you do not have access to. The accessibilists should say that if you justifiably believe, say, that someone is at the door on the basis of seeming to hear a knock, the adequacy of your reason does not depend upon external factors inaccessible to you (e.g., whether there is a high objective probability that someone is there given that it seemed you heard a knock). In a world without doors and knocks, an evil demon might induce in someone conscious experiences that lead her to think that she hears a knock. An access internalist might say (depending upon what they take accessibility to be) that the subject's belief is justified in this world. Alston and Swain might say that the right external connections are not in place for the accessible reason to be an adequate justifier.[32]

Because access is a technical notion, the accessibilists have to tell us what the accessibles are. Ginet characterizes access in terms of "direct recognizability":

This requirement of direct recognizability means that every fact belonging to a set that minimally suffices for S's having justification for being confident that *p* must be such that if it obtains then the only possible way in which S could fail to know that it obtains would be through either (a) failure to consider sufficiently carefully the question whether or not it obtains or (b) failure to possess the concept of that sort of fact. A proposition that gives one justification for being confident of a proposition must be such that, given sufficient intelligence, one could acquire an ability to recognize that position whenever one is in it.[33]

---

[30] See Audi 1993, p. 332.
[31] Alston 1989, p. 233 and Swain 1981, p. 74.
[32] Which is not to say that if you have access to more than your non-factive mental duplicates do, your beliefs are better justified than theirs. Accessibilists could say that you have access to whatever you know, believe that non-factive mental duplicates know different things, but also think that these differences in what is known do not benefit the subject in the good case.
[33] Ginet 1975, p. 33.

This is a very stringent requirement. Suppose Coop sees that it is snowing. The fact that it is snowing is not directly recognizable to him, Ginet says, because he could have had some reason to think he is hallucinating and this is a problem that, "no amount of clear-headed reflection on his position or understanding of what it is to see snow falling could remedy."[34]

Audi suggests that reflective knowledge suffices for access:

> The "internal," in the relevant sense, is that to which one has introspective, and thus internal, access; it includes beliefs, visual and other sensory impressions, and thoughts. To have such access to something is to be aware of it or to be able through self-consciousness or at least by introspective reflection to become aware of it.[35]

The reason that Audi's requirements for access are less demanding than Ginet's is that much of what we know via introspection is defeasible. You could, for example, have evidence of the unreliability of introspection that defeats the justification you have for beliefs about your own mental states, in which case Ginet's account implies that what we introspect is not accessible to us even when our introspective knowledge is not defeated.[36] For Audi, if you know via introspection that you believe or seem to see something, you have all the access you need to your beliefs and experiences.[37] I see no reason for accessibilists to defend anything more demanding since externalists often object to even this modest access requirement on justification.

Should accessibilists say that the factors that determine whether your beliefs are justified are limited to those factors that you have accessed, or can something contribute to justification if it is merely accessible? There is a worry that an actual awareness requirement generates a regress problem. If the fact that p can only have some bearing on justification if you have awareness of that fact and the awareness of that fact can only make you better off epistemically if you have access to the fact that you are aware of this fact, it seems that you would need to have awareness

---

[34] Ginet 1975, p. 34.

[35] Audi 1993, p. 332.

[36] I shall assume that you can know p directly via introspection even if p is not directly recognizable in Ginet's sense. It seems to me that someone who has the required concepts and gives the matter sufficient attention can fail to know p because she has defeating evidence even if she could have known p via introspection if she did not have this evidence. For discussion of such cases, see Armstrong 1963.

[37] It would be better for accessibilists to understand the notion of access in terms of knowledge or some factive notion rather than justification for two reasons. First, there are circularity worries. Second, you cannot access what is not there. On most views, you can justifiably believe what is not so.

of your awareness of p for p to make a justificatory difference. A regress looms. In my view, accessibilists should say that potential access is all that is needed for something to contribute to justification.[38] Even if the subject has not accessed some factor by becoming introspectively aware of it or forming some second-order belief about it, the subject can be properly guided by internal factors. When you chop vegetables or juggle you are guided by internal, accessible representations that you typically do not access. If justifications are supposed to guide us in determining what to believe, there is a plausible rationale for thinking that potential access is all we need since this is all the access we need to be guided thoughtfully and skillfully by these representational states in the pursuit of our ends.[39]

Let's say that Generic Internalism is the view that justification supervenes upon (i) the subject's non-factive mental states or (ii) that which is available to introspection and reflection. Generic Externalism is the denial of Generic Internalism. Externalism implies that it is possible for beliefs held by epistemic counterparts (i.e., subjects that are internally the same either in terms of their non-factive mental states or what they can access) to differ justificationally.

Which external factors do externalists think matter to justification? According to process reliabilists, doxastic justification depends upon whether the cognitive processes that produce or sustain a belief are reliable. For Goldman, a process is reliable if it produces a sufficiently high ratio of true beliefs to false beliefs.[40] According to the reliable indicator theory, the justification of a belief depends upon whether the belief's basis is a reliable indicator of the truth of that belief.[41] These indicators are typically taken to be a reason on which your belief is based, an internally accessible psychological state such as an experience or belief.[42] Alston suggests that the reliability of an indicator is best understood in terms of

---

[38] For an early discussion of this worry, see Alston 1989, p. 233. Alston dismisses the idea that there is a difference between reasons and various other enabling conditions that determine whether a belief is justified. I think accessibilists can blunt his regress objection if they say that we only needed access to reasons, not the total set of conditions necessary for justified belief. Bergmann 2006 raises a similar objection and argues that a weak access requirement (i.e., that sometimes justifiers are accessible, but not necessarily accessed) is unmotivated. For a response, see Matheson and Rogers 2011. Ultimately, I agree with Bergmann that the access requirements are unmotivated, but for reasons that differ from his. See Chapter 4 for discussion.

[39] See Pollock 1987 and Pollock and Cruz 1999 for discussion of a guidance conception of justification.

[40] Goldman 1979.   [41] Alston 1989 and Swain 1981.

[42] For Swain, these indicators will be psychological states. Although he says these states are reasons, he distinguishes causal reasons from justifying reasons and takes the latter to be propositions. See Swain 1981, p. 75.

some objective notion of probability. For a belief to be justified, he would say that the objective probability that the belief is true given the indicator on which it is based has to be sufficiently high.[43]

Reliability is not always characterized probabilistically. Leplin says that a process is reliable if it would not produce false beliefs under normal conditions.[44] This view differs from standard reliabilist accounts of reliability in two ways. First, the fact that some process results in a high truth-ratio does not entail that the process would not produce false beliefs under normal conditions. Second, the fact that some process would not result in false beliefs under normal conditions does not entail that the process produces a high truth-ratio. Since most reliabilists do think of reliability in terms of probability, I shall follow their lead. I will note one advantage of Leplin's approach, which is that it accommodates the intuition that you cannot justifiably believe a lottery ticket to be a loser if you do not have insider's information or learn about the outcome of a drawing by reading about it in the paper. His account accommodates this intuition easily, but more traditional formulations of Reliabilism do not.

Some virtue theorists say that justification depends upon whether your beliefs were acquired by means of the exercise of an intellectual virtue. On Sosa's view, an intellectual virtue must produce a sufficiently high ratio of true beliefs under suitable circumstances.[45] Intellectual virtues are rooted in something internal to us if, as Sosa suggests, they are identified with our cognitive faculties.[46] Whether these faculties are exercised virtuously depends upon whether they reliably lead to truth. That depends

---

[43] Alston 1989, p. 269.

[44] Leplin 2009, p. 35. His account of reliability is inspired by Nozick's 1981 account of knowledge. Nozick held that to know *p*, your belief has to be sensitive (i.e., it must have been produced by a method M such that if *p* were false, you would not come to believe *p* via M). Leplin's view cannot be that justified beliefs are sensitive, because he holds that justified beliefs can be false. (False beliefs cannot be sensitive. Because subjunctive conditionals entail their corresponding material conditionals, the subjunctive conditional "if it were the case that -*p*, you would not believe *p*" is incompatible with "-*p* and you believe *p*". So, if you believe *p*, *p* must be true. See Williamson 2000a, p. 148.) Leplin's view is that reliability is understood in terms of sensitivity under normal conditions and allows that beliefs formed in abnormal conditions can be formed by reliable processes and justified as a consequence. So, his view is that in normal conditions, the processes that lead you to form the belief that a building is a barn by looking at it can justify your belief if the process would not have led you astray in such normal conditions. In such conditions, justified beliefs always turn out to be true. In abnormal conditions, however, this same process can lead you astray, but the process can justify your belief nevertheless.

[45] Sosa 1991.

[46] Greco argues (persuasively, I think) that we need to build in this restriction to deal with cases of strange and fleeting processes (e.g., Plantinga's 1993 serendipitous brain lesion, a lesion that causes you to believe that you have this lesion. The lesion reliably leads to truth, but your belief that you have this lesion is not justified). See Greco 2010, p. 175.

upon matters external to us. For the purposes of our discussion, virtue theorists who work with Sosa's conception of an intellectual virtue can be classified as reliabilists.[47]

There are further externalist views to consider, such as the view that takes doxastic justification to be knowledge, but I will hold off discussing this view until later chapters because the arguments for this view have played no role in shaping the Internalism–Externalism debate.[48] For the most part, externalists have defended views with some kind of reliability requirement, and so, in this chapter, we shall focus primarily on externalist views that say that your beliefs are justified only if the processes that produce them or the grounds on which they are based are reliable either in the circumstances under which they were produced or some specified set of circumstances. The internalists maintain that even if our justified beliefs turned out to be reliably connected to the truth, this is not why they are justified.

1.4 THE ARGUMENTS FOR EXTERNALISM AND INTERNALISM

In this section, I want to discuss some of the standard arguments for the standard externalist and internalist views. In reviewing these arguments, I think we can start to see why the debate has reached an impasse.

1.4.1 *The argument from epistemic poverty*

Our first argument for Externalism is Alston's argument from epistemic poverty. Let's start by considering an example:

S has lived all his life in an isolated primitive community where everyone unhesitatingly accepts the tradition of the tribe as authoritative. These have to do with alleged events distant in time and space, about which S and his fellows have no chance to gather independent evidence. S has never encountered anyone who questions the traditions, and these traditions play a key role in the communal life of the tribe. Under these conditions it seems clear to me that S is in no way to blame for forming beliefs on the basis of the traditions. He has not failed to do

---

[47] In more recent work, Sosa (2010, p. 7) says that aptness requires success that results from the manifestation of a competence seated in the agent. The older notion of aptness tolerated false belief, but the most recent account of aptness does not. In Chapter 7, I argue that this new notion of aptness (aptness* henceforth) plays an important role in an account of justification.

[48] See Haddock 2010 and Sutton 2007. This also seems to be the view of Adler 2002a. Bird 2007 and Williamson 2000a argue that you should not believe what you do not know, but they insist that there can be false, justified beliefs.

anything he could reasonably be expected to do. His beliefs about, for example, the origins of the tribe stem from what, so far as he can see, are the best grounds one could have for such beliefs. And yet, let us suppose, the traditions have not been formed in such a way as to be a reliable indication of their own truth. S is deontically justified, but he is not believing in a truth-conducive way.[49]

Alston believes that the ubiquitous S meets his obligations, but thinks his beliefs are not justified, because they are not based on truth-conducive grounds. If this is correct, the deontological view is mistaken since this view says that you justifiably believe *p* if you believe *p* while meeting your epistemic obligations. While there are internalists who are not deontologists and deontologists who are internalists, I think that if Alston's objection to Deontologism is sound it should apply with equal force to any internalist view.[50] I do not think internalists have the resources to explain why someone in S's position would not have sufficient justification if Alston is correct and S has met his obligations.

If Alston's argument can be extended in this way, we have our first argument for Externalism:

1. S meets his epistemic obligations.
2. If so, Deontologism implies S's beliefs are justified.
3. (Therefore) Deontologism implies that S's beliefs are justified.
4. Internalism should deliver the same verdict.
5. (Therefore) Internalism implies that S's beliefs are justified.
6. S's beliefs are not justified.
7. (Therefore) Internalism delivers the wrong verdict in cases of cultural isolation.

The crucial premises are (1) and (6). Alston thinks (6) is intuitively compelling. As for (1), Alston argues that S's beliefs must be justified because S cannot be blamed for believing what he does:

Deontological justification is sensitive to cultural differences because it depends on what can reasonably be expected of one, and that in turn depends on one's social inheritance and the influences to which one is exposed. But truth conductivity does not so depend. Hence they can diverge.[51]

I do not think that the argument from epistemic poverty is dialectically effective. Since Alston has not yet argued that there are no epistemic

---

[49] Alston 1989, p. 145.
[50] A number of writers have argued that Deontologism supports Internalism. See Cohen 1984; Ginet 1975; Huemer 2006; Plantinga 1993; Pollock and Cruz 1999; and Steup 1999. Bergmann 2006; Brueckner 1996; and Gibbons 2006 argue that Deontologism is compatible with Externalism.
[51] Alston 1989, p. 146.

obligations, he has to grant for the sake of this argument that there are and that S has met them.[52] He insists that S has met his obligations, accuses those who disagree of insensitivity, and insists that S's beliefs are not justified. The success of the argument depends upon whether it would be right to say (as Alston does) that S has no obligation to refrain from believing p, but does not justifiably believe p. In other words, Alston has to say that S permissibly believes p, but S's belief is not justified. The problem with this is that if you have any epistemic obligation at all, it is to refrain from believing without adequate justification. Deontologists should say that Alston's argument is unsound because (1) and (6) are incompatible. They should also say that Alston's case is underdescribed. If we imagine that S has lived up to the canons of good reasoning by following the available evidence, it is somewhat intuitive to say that (1) is true, but then (6) is not intuitively compelling. If, however, we imagine that S has not lived up to the canons of good reasoning, (6) seems somewhat intuitive, but (1) does not.

A further problem with his objection to Deontologism is the assumption that your obligations are limited to what can be reasonably expected of you given your circumstances. Apart from the cultural relativists, nobody should accept this.[53] Suppose our moral standards better track the truth than the standards of some alien culture. We cannot expect those who were raised in this culture to appreciate the superiority of our moral views and so we cannot reasonably expect them to believe what we believe and to act as we would act. If they woke up one morning and started acting like we did without changing their beliefs, they would be unreasonable. If they changed their beliefs without having new insights, different intuitions, considering new forms of life, reflecting on the arguments that we reflect on, they would be unreasonable. Yet, this is what morality requires them to do. They habitually violate correct moral standards because of what they believe and because they act on their beliefs in just the way any reasonable person would. In rejecting the cultural relativist's claim that moral standards 'shift' so as to accommodate a plurality of incongruous views of the good and the right, we should reject Alston's suggestion that standards of epistemic obligation shift from culture to culture. Cultural influences might excuse someone from failing to meet her obligations (e.g., if there is a duty to follow the evidence and

---

[52] We shall see that Alston does reject Deontologism, but the success of this objection does not depend upon the success of his argument against Deontologism.
[53] Not that the cultural relativists should accept it, mind you.

to refrain from believing without evidence, those raised in cultures that believe that there are matters where you should believe without or against the evidence might be excused for so doing), but they do not thereby change the standards that determine whether you meet your obligations. What goes for the standards of obligation goes for the standards of justification. Justification is just permissibility.

1.4.2 The argument from explanatory poverty

Let's consider a second argument for Externalism, the argument from explanatory poverty:

1. A theory of justification that provides a unifying explanation as to why our justified beliefs are justified is preferable to a theory that offers no such explanation.
2. Such an explanation will explain why certain epistemic principles that identify conditions under which beliefs are justifiably held are genuine and others are spurious.
3. Whereas the externalist can offer a unifying explanation of these principles, internalists cannot.
4. (Therefore) Externalism is preferable to Internalism.[54]

In support of (3), Goldman tries to show two things. First, that reliabilists can explain the difference between genuine and spurious epistemic principles:

Consider some faulty process of belief-formation, i.e., processes whose belief-outputs would be classed as unjustified. Here are some examples: confused reasoning, wishful thinking, reliance on emotional attachment, mere hunch or guesswork, and hasty generalization. What do these faulty processes have in common? They share the feature of *unreliability*. They tend to produce *error* a large proportion of the time. By contrast, which species of belief-forming (or belief-sustaining) processes are intuitively justification-conferring? They include standard perceptual processes, remembering, good reasoning, and introspection. What these processes seem to have in common is *reliability*: the beliefs they produce are generally reliable.[55]

Second, that the internalists cannot offer their own explanations of these principles. He surveys some of the ways internalists have tried to identify what is distinctive of genuine epistemic principles (e.g., principles that say that we can justifiably believe what is indubitable, self-evident,

---

[54] See Goldman 1979.   [55] Goldman 1979, p. 10.

incorrigible, etc.) and argues that none of these features are distinctive of genuine epistemic principles.[56] Thus, it seems that the externalists can do a better job explaining why justified beliefs are justified.

Goldman rightly rejects the internalist explanations he considers, but internalists can say two things in response. First, they can argue that the externalist explanation he provides is inadequate by showing that genuine epistemic principles do not always reliably lead to truth. (We shall see below that internalists have persuaded a number of externalists [including Goldman] that you can justifiably believe something even if you form your beliefs in an environment in which the processes that produce your beliefs do not produce any true beliefs at all.) Second, internalists can try to find some ways to distinguish genuine epistemic principles from spurious ones that Goldman did not anticipate. In so doing, they might show that internalists can do a better job explaining why genuine epistemic principles confer justification and so they might rightly reject (3).

Wedgwood, for example, argues that it 'makes sense' to follow certain epistemic rules with internally specified application conditions (e.g., "Believe *p* if it looks to you as if *p* and you have no available reason to believe ~*p* or think things are amiss") given that the aim of belief formation and revision is to believe correctly. If it makes sense to pursue your aim in this way, the beliefs you form by following these rules should count as rational.[57] Plausibly, what is rational to believe or do depends upon your perspective, which means to your ends it makes sense to pursue given your perspective, and whether your aims are intelligible, but not whether your means are reliable. If rational beliefs are justifiably held, these rules confer justification and we can explain why these rules confer justification without appealing to any of the conditions that figure in externalist accounts of justification (e.g., reliability or proper function).[58]

---

[56] Goldman 1979, p. 9. One defect in these internalist approaches is that none of the internalist principles he considered places any restriction on the cause of your beliefs. If, say, you believe something that happens to be self-evident or incorrigible on the basis of what your horoscope says, you can conform to the internalist principles without your beliefs being justified. This worry is distinct from the worry that underlies the argument from explanatory poverty, which is that the internalist cannot explain why it is that our beliefs are justified if formed by following certain rules or principles. It also seems that the internalist can try to deal with Goldman's worry by saying that theirs is a view of propositional justification and conceding to him that a further basing requirement needs to be introduced. Either this basing requirement can be understood along internalist lines or the internalist can admit without too much embarrassment that doxastic justification involves an external element because of the basing requirement without abandoning the view that the justification of each belief is understood in an internalist way.

[57] See Wedgwood 2002a.

[58] Audi 2001; Cohen 1984; Conee and Feldman 2004; Foley 1987; Langsam 2008; Madison 2010; and Wedgwood 2002a all hold that rationally held beliefs are justifiably held beliefs.

Thus, unless Goldman can show that it is not rational to follow these rules for belief formation and revision or show that you can rationally believe without believing with justification, the internalists can reject (3).

1.4.3 The argument from stored beliefs

Let's consider another of Goldman's arguments for Externalism, the argument from stored beliefs:

1. Internalism says that the only facts that contribute to the justification of an individual's beliefs at this moment are reflectively accessible or retrievable from memory.
2. Given this constraint, internalists cannot account for the intuition that many of the things we justifiably believe currently we believe without being able to identify the reasons we needed to justifiably form these beliefs initially.
3. (Therefore) Internalism delivers the wrong verdict, classifying justified beliefs stored in memory as unjustified.[59]

Internalists often respond by saying that they can account for the intuition that many of the things you currently justifiably believe you believe without being able to recall any of the justifying reasons you had initially. Conee and Feldman say that you often have a justification for beliefs stored in memory constituted by "conscious qualities of its recollection, such as its vivacity … and associated feeling of confidence."[60] Pollock and like-minded foundationalists about memory say that seeming to remember *p* can provide you with a *pro tanto* reason to believe *p*.[61] If they can accommodate the crucial intuition in this way, internalists can reject (2).

Goldman anticipated this response and argued that these approaches lead to absurdly permissive views of justification. Suppose Sally reads about the health benefits of broccoli in the *New York Times* and retains the belief that broccoli is healthy without remembering where she read this or what evidence supports this belief. Contrast this case with one in which Sally comes to form the same belief having read the *National Inquirer*. Goldman says:

---

[59] Goldman 1999a. Greco 2005 offers a similar argument.
[60] Conee and Feldman 2001, p. 9. They flirt with the idea that the feelings of confidence can serve as evidence that provides inductive support for beliefs formed in the past. Foundationalists about memory say that apparent recall can provide a *pro tanto* reason for belief, one that might justify without figuring in an inductive inference from past success.
[61] See Audi 2005 and Pollock and Cruz 1999 for discussion and defense of such a view.

[Sally's] broccoli belief was never acquired, or corroborated, in an epistemically sound manner. Then even with the indicated current background belief, Sally cannot be credited with justifiably believing that broccoli is healthful. Her past acquisition is still relevant – and decisive. At least it is relevant as long as we are considering the "epistemizing" sense of justification, in which justification carries a true belief a good distance toward knowledge. Sally's belief in the healthfulness of broccoli is not justified in that sense, for surely she does not know that broccoli is healthful, given that the *National Inquirer* was her sole source of information.[62]

The general lesson he takes from this is that if your beliefs are defective when initially formed they remain defective until you find adequate reasons for holding them.

Although I find his argument rather persuasive, I think Goldman's examples support externalist views far more radical than those he would defend. Suppose Windom exploits Leo's gullibility and tricks him into entering the experience machine. Once trapped inside, Leo knows that the machine will induce in him a series of hallucinations and so he knows that things will not be what they seem. So, he initially knows that the reasons he will be given are defective and knows that he will be supplied with these defective reasons because of his gullibility. Windom tells him that if he starts to display sufficient epistemic virtue over the coming months, he will be released from the machine. Otherwise, he will never escape. This machine only erases Leo's memories of being forced into the machine a day or two after he has been strapped in, but it does not prevent him from recalling the hallucinatory experiences he had during these initial days. On the first day, it seems to him that he is going to work but he knows better than to believe that he is. On the third day, he seems to recall going to work two days ago and now believes that he did go to work that day. What should we say about Leo's belief (B1) based on the apparent memory of having gone to work two days earlier? It is based on defective reasons and it is based on those reasons because of Leo's gullibility. What about the beliefs Leo forms in response to his experience two weeks after being strapped into the machine: should we say that his belief (B2) that he is eating breakfast is justified by the apparent experience of eating his cereal and drinking his coffee? Remember that Leo receives his defective reasons because of his epistemic vices (e.g., his gullibility, his disposition to rush to judgment, his lack of critical skills, etc.).

---

[62] Goldman 1999a, p. 280.

Intuitively, to me, B1 and B2 are on par. I hold the radical view that the veridicality of particular experiences matters to the justification of your experiential beliefs, so I would be willing to say that neither B1 nor B2 is justified. I suspect that few epistemologists would agree, however, that B2 is unjustified, but I think many would agree that B1 and B2 are justificationally on par. It would be irrational for Leo to reflect on B1 and B2 and take different attitudes towards them given the information available to him. If B1 and B2 are both regarded as justified, then Goldman needs to explain how Leo's situation is different from Sally's. It seems to me that Leo's situation is similar to Sally's in this important respect – because of earlier epistemic vices, both later come to have defective reasons that would be rational to form beliefs in response to. In Sally's case, she recalls testimony that was based on a source that is not to be trusted, but is no longer in any position to appreciate that fact. In Leo's case, he recalls experiences that are not to be trusted, but is no longer in any position to appreciate this fact because his epistemic vices stand in the way of discovering that his reasons are defective. If, in spite of this, Leo's beliefs are justified, it is not clear that Sally's beliefs are unjustified and it is not clear that earlier epistemic vices will continue to undermine justificatory status indefinitely.

Goldman does raise an important challenge that internalists should address if they say that Sally's beliefs are justified:

Suppose I adopt a belief in P in an unjustified fashion, for example, by wishful thinking. The next day I seem to remember that P but have no recollection of how I originally formed it. According to the foundational theory, assuming there are no defeaters, I am now justified in believing P. But that seems counterintuitive: Why should the mere passage of time – plus some forgetfulness on my part – suddenly make me justified in believing P although initially I was unjustified?[63]

Unfortunately, I think internalists can meet this challenge. They should not say that the mere passage of time improves justificatory standing. They should appeal to the (alleged) principle that if you have reason to believe *p* and no reason to doubt or disbelieve *p*, this reason might be sufficient to believe *p*.[64] For them, the relevant reasons are available. What changes with time is the availability of the defeating reason. The fact the

[63] Goldman 2009a, p. 324.
[64] This is supposed to be analogous to the seemingly platitudinous claim that you can justifiably act if you have a reason to act and no reason not to. It is not. The epistemic principle just stated assumes that the reasons not to act have to be available for them to have any bearing on justificatory status.

information came from a disreputable source defeats justification initially, but the defeater does not continue to threaten the justificatory status of a belief if it is not available.

Many people have the intuition that it would be rational to believe what you seem to recall when you have no available reason to question the veracity of your memory even if your belief was defective when initially formed. Indeed, I suspect that this will be nearly as widely held as the view that the veridicality of your experiences does not determine whether your perceptual beliefs are rationally held. If so, internalists can say that these beliefs stored in memory are justified currently even if defective when initially formed. As we saw with his previous argument, if Goldman is going to overcome this kind of intuition he needs to show that what is rational to believe is not always something you have sufficient justification to believe. He also needs to show that justification defeaters can defeat justification even if they are not available to a subject. Without defending these two controversial claims, intuitions about beliefs stored in memory will do little to advance the externalist cause.

1.4.4 *The argument from the truth-connection*

Perhaps the strongest argument for Externalism is the argument from the truth-connection:

1. The conditions that justify belief have to be sufficiently indicative of the truth or make it sufficiently likely that the belief is true.
2. Internal conditions alone cannot make it sufficiently likely that your belief is true or provide an adequate indication that your belief is true.
3. (Therefore) Justification is an externalist notion.[65]

What is distinctive of *epistemic* justification is that having it puts you in the proper relation to truth. As BonJour remarks:

If epistemic justification were not conducive to truth in this way, if finding epistemically justified beliefs did not substantially increase the likelihood of finding true ones, then epistemic justification would be irrelevant to our main cognitive goal and of dubious worth. It is only if we have some reason for thinking that epistemic justification constitutes a path to truth that we as cognitive beings

---

[65] See Alston 1989; Bach 1985; Engel 1992a; Goldman 1979; Majors and Sawyer 2005; and Swain 1981. Sosa 1991, p. 274 suggests that the virtues that we exercise in acquiring justified beliefs have to be truth-conducive, but distinguishes justification from aptness to accommodate intuitions about deception cases.

have any motive for preferring epistemically justified beliefs to epistemically unjustified ones.[66]

Remember that both sides agree that if your beliefs are justified, your belief is better than a guess or baseless hunch. It is better, externalists say, because your justified beliefs are likely true. The conditions that determine whether it is likely that your beliefs are true do not seem to supervene upon the accessibles or non-factive mental states, as it seems that some of your internal duplicates will have nothing that supports their beliefs that is conducive to truth. Think about your systematically deceived internal duplicate. There is nothing in her situation that substantially increases the likelihood her beliefs are correct. However, the standard line for internalists to take is that her beliefs are just as justified as yours. Thus, if justification provides you with a proper connection to the truth, it depends upon more than just relations between accessibles or among mental states.

The trouble with this argument for (1) is that it uses the notion of a *proper* connection to truth. You can cash this notion out in externalist terms, but internalists can resist this argument by offering an alternative notion of propriety (e.g., as epistemic responsibility or conforming to the right rules of belief revision). If some alternative notion of propriety can be understood in internalist terms, the externalists have to say that their notion is the notion that matters to justification. Now we have to decide which notion of propriety is the one that matters to justification.

Externalists could say that what constitutes your justification has to properly connect you to the truth in the sense that it provides a non-accidental connection to the truth. If your beliefs are justified, they might say, when they turn out to be true they will not fail to constitute knowledge for Gettierish reasons.[67] Doxastic justification does not put you in a position to know because there can be false, justified beliefs and you are only in a position to know what is true, but justification moves you a fair distance in the direction of knowledge.

If propriety is understood in this way, it makes sense to think of justification in externalist terms insofar as internal conditions alone do not provide a non-accidental connection to truth. The problem with this line of argument is that it rests on a controversial assumption about the role justification plays in the acquisition of knowledge. Pollock and Cruz say that anyone who claims that justification provides a non-accidental connection to the truth has either failed to learn the lesson of Gettier's cases or has changed the subject from justification to warrant (i.e., that condition

---

[66] BonJour 1985, p. 8.   [67] See Swain 1981.

that distinguishes true belief from knowledge).[68] If there is some other rationale for thinking of propriety in externalist terms, it is not yet clear what it is.

1.4.5 The argument from unusual faculties

I want to shift gears and look at arguments for Internalism, starting with the argument from unusual faculties. BonJour offers an example that is supposed to show that justification should be understood along internalist lines:

> Norman, under certain conditions that usually obtain, is a completely reliable clairvoyant with respect to certain kinds of subject matter. He possesses no evidence or reasons of any kind for or against the general possibility of such a cognitive power, or for or against the thesis that he possesses it. One day Norman comes to believe that the President is in New York City, though he has no evidence either for or against this belief. In fact the belief is true and results from his clairvoyant power, under circumstances in which it is completely reliable.[69]

BonJour thinks it is intuitive to say that Norman's beliefs are not justified and that if this is correct, we can see that justification is not an externalist notion:

1. If Norman happened to be a reliable clairvoyant, Externalism would classify the beliefs that result from his clairvoyant power as justified even if he did not have any reason to think that he had these powers.
2. Norman's beliefs, however, would not be justified.
3. (Therefore) Externalism delivers the wrong verdict by classifying unjustified beliefs as justified.

Externalists sometimes bite the bullet and deny (2):

> [M]any reliabilists would allow that an appropriate input could be something external to the person, so long as that thing non-deviantly caused the belief in a reliable way. For example, many reliabilists would allow that (if God exists) it is possible for people to know things via divine revelation. Such revelation could result from God directly (and reliably) causing true beliefs to be formed in the believers, without using states internal to the believers as intermediate causes of those beliefs. The input that is non-deviantly causing these beliefs is some state or activity in God, which we can plausibly think of as being external to the believer.[70]

---

[68] Cruz and Pollock 2004, p. 135.
[69] BonJour 1980, p. 62. [70] Bergmann 2006, p. 52.

If we stipulate that BonJour's clairvoyants received their powers from the gods, I would still side with BonJour. Norman seems plainly irrational. If you asked him where he thought the President was he would say that the President was in New York City. If you asked him why he thought that, he would say "Oh, no reason, but that is where he is." Bergmann's response only serves to confirm BonJour's worry that, "on the externalist view, a person may be ever so irrational and irresponsible in accepting a belief, when judged in light of his own subjective conception of the situation, and may still turn out to be epistemically justified."[71] It is not clear whether Bergmann would say that Norman's beliefs (which I take to be on par with his subject's divinely induced beliefs) are irrationally held, but I think that many would have this intuition. If so, he either has to defend the idea that your justified beliefs can be irrationally held or explain away the intuition that Norman is irrational much in the way that people who claim to receive messages from the gods are.

The mistake in BonJour's argument is (1). Externalists should build an internalist element into their theory of justification. Doxastic justification requires personal justification. You cannot justifiably believe what you are not justified in believing. If personal justification is a matter of forming beliefs in rational and responsible ways, doxastic justification requires that you form your beliefs in rational and responsible ways. As Wedgwood suggests, a person is non-inferentially justified in believing something if she forms her belief in response to some representational state (e.g., an experiential state in which it seems to the subject that *p*) where it makes sense for her to form that belief when she is in such a state given the aim of believing only what is true. The problem with Norman is that there is nothing that plays the role for him that experience plays in the production of our perceptual beliefs. It does not make sense for him to form the beliefs that he does given the goal of believing only what is true. The important point is that externalists can accommodate BonJour's intuition by insisting that doxastic justification requires personal justification and offering an internalist account of personal justification.

1.4.6 The argument from internal reasons

Conee and Feldman argue for Internalism on the grounds that it provides the best explanation for intuitions about pairs of cases like these:

[71] BonJour 1980, p. 59.

Bob and Ray are sitting in an air-conditioned hotel lobby reading yesterday's newspaper. Each has read that it will be very warm today and, on that basis, each believes that it is very warm today. Then Bob goes outside and feels the heat. They both continue to believe that it is very warm today. But at this point Bob's belief is better justified.

Hilary is a brain in a vat who has been abducted recently from a fully embodied life in an ordinary environment. He is being stimulated so that it seems to him as though his normal life has continued. Hilary believes that he ate oatmeal for breakfast yesterday. His memorial basis for his breakfast belief is artificial. It has been induced by his "envatters." Here are two versions of relevant details. 5a) Hilary's recollection is very faint and lacking in detail. The meal seems incongruous to him in that it strikes him as a distasteful breakfast and he has no idea why he would have eaten it. 5b) Hilary's recollection seems to him to be an ordinary vivid memory of a typical breakfast for him.[72]

Internal differences between Bob and Ray are supposed to explain why Bob's beliefs are better justified. The mental differences in (5a) and (5b) are supposed to explain why Hilary is better justified in (5b).[73]

After discussing their cases, Conee and Feldman issue a challenge to externalists:

It is reasonable to generalize from these examples to the conclusion that every variety of change that brings about or enhances justification either internalizes an external fact or makes a purely internal difference. It appears that there is no need to appeal to anything extramental to explain any justificatory difference. These considerations argue for the general internalist thesis that these epistemic differences have an entirely mental origin.[74]

I disagree. It is not reasonable to draw any conclusions from these examples. First, their intuitions do not favor Internalism over Externalism since externalists do not deny that internal differences between two subjects can explain differences in the justificatory status of their beliefs. Reliabilists can say, for example, that internally available evidence can improve your epistemic situation because following such evidence is one reliable way of forming beliefs. Externalists about evidence can say that Hilary's beliefs are better justified because what Hilary knows in (5b) better justifies his beliefs than what Hilary knows in (5a). Second, the generalization is not reasonable because their sample is not representative. They focus on cases where there are internal differences between subjects, but they do not discuss cases of internal duplicates that differ in the ways externalists say matter to justification.

---

[72] Conee and Feldman 2004, p. 59.
[73] Conee and Feldman 2004, p. 59.
[74] Conee and Feldman 2004, p. 59.

Are there cases where external differences make a justificatory difference? I think so. If you see that p is true, you have better reasons than someone who mistakenly believes p is true on the basis of a subjectively indistinguishable hallucination. Why? You are better off because you have an excellent reason for rejecting the hypothesis that p is false – p is true, as you saw earlier. Your counterpart in a ~p-world might have her reasons for rejecting the hypothesis that p is false, but her reasons will be weaker than yours since her reasons will include neither p nor any proposition that entails p.[75]

Conee and Feldman try to draw a general lesson from their examples, but their examples only support the modest claims that internal differences between subjects can make a difference to justification without supporting the internalist view that these are the only differences that matter to justification. Obviously, Conee and Feldman will deny that my example shows that there can be justificatory differences without internal differences, but the important point is that their intuitions about their examples do not conflict with my intuitions about my example. Since my intuitions about my example are incompatible with Internalism, their argument lends little support to Internalism.

1.4.7 The argument from guidance

Pollock argues that justification is an internalist notion on the grounds that justification is supposed to guide you in deciding what to believe:

1. Your beliefs are justified iff you comply with the correct epistemic norms in forming these beliefs.[76]
2. These epistemic norms play a dual role, determining whether your beliefs are justifiably held and guiding you in forming beliefs.
3. These norms cannot fulfill their guiding function unless they have internalist application conditions and they are justified in internalist terms.
4. (Therefore) Neither your justifying reasons nor their adequacy can depend upon anything external to you.
5. According to Externalism, either your justifying reasons or their adequacy can depend upon something external to you.
6. (Therefore) Justification is not an externalist notion.[77]

[75] I defend these points in Chapters 3 and 4.
[76] Pollock and Cruz 1999, p. 131. In Chapter 7, I argue that norms do not require compliance.
[77] Pollock 1987 and Pollock and Cruz 1999.

Using terminology that differs from Pollock's, let us say that you *conform* to a norm that says that you should Φ iff you Φ. *Compliance* is a matter of conforming to a norm by being appropriately guided by it. For Pollock, justification requires complying with epistemic norms where this compliance manifests a kind of procedural knowledge in the way that riding a bike does. The key premises in his argument are (2) and (3). I do not think we should accept either of them.

Let us look at (2) first. If norms are normative, they tell you what your (*pro tanto* or all things considered) duty is. Why think that they also play a procedural or guiding role? Pollock says this:

> It is important to distinguish between two uses of norms (epistemic or otherwise). On the one hand, there are third-person uses of norms wherein we use the norms to evaluate the behavior of others. Various norms may be appropriate for third-person evaluations, depending upon the purpose we have in making the evaluations. For example, we may want to determine whether a person is a good scientist because we are trying to decide whether to hire her. To be contrasted with third-person uses of norms are first-person uses. First-person uses of norms are, roughly speaking, action-guiding. For example, I might appeal to Fowler's *Modern English Usage* to decide whether to use "that" or "which" in a sentence. We will call such action-guiding norms "procedural". Epistemological questions are about rational cognition – about how cognition rationally ought to work – and so are inherently first-person. The traditional epistemologist asks, "How is it possible for me to be justified in my beliefs about the external world, about other minds, about the past, and so on?" These are questions about what to believe. Epistemic norms are the norms in terms of which these questions are to be answered, so these norms are used in a first-person reason-guiding or procedural capacity.[78]

Pollock's view is that when we evaluate someone's actions or attitudes using information unavailable to them (i.e., a third-person use), we are not using the norms to determine the deontic status of this agent's actions or attitudes. These norms are used to determine deontic status only when we use them using just the information available to the subject at the time of action or belief formation. I think externalists should contest this point. In cases of moral evaluation, I would argue that ignorance or mistaken belief might excuse someone who did not conform to moral standards whereas Pollock's view seems to be that the standards only apply to agents who have the non-normative information they need to see what it takes to conform to these standards.

---

[78] Pollock and Cruz 1999, p. 124.

There is a lot packed into the passage I quoted. It contains a number of potential explanations as to why Pollock accepts (2):

(i) Epistemic norms are procedural norms because they address questions about what to believe.
(ii) Epistemic norms are procedural norms because they should guide belief formation.
(iii) Epistemic norms are procedural norms because they have to do with rational cognition.
(iv) Epistemic norms are procedural norms because traditional epistemological questions have been about procedural norms.

I think (i) offers little support to (2). We have no reason yet to think that a norm's status as a norm depends upon whether it identifies right-making features and provides a suitable doxastic decision procedure.[79] In ethics we often find that the norms that help us understand what makes right acts right will not give us a decision procedure that takes us from where we are to a decision about what to do. We need an argument for (i) before we use (i) to justify (2).

Turning to (ii), it says that epistemic norms are procedural norms because they guide belief formation. If we had a reason to think that genuine epistemic norms *must* guide belief formation for our beliefs to be justified, we would have our argument for (2). The problem is that we do not have an argument for the claim that epistemic norms must guide belief formation in order for our beliefs to be justified. While I do not see how anyone could accept (ii) and deny (2), this is because I see no difference between these two claims.

As for (iii), it might seem to fare better than (i) or (ii) as a justification for (2) because it is clear that rational cognition has to do with what is internal to you. The problem is that it is doubtful that rational cognition is all that is required for meeting your epistemic obligations. Rational cognition alone will not ensure that you meet your practical obligations. Not if rational moral disagreement or consequential moral luck is possible. If rational cognition alone will not ensure that you meet your practical obligations, why should we assume that rational cognition alone ensures that you meet your epistemic obligations? What if there was a nexus here and meeting your epistemic obligations depends upon whether your beliefs put you in a position to meet your practical obligations? Rationality requires that you do what you rationally judge you ought to do. Thus, if

---

[79] See Goldman 1980 and Jacobson 1997.

we assume that rationality is normative in the weak sense that you cannot be obligated to do what it is not rational to do, we have to assume that there is a nexus and that your epistemic obligations will include the obligation to refrain from forming false beliefs about what you ought to do. Thus, Pollock cannot say that rational cognition is all you need to meet your epistemic obligations unless he is prepared to deny that consequential moral luck is possible and deny that rational moral disagreement is possible.

Finally, (iv) does not look very promising. Why think that the ordinary notion of justification we use when determining whether someone has met her epistemic obligations would play an important role in discussions of traditional philosophical problems such as skeptical arguments concerning our knowledge of the past or of other minds? On its face, it seems that if you want to solve the problem of other minds, you need something more impressive than what you have available to you when you know that your friend has a headache. It seems we do not have a compelling reason to accept (2).

The second crucial premise in Pollock's argument is (3). Norms tell you what your (*pro tanto* or all things considered) duty would be under certain conditions. Externalists could say that some of the conditions that figure in such norms are external conditions (e.g., "You should not form beliefs on the basis of non-veridical experiences"; "You should not believe what the experts deny"). In Pollock's jargon, *belief externalists* say there are such norms. The externalist could also say that the condition that figures in the specification of the norm is an internal condition while insisting that the reason why that condition figures in the specification of a norm has to do with some external condition (e.g., the externalist could say "It is permissible to believe *p* if it seems to you perceptually that *p*" and say that this is true because such appearances reliably lead to truth). To introduce more jargon, *norm externalists* say that some epistemic norms are justified by appeal to external conditions such as reliability. Pollock rejects both Belief and Norm Externalism.

His reason for rejecting Belief Externalism is that belief externalists say that the application conditions for some epistemic norms make reference to conditions external to you. If epistemic norms are procedural norms, he says, their application conditions should be made up exclusively of conditions directly accessible to you. He suggests that only your non-factive mental states are directly accessible to you, in which case Externalism is mistaken.

Since there is not a compelling case for (2) and the argument against Belief Externalism assumes that epistemic norms are procedural norms, the belief externalist can block the argument by denying that epistemic norms are procedural norms. Even if we grant that epistemic norms are procedural norms, it is not obvious why we should reject Belief Externalism. First, it is not clear why only internal conditions are directly accessible to you. In some perfectly good sense, you might think that what you see is directly accessible to you when you see it. If you see that *p*, perhaps you can know non-inferentially that *p*, and why think what you can know non-inferentially is not directly accessible to you? True, there are technical notions of accessibility on which what is accessible to you is accessible only via reflection, but this privileges introspection over perception as a source of reasons and evidence. If both introspection and perception are fallible, the difference between perception and introspection is a psychological difference, not a principled epistemic difference.

Second, consider the norm that says that you should not believe what you do not know. You are always in a position to conform to this norm. If you refrain from believing *p*, you will not violate this norm whether you were in a position to know that *p* or not. While this is a procedural norm, it has external application conditions. It tells you what not to believe by telling you not to believe when certain external conditions obtain (i.e., if the fact that *p* is true is one that does not supervene upon conditions internal to you, whether you are in a position to know *p* depends upon conditions external to you). Thus, even if epistemic norms are procedural norms, it is not clear why Belief Externalism is false.

The knowledge norm tells us what is prohibited, but it offers no positive guidance. Presumably, Pollock rejects Belief Externalism because he thinks there are procedural norms that offer positive guidance by identifying conditions under which we are permitted to believe something. Should we say that there are procedural norms that provide positive guidance that tells us what we have the right to believe when we are in certain internal states? The intuition that there must be such norms is widely shared. Here, Jackson makes his pitch for procedural norms in ethics:

The ... problem arises from the fact that we are dealing with an *ethical* theory ... a theory about *action*, about what to *do* ... Now, the fact that an action has in fact the best consequences may be a matter which is obscure to an agent ... Hence, the fact that a course of action would have the best results is not in itself a guide ... for a guide to action must in some sense be present to the agent's mind. We need ... a story from the inside of an agent to be part of any theory which is properly a theory in ethics, and having the best consequences is a story from the outside.[80]

I think we should be skeptical of any suggestion that there could be such procedural norms that offered positive guidance.

The first thing to ask about this "story from the inside" is whether this story provides guidance for all of us. I think that if a person is sufficiently confused, wicked, or inconsistent, there is no story to tell that takes them from where they are now (where that is characterized in terms of their subjective states) to where they ought to be where they can see that they are being led down the right path. If not, then whatever reasons these procedural norms issue, they would not have both rational authority and universal applicability. If you are in bad enough shape, maybe there is just no helping you.

We see this worry play out in ethics when we look at two alternatives to an objectivist approach to obligation. According to the objectivist, your obligation is to Φ iff Φ-ing is the best option you have (i.e., the option that would maximize actual deontic value). According to the prospectivist, your obligation is to Φ iff Φ-ing is prospectively best. The prospectively best option can be thought of as the option that maximizes *expected value* or *expectable value*.[81] Expected value is a function of the actual value of an outcome and the evidential probability that the outcome would eventuate if you performed an action. Expectable value is a function of the evidential probability that the outcome will eventuate if you perform an action and the probable value associated with these outcomes, where the probable value of an outcome is understood in terms of the evidential probability that some outcome has some deontic value.

Because the first version of the prospectivist view of obligation ranks options in terms of actual values and these values might be obscure to you, the first prospectivist view does *not* provide a story from the inside except to those who have all and only the right values. If you assign too

---

[80] Jackson 1991, p. 467.
[81] Jackson 1991 defends the view that there is a sense in which you ought to act in such a way as to maximize expected value. Zimmerman 2008 defends the view that you ought to act in such a way as to maximize expectable value. Suppose the action that would maximize expected value would, if performed, kill your patient. Suppose you intend to perform this action but, as luck would have it, your attention slips and you perform some alternative course of action and your patient is saved. On Jackson's view, there is a sense in which you failed to do what you ought, but he recognizes that there is another sense in which you did not fail to do what you ought. He thinks that there are subjective and objective readings of 'ought'. The subjective reading is, he suggests, the one that is a guide for action. Zimmerman rejects the idea that 'ought' is ambiguous for reasons we consider below.

much or too little value to something, fail to see the value in something, or seem to see value where none can be found, there is no story from the inside that tells you what to do. So, the first prospectivist view is not adequate to the task of identifying procedural norms that give positive guidance.

On the second version of the prospectivist view, there might be a way that an ideally rational version of you could work out what to do in any given situation, but as the ranking of options is done in terms of what your values are, gaps in your evaluative evidence might mean that the options that are prospectively best are nevertheless morally abhorrent.[82] If the subject's evaluative evidence is taken to be evaluative propositions the subject has in mind (e.g., that the subject finds intuitive [be they true or false]), then we have to say that subjects that have what we would regard as abhorrent values are obliged to do unspeakable things to others and would be acting in morally repugnant ways if they failed to act on their abhorrent moral beliefs. (Imagine, for example, lazy cannibals or apathetic terrorists. Would we condemn them for eating too little human flesh or failing to kill as many non-combatants as they think they should? Or, consider someone befuddled by sophistical arguments about the moral status of the fetus. Suppose she is torn between the view that the fetus has the same value as an infant and the view that an early-term fetus has the same value as an unfertilized egg. Should we say that it would be worse for such a subject to have an abortion than to play Russian roulette with sleeping infants? On the hypothesis that the fetus has no more value than a sperm or egg, this version of the prospectivist view would still say that it would be worse to have an abortion than to play Russian roulette with sleeping infants using a six-shooter loaded with a single bullet.) If the subject's evaluative

---

[82] Zimmerman acknowledges this and says that while it might have been that Hitler committed no wrongs (depending upon what evaluative evidence he had), his actions might have been evil. See Zimmerman 2008, p. 49. I have a hard time understanding what evil without wrongdoing amounts to. Evil is not understood in terms of moral culpability. On his view, you are not morally culpable for Φ-ing if you non-culpably judge that it would be right for you to Φ. I'm not sure that this is the right way to think of culpability, but I think that if you know that it would be right to Φ and you are motivated by your sense of right and wrong you cannot be culpable for what you do. If Hitler could have acted rightly on the prospectivist view, I see no reason to think that he could not work out that his actions were right. Should we say that Hitler's actions were evil not because they were wrongful and not because he was culpable, but simply because of what they brought about? If so, it seems his actions are evil in the way that earthquakes, plagues, and forest fires are. I think earthquakes are only evil if they have a morally responsible agent as their cause. Zimmerman cannot say that Hitler's actions were wrongful objectively speaking because he rightly rejects the idea that there are objective and subjective obligations. Better, I think, to let intuitions about whether someone did something evil to determine whether someone met his obligations.

evidence is limited to true propositions that the subject has in mind in some way (fill in the details however you like), a sufficiently misguided agent could be obliged to do next to nothing because there would be too few true propositions in her evaluative evidence to rank available worlds in such a way as to require her to act. She would be permitted to fiddle while Rome burned, so to speak. Moreover, if there is a truth-condition on evidence, the subject's rational judgments about what to do could diverge radically from correct judgments about what is prospectively best since what would be rational to believe about what to do would be a function of both the true and false evaluative propositions the subject accepts. There is no story from the inside on this account, either.

Suppose whatever procedural norms there are cannot help everyone, only the select few. How do we select the select few? Should we say that procedural norms help those who are sufficiently rational or have sufficiently decent values? Perhaps, but then Pollock faces a dilemma. If we do not assume that all it takes to form justified beliefs is for the rational cognizer to cognize rationally, there is no reason to think that these procedural norms will lead the rational cognizer to form justified beliefs. If, however, we assume that the rational believer is the one who forms rational beliefs and take the rational to be characterized in terms of the justified, the resulting view is that procedural norms provide guidance only to those who are in a position to form justified beliefs. If it turns out only those in suitably friendly external environments are in a position to form justified beliefs, the procedural view lends no support to Internalism. Pollock needs to show that features of the external environment can never stand in the way of believing with justification. To show that, you first have to show that justification is an internalist notion. Once he does that, his current argument would be superfluous.

There is a further related worry that Pollock needs to address. Consider the norm that enjoins you to refrain from believing what you do not know. This is just the sort of norm that belief internalists say is no norm at all. If there were such prohibitions, there could not also be norms that told you that you were obligated or permitted to believe that things are what they appear to be unless things are invariably the way they appear to be (which, as you know, they are not). Thus, to show that Belief Internalism is true and that there are procedural norms that offer positive guidance, you have to show that there are no additional norms that prohibit us from forming beliefs when certain external conditions obtain. Once again, the argument for Internalism is incomplete without this and unnecessary once you have it.

1.4.8 Huemer's peritrope

Huemer defends an internalist account of justification that has the principle of Phenomenal Conservatism as its centerpiece:

> PC: If it seems to you that *p*, then, in the absence of defeaters, you thereby have at least some degree of justification for believing *p*.[83]

He maintains that it would be self-defeating to deny PC, which suggests that it might be self-defeating to deny his internalist view that justification is determined by seeming or appearance states and not further conditions external to you.

In this passage Huemer explains why he thinks it would be self-defeating to deny PC:

> [T]he rejection of Phenomenal Conservatism is self-defeating, roughly, because one who rejected Phenomenal Conservatism would inevitably do so on the basis of how things seemed to himself; he would do so because Phenomenal Conservatism did not seem to him to be correct, or because it seemed to him to be incompatible with other things that seemed correct. Therefore, if this opponent of Phenomenal Conservatism were right, his belief in the negation of Phenomenal Conservatism would itself be unjustified.[84]

The self-defeat argument (SDA) comes to this:

1. Your beliefs are based on the way things seem to you.
2. If your belief in *p* is based on X and you believe that X is not a source of justification, your belief in *p* is not justified for reasons of self-defeat.
3. If you believe PC is mistaken, you believe that the way things seem to you is not a source of justification and believe this on the basis of the way things seem to you intuitively.
4. (Therefore) If you believe that PC is mistaken, your belief is not justified for reasons of self-defeat.

Each premise of this argument is open to challenge.

Let's focus on (2) first. Audrey thinks that the word of a gambler is worthless. Ben is a gambler and he tells Audrey that *p* is true. Audrey believes *p* on the basis of Ben's testimony and believes she believes *p* on the basis of his testimony. Is the justification for her belief in *p* defeated for reasons of self-defeat? No, because she does not know that Ben is a gambler. Thus, (2) is false. The self-defeat charge sticks only if you take

---

[83] Huemer 2007a, p. 30.   [84] Huemer 2007a, p. 39.

X to be your only basis for belief and take it that X is not a source of justification.

To see why this matters, suppose you believe that PC is false and suppose Huemer is right that you believe this on the basis of how things seem to you. If you believe that you believe PC is false because you see that it is false or because of some fact that does not supervene upon facts about how things seem to you (e.g., the fact that, say, PC entails some proposition you know is false), you do not lack justification for reasons of self-defeat. If you believe your beliefs are based, in part, upon something other than seeming states, you might harbor mistaken views about what justifies your beliefs, but that does not mean that your beliefs are self-defeating.

The self-defeat charge sticks only if you believe that PC is false and take yourself to believe it on the basis of how things seem and not anything further:

> Seeming Basis: If your beliefs are based on anything, they are based on appearances or seemings and nothing further.

Even if Huemer's targets accepted Seeming Basis, there is a second problem with the SDA. Externalists can accept PC and Seeming Basis with equanimity. Consider the view that you justifiably believe all and only what you know. Since you can know things on the basis of how things seem to you, the combination of Seeming Basis and PC does not commit you to Internalism.

For the SDA to succeed as an argument for Internalism, Huemer also has to persuade his targets to accept:

> Mental Dependence: The justification of your beliefs depends in a broad sense entirely upon the bases for your beliefs and your non-factive mental states.

Justification depends positively upon the quality of your reasons and negatively upon the absence of defeaters. Unless we all accept that defeaters and reasons to believe supervene on appearances or seemings, it would not be self-defeating to reject Internalism. Unless there is a compelling rationale for Mental Dependence and Seeming Basis that actually persuades externalists, the SDA fails. I do not expect any externalists to accept Mental Dependence and Seeming Basis since Internalism seems to follow from these theses on its own.

Before turning to the next argument, I want to briefly discuss Huemer's argument for (1):

My first premise is an empirical one, to the effect that, when we form beliefs ... our beliefs are based on the way things seem to us. Indeed, I think that the way things appear to oneself is normally the only (proximately) causally relevant factor in one's belief-formation. In other words, in normal contexts, including that of the present discussion of epistemic justification, one would not form different beliefs unless things appeared different to oneself in some way (belief content supervenes on appearances, in normal circumstances). Furthermore, in normal conditions, the way appearances determine beliefs is by inclining one towards believing what appears to oneself to be so, as opposed, say, to our being inclined to believe the things that seem false.[85]

Huemer is right that the proximate cause of your beliefs will be some combination of mental states. The crucial question, however, is not whether these mental states are the *causal* basis for your beliefs, but whether they are the *justificatory* basis for your beliefs. If I said that my basis for firing you was that I believed you were stealing office supplies, you could say rightly that I had no basis for firing you if you stole nothing. My belief and subsequent action would have had a causal basis (i.e., my belief that you stole something), but it might not have any justificatory basis.

In later chapters, I argue that the relata of the causal basing relation are not the same as the relata of the justification relation.[86] The causal basis for your beliefs are mental states, but the justificatory basis of what you believe will be things you believe or experience, not your experiencings or believings. There are two common strategies for trying to refute this view and show that the relata of these relations are the same. Some argue on broadly Davidsonian grounds that motivating reasons are causes and then try to show that when you believe with justification, your reasons for believing had to be good reasons. Some argue by appealing to intuitions about error. These arguments play an important role in motivating Internalism. Without them, the observation that the proximate causes of our beliefs are mental states does not give us any reason to accept Internalism or the idea that your justificatory basis consists of seemings or appearances as opposed to what seemed or appeared to be true (i.e., facts or propositions you had in mind).

---

[85] Huemer 2007a, p. 39. Wedgwood 2002a offers a similar argument.
[86] Swain 1979, p. 27, distinguishes between two kinds of basing, causal and evidential. He says that mental states are the causal basis of belief and that propositions are the evidential basis.

1.4.9 The argument from Deontologism

A common argument for Internalism appeals to the idea that justification is a deontological notion:

1. Your beliefs are justified iff they are permissibly held.
2. Internal factors alone determine whether your beliefs are permissibly held.
3. (Therefore) Internal factors alone determine whether your beliefs are justified.

Both premises are controversial. While (1) is defensible, (2) is not.

Someone might take issue with (1) because they think that justification depends upon whether your beliefs promote something of epistemic value rather than whether you do what epistemic duty requires. This objection is misplaced. The question as to whether there are any epistemic obligations is distinct from the question as to what the grounds of these obligations might be. Even if you think that justified beliefs are justified because they promote something of epistemic value, you might say that our obligation is to promote what has epistemic value, in which case justification would still be understood in deontological terms. I intend to defend Deontologism only in a very attenuated sense. If you should not believe *p*, you cannot justifiably believe *p* for the very same reason you should not believe *p*. Deontologism commits you to no substantive views about the grounds of epistemic obligation. As it is understood here, it does not assert that the right is prior to the good. It simply recognizes the existence of epistemic obligations, says that justification should be understood in terms of permissibility, and leaves it open as to whether these obligations should be understood in terms of conforming to norms, promoting the good, believing as the virtuous would believe, etc.

Some object to the very idea of epistemic obligation. They say that there is no obligation to promote what has epistemic value, to follow the right rules of belief revision, or to avoid holding contradictory beliefs. Skepticism about epistemic obligation seems to derive mainly from Alston's attack on Deontologism. He rejects Deontologism because he thinks there could only be epistemic obligations if it would be possible to exercise voluntary control over what you believe. Since, he says, you do not have voluntary control over your beliefs, there are no epistemic obligations.

In arguing that deontologists are committed to doxastic voluntarism (i.e., the view that you have voluntary control over your beliefs), he appeals to the principle that 'ought' implies 'can' (OIC), saying that you can be obligated to refrain from believing p only if you have effective choice as to whether to believe or not:

> OIC: In circumstances under which S ought/ought not Φ, S can Φ and can refrain from Φ-ing.[87]

A common response to Alston's argument is to say that we can exercise various kinds of control over our beliefs and that the kind of control we exercise over our beliefs is sufficiently robust for us to meaningfully talk about epistemic obligations.[88] More recently, a number of authors have argued that OIC does not commit you to doxastic voluntarism.[89] If Coop should not believe Ben's lies and Coop does not believe what Ben says, Coop meets his obligations even if he cannot believe/refrain from believing voluntarily. It is one thing to say that your obligations are limited to what you are able to do and quite another to say that your obligations are limited to what you can do voluntarily. Andy's fear of butterflies and Ben's feelings of entitlement are not under their voluntary control, but Andy should not fear butterflies and Ben should not feel so entitled. Since beliefs do seem to be responsive to reasons and since there are intuitively plausible cases of obligations without voluntary control, I think it is not obviously incoherent to say that we have epistemic obligations.

The problem with the deontologist's argument for Internalism is not (1), but (2). To see why some deontologists accept (2), we have to understand what deontological internalists take epistemic duty to be. Steup says:

> I take the concept of epistemic justification to be a *deontological* one. I believe that epistemic justification is analogous to moral justification in the following sense: Both kinds of justification belong to the family of deontological concepts, concepts such as permission, prohibition, obligation, blame, and responsibility … A belief that is epistemically justified is a belief that is epistemically permissible, a belief for which the subject cannot justly be blamed, or a belief the subject is not obliged to drop.[90]

Before him, Alston said:

> The terms, 'justified', 'justification', and their cognates are most naturally understood in what we may term a 'deontological' way, as having to do with obligation, permission, requirement, blame, and the like.[91]

---

[87] Alston 1989, p. 118.
[88] See Hieronymi 2008; Ryan 2003; Steup 2008; and Weatherson 2008.
[89] See Chuard and Southwood 2009 and McHugh in press.
[90] Steup 1999, p. 375. [91] Alston 1989, p. 257.

And before him, Ginet wrote:

One is *justified* in being confident that *p* if and only if it is not the case that one ought not to be confident that *p*: one could not be justly reproached for being confident that *p*.[92]

These authors agree that if you believe without justification, you can be blamed for so doing. If this is how we should understand epistemic obligation, is a sound argument for Internalism in the offing?

It is plausible that the conditions that determine whether you are blameworthy are internal to you, but not plausible that justification depends only upon whether you can be blamed for your beliefs. Suppose you have been brainwashed into believing that aliens have infiltrated your body and are responsible for your urge to smoke. Your belief is not justified just because the brainwashing makes it impossible to give the belief up, but you might be blameless in believing what you do. Deontologists should distinguish justification from mere blamelessness.[93]

Deontologists might instead defend (2) by saying that rational beliefs are justified beliefs. Assuming that external conditions have no direct bearing upon whether your beliefs are rationally held, perhaps there is a plausible argument from Deontologism to Internalism.

The problem with this approach is that you can believe and act rationally without believing or acting with justification. To see this, it would be helpful to consider Gardner's statement of the serial view of defenses:

[I]t is best of all if we commit no wrongs. If we cannot but commit wrongs, it is best if we commit them with justification. Failing justification, it is best if we have an excuse. The worst case is the one in which we must cast doubt on our own responsibility. When I say 'best' and 'worst' here I mean best and worst for us: for the course of our own lives and for our integrity as people.[94]

There are (at least) three ways of removing blame. In the worst case, he says, you are blameless because you cannot assume responsibility for what you do or think. In arguing that you lack the rational capacities to assume responsibility, we offer an exemption or denial of responsibility.[95] In the best case, there is no breach of duty and no wrong is committed. Excuses are supposed to fall somewhere in the middle.

---

[92] Ginet 1975, p. 28.
[93] As Moser 1991 stresses in his discussion of Alston's objections to Deontologism.
[94] Gardner 2007, p. 88.
[95] For a helpful discussion of the distinction between exemptions and excuses, see Gardner 2007; Horder 2004; and Strawson 1962.

In cases of excusable wrongdoing, you have the capacities required to assume responsibility for what you do, but *this* wrongful deed does not reflect badly on your character. This does not happen when you have overriding reason to commit the wrong. When you have such reasons your actions are justified, not just excused. The reason excusable wrongs do not reflect badly on your character is that you acted responsibly and did what a virtuous person would in your situation. To do that, you had to be rational in taking yourself to have acted rightly without acting permissibly. Thus, if excusable wrongdoing is possible, the rational is *not* the mark of the permissible.[96]

An example should help. There is a difference between not returning a book on time to the library because you had to perform an emergency tracheotomy (justification), because you were drugged and your capacities needed to make responsible decisions were undermined (denial of responsibility or exemption), or because you were mistaken about the library's location because you had a non-culpably mistaken belief about the library's location (excuse). If we classify the last case with justifications, we would say that you should not have done things differently and you do not owe any sort of reparation or compensation for a wrong. If we classify the last case with exemptions, we would try to get you off the hook by saying that you were not answerable for your deeds. Neither claim seems right. If you think that there really are three distinct ways of removing blame and agree that excuses are only appropriate when someone has acted responsibly, then since you cannot act responsibly without acting rationally, rational action motivated by rational belief is required for an excuse.

It takes considerable effort to persuade people that non-culpably held mistaken beliefs and non-culpable ignorance excuse wrongdoing rather than obviate the need to justify an action. Rather than argue for that view now, I want to describe what seems to be a plausible and coherent view on which something could be rational without being justified. Even if I am wrong in saying that mistaken beliefs excuse, there is good reason to distinguish rationality from justification:

---

[96] In the few cases where I have seen epistemologists discuss excuses, their examples of excusable behavior involve agents who have gone insane and are moved to act by their delusions rather than cases where a sane and rational agent is motivated to act on a consideration that a reasonable person might take to show that the agent's conduct was right. (See Audi 1993 and Wedgwood 2002a, for examples of this.) In ordinary contexts, if someone said that somebody's behavior should be excused because they were prompted to act by an insane delusion, I would not object. I would object to the idea that there are but two ways of trying to show that someone is blameless for what they have done.

1. If you Φ rationally iff you justifiably Φ, when only one rational option is available, it would become obligatory.
2. There are situations in which it would be irrational to withhold judgment as to whether *p* and irrational to disbelieve *p*.[97]
3. (Therefore) If you rationally Φ iff you justifiably Φ, situations could arise in which you would be obligated to believe *p*.
4. There are no positive epistemic obligations.
5. (Therefore) It is not true that you justifiably Φ whenever you rationally Φ.

In support of (2), think about situations in which you have strong evidence for *p*. If your evidence is sufficient for knowledge, you are aware of this evidence, you are not aware of any defeaters, and you are concerned with settling the question whether *p*, it seems irrational for you to withhold judgment or to judge that ~*p*. Nevertheless, this is not a situation in which you are epistemically obligated to believe *p*. If this is right, we have our conclusion.

What is wrong with the idea of positive epistemic obligations? First, it is hard to see what wrong you could be guilty of if you do not bother to draw some of the obvious conclusions from your evidence.[98] If you do not form beliefs concerning the obvious logical consequences of things you believe, what of it? Not forming these beliefs is not like not bothering to lift a finger to save a life that could easily be saved. To be sure, there are those who will not believe what the evidence strongly indicates where it seems the subject is guilty of some epistemic wrong. Think of global warming skeptics. While it is clear these skeptics are guilty of some epistemic wrong, it is not clear that the wrong is simply one of omission. These skeptics typically believe lots of things they should not (e.g., novelists with no scientific credentials are experts because their novels are about scientists, planets other than our own are seeing temperature increases that match our own, that God promised not to kill us [again] with a flood, etc.) or are swayed by non-rational considerations, and these seem to be the sins they commit. If they were not guilty of these sins, they would not be global warming skeptics unless they harbored a more widespread skepticism. If global warming skeptics were simply risk averse and believed next to nothing about the external world, say, they might strike us as odd, but consistent skeptics do not seem to be guilty of any

---

[97] Silins 2005, p. 392.
[98] Goldman 1986; Nelson 2010; and Sutton 2007 agree.

wrong simply by virtue of their risk aversion. Similarly, those who are lazy and lack curiosity do not seem to be guilty of any epistemic wrong for failing to go regularly to a library.

Second, it is hard to imagine what a plausible account of positive epistemic obligation would look like. If there were positive epistemic obligations, there should be some principle that identifies some condition, C, and says that you ought to form C-beliefs. What might that condition be? Suppose the condition is truth. Since we cannot believe all the true propositions, the principle violates OIC. The same problem arises for other principles in the neighborhood (e.g., the principle that says that you ought to believe all the obvious consequences of what you know).

What if instead the principle said that you ought to form as many C-beliefs as you can? This principle cannot violate OIC, but it still seems problematic. Suppose you have two options. You can head to the library to study history or you can head to the laboratory to do chemistry experiments. You can acquire C-beliefs in either place, but they are easier to come by in the library. Thus, the number of C-beliefs you could form in the library is greater than the number of C-beliefs you could form in the lab. Suppose you head to the lab. The beliefs you form constitute knowledge, but forming those beliefs prevents you from forming a greater number of C-beliefs in the library. Thus, you would not satisfy the principle that says that you ought to form as many C-beliefs as you can even if your beliefs constitute knowledge. So, you would violate the principle even if you have knowledge. I think this means the alleged principle is not a principle since you justifiably believe what you come to know in the lab. Acting in such a way as to acquire fewer justified beliefs is not like acting in such a way as to save fewer lives.

Is there still a way to make sense of the notion of positive epistemic obligation? What if we tried to specify positive epistemic obligations as relative to some end of yours (e.g., you should form C-beliefs if this serves some end of yours)? The main problems with this proposal seem to be these. First, it is not clear how this could explain how you could have positive obligations to form C-beliefs because it is not clear that you can have categorical reasons to form beliefs simply because they suit some end if you do not have categorical reasons to pursue this end. Thus, to make this proposal work, we would have to limit the ends to ends you have categorical reason to pursue. I doubt there is a sufficient stock of ends to cover all of the relevant beliefs. We would have to assume that for any belief it would be irrational for you not to hold given your evidence there is some end that you have categorical reason to pursue that requires this belief. I cannot think of any justification for that assumption. Second, if the ends were not epistemic in nature, it is not clear why there would be distinctively epistemic obligations to form the beliefs that suited these non-epistemic ends. If the ends were epistemic in nature and they were ends you had categorical reason to pursue, I suspect that this proposal would suffer the same sorts of problems that arose earlier for the view that said that you ought to form as many C-beliefs as you can. That view identified an epistemic end (i.e., acquiring as many C-beliefs as you can) and that view implied implausibly that you could not justifiably form beliefs that prevented you from forming a greater number of C-beliefs.

If you still think that rationality and justification come to the same thing, consider one more argument:

1. A person from a different culture can rationally judge that the right thing for them to do is to Φ even if by our standards it would be morally abhorrent for them to Φ.
2. If such a person rationally judged that the right thing for them to do is to Φ, assuming that this person is morally conscientious and there is no overriding non-moral reason for them to refrain, it could be rational for them to Φ.
3. (Therefore) It would be rational for this person to Φ.
4. If it is rational for this person to Φ, this person is permitted to Φ.
5. (Therefore) This person is permitted to perform morally abhorrent actions, such as Φ-ing.

The argument's conclusion is absurd. If the agent's actions were truly abhorrent, they could not be justified. So, which premise should we reject? Rational and morally conscientious subjects who were raised in sufficiently different cultures can be rational in believing that they ought to conform to the prevailing moral standards. Some of these standards, however, permit or require agents to perform morally abhorrent actions, so (1) looks unassailable. If we distinguish the rational from the justified, we can say that these subjects act rationally and are morally conscientious without condoning their behavior or (worse) saying that they should have been more wicked on those occasions when they were akratic and failed to act on their own normative judgments. Unless you deny (4), it seems (1) and (2) commit you to a rather crude form of cultural relativism. (Of course, you might prefer condoning cannibalism to drawing a distinction between rationality and justification. Who am I to judge?)

The argument from Deontologism to Internalism fails if it assumes that rational beliefs are justified beliefs. Not every deontological argument for Internalism assumes this. Huemer, for example, says this in support of the idea that deontologists should be internalists:

> In John Steinbeck's novel, *The Pearl*, the protagonist, a fisherman, discovers an enormous pearl. He thinks that the pearl will bring wealth and comfort to his family ... By the end of the novel, it has become clear that the pearl was far more trouble than it was worth. An English teacher of mine once posed the following essay question ... "True or false: When the fisherman discovered the pearl, he should have just thrown it back in the ocean." ... What's the right answer? Well, (*pace* the English teacher) the question was ambiguous. *From the fisherman's point of view* ... he should have done just as he did, try to sell the pearl. On the other hand, from the point of view of the omniscient observer ... the fisherman should have thrown the pearl back into the ocean.[99]

Deontological internalists who pursue this line can say that even if there is a sense in which we 'should' not believe what is not true, this is not the sense of 'should' that matters to epistemology. The sense of 'should' that matters to justification is a subjective one.

There are two problems with this argument. First, it trivializes Internalism. If we stipulate that the sense of 'should' that matters to justification is a subjective one, who could have thought that it was an open question whether justification is an internalist notion? Unless the Internalism–Externalism debate rests on a very silly mistake, the debate cannot be about whether the subjective sense of 'should' involves an objectivist element. Second, the hypothesis that there is a subjective and objective sense of 'should' is implausible.[100] To paraphrase Thomson, if someone came to you and wanted to know what she should do and you answered, "Well, in one sense of 'should' you should do this and in another sense of 'should' you should do that instead" you have not answered her question. She now has to decide whether she should$_{really}$ do the first things or the second. You have refused to answer an unequivocal question. Rather than say that there is a subjective and an objective reading of 'should', it is more fruitful to think of the issue this way. There is one notion of 'should', what you should$_{really}$ do or think in light of all the relevant facts. The question is whether external facts can have some bearing on what you should$_{really}$ do or think, so it is a question about which

<hr/>

[99] Huemer 2001, p. 22.
[100] For discussion, see Thomson 2001, p. 50, and Zimmerman 2008, p. 7.

facts are relevant to the question you have in mind when you wonder what to believe.

Let's look at one final attempt to derive Internalism from Deontologism. Ginet appeals to OIC in arguing that deontologists should be internalists:

> Assuming that S has the concept of justification for being confident that p, S *ought* always to possess or lack confidence that p according to whether or not he has such *justification*. This is simply what is meant by having or lacking justification. But if this is what S ought to do in any possible circumstance, then it is what S *can* do in any possible circumstance. That is, assuming that he has the relevant concepts, S can always tells whether or not he has justification for being confident that p. But this would not be so unless the difference between having such justification and not having it were always directly recognizable to S. And that would not be so if any fact contributing to a set that minimally constitutes S's having such justification were not either directly recognizable to S or entailed by something directly recognizable to S.[101]

Alston offers this reconstruction of Ginet's argument:

1. S ought to withhold belief that p if S lacks justification for p.
2. What S ought to do S can do.
3. (Therefore) S can withhold belief wherever S lacks justification.
4. S has this capacity only if S can tell, with respect to any proposed belief, whether or not S has justification for it.
5. S can always tell this only if justification is always directly recognizable.
6. (Therefore) Justification is always directly recognizable.[102]

Alston objects to (5). Arguing by analogy, he says that since we cannot always directly recognize whether our actions are justified we ought to be skeptical of Ginet's claim that we can always directly recognize whether our beliefs would be justified:

> Consider the ethical analogy that is inevitably suggested by Ginet's argument. There is an exactly parallel argument for the thesis that the justification of actions is always directly recognizable. But that is clearly false ... Would I be morally justified in resigning my professorship as late as April 12 in order to accept a position elsewhere for the following fall? This depends, inter alia, on how much inconvenience this would cause my present department ... There is no guarantee that all these matters are available to me just on simple reflection. Why should we suppose, without being given reasons to do so, that the justification of beliefs is different in this respect?[103]

---

[101] Ginet 1975, p. 35.   [102] Alston 1989, p. 217.   [103] Alston 1989, p. 218.

While I agree with Alston that the justificatory status of your actions does not depend entirely on what you can directly recognize, Ginet has a response available. Suppose Alston knew that the permissibility of resigning depended upon facts that he did not now know and could easily obtain. Suppose he decided to resign without first checking these facts. It seems he would not be justified in acting without first checking these facts. If, however, he did not know that he needed to check these facts before making a decision, it seems plausible that he could justifiably make a decision without first considering these facts. It might turn out that his resignation is regrettable, but many internalists (and externalists) think that facts you are non-culpably ignorant of cannot undermine the justification you had for acting.[104]

Even if Alston is wrong and (5) is correct, Ginet's argument is unsound because of (4). Suppose we sometimes do have the power to withhold judgment as to whether p is true. Whether you have this ability and can exercise it does not depend upon normative facts (e.g., the fact that you do/do not have sufficient justification for believing p). Even if justifying reasons were invisible or inaccessible, their presence or absence would have no bearing on what you are able to do. So, while we can withhold when reasons for withholding are absent, this lends no support to the thought that we can also identify whether we have reasons to withhold.

Ginet either conflates 'ought' implies 'can tell that you ought' with 'ought' implies 'can' or thinks OIT is a consequence of OIC:

OIC: In circumstances under which S ought/ought not Φ, S can Φ and can refrain from Φ-ing.

OIT: In circumstances under which S ought/ought not Φ, S can tell whether or not she ought to Φ.[105]

OIT is false, so either OIC does not entail it or we should reject (2) as well as (4).

Consider three objections to OIT. First, think about cases of conflicting reasons. If there is a case for Φ-ing and against Φ-ing, you might know of the relevant reasons without knowing which reasons are stronger. You should act for the stronger reason. The weight of these reasons does not depend upon your epistemic position. If you were reflective and realized that you were in the kind of situation where you cannot know which

---

[104] See Ginet 1990, p. 97.

[105] Ginet is not alone in building epistemic requirements into OIC. See R. Lemos 1980.

reason is stronger, you are not thereby in a position to see that the reasons for and against Φ-ing apply to *you* with equal force. When in a quandary, you are not free to decide to Φ or refrain from Φ-ing without being in danger of doing wrong. Ignorance of the comparative strength of reasons does not subvert the obligation to act on the stronger, contrary to what OIT implies.

Second, there is a structural problem with OIT. Suppose you have an obligation to remove the left kidney. If so, OIT tells us that you can tell that you have an obligation to remove the left kidney. If your obligation is, inter alia, the obligation to remove the left kidney only if you can tell that this is your obligation, OIT tells us that you are under this obligation only if you can tell that you can tell that your obligation is to remove this left kidney. So, your obligation to remove the left kidney depends upon whether you can know that you know that you know, etc. Assuming, as is plausible, that you can have obligations to Φ where you are not in a position to know that you are in a position to know that you are in a position to know that you ought to Φ, we have to reject OIT.

Third, anyone who accepts OIC ought to reject OIT. Because Zorro is Don Diego, you cannot kill Zorro and spare Don Diego. Thus, if you ought to bring someone the head of Zorro, you ought to bring them the head of Don Diego. If you ought to protect Don Diego from harm, you must protect Zorro. According to OIT, if you ought to protect Don Diego, you can know that you ought to protect Don Diego, which I take involves refraining from killing him. This also involves protecting Zorro. Thus, according to OIT and OIC, nobody can be obliged to protect Don Diego unless they can tell that they ought to protect Zorro. It seems to me that someone can promise to protect Don Diego and thereby be obliged to do so without thereby unmasking Zorro.

We have not seen any compelling reason to think that Internalism follows from Deontologism. Alston was right that our practical obligations do not depend exclusively upon what we share in common with our epistemic counterparts. There is nothing to the concept of obligation that requires us to be internalists about the grounds of obligation. If epistemic obligations are determined exclusively by internal conditions, it must be because there is nothing external to us of epistemic concern or there is something special about epistemic obligations. The former seems implausible since both truth and knowledge seem to be matters of epistemic concern. The latter seems implausible since there seems to be no explanation as to why epistemic obligations would be special in this regard.[106] In later chapters I shall argue that we ought to be externalists because justification is a deontological notion. If we list our epistemic obligations, we will see that epistemic counterparts do not do equally well in meeting them. If internalists disagree, their list is too short.

1.4.10   The new evil demon argument

To my mind, the strongest argument for Internalism is the new evil demon argument.[107] In evaluating the arguments for Internalism we have seen that the arguments support conclusions that the externalists can accept, and that the externalists can say that the internalist arguments have failed to rule out the possibility that justification depends negatively upon external conditions. If the new evil demon argument is sound, the internalists can rule out the possibility that external conditions could undermine justification and shore up many of the arguments we have considered above. If, however, the new evil demon argument fails, I think none of the arguments for Internalism could succeed. Thus, the new evil demon argument plays a crucial role in the case for Internalism.

The new evil demon argument is based on Cohen's objection to a simple version of Reliabilism:

> R: S's belief that *p* is justified iff the processes that produced S's belief are reliable in the kind of environment in which S's belief was formed and there is no reliable process the subject has such that if this process were used as well this would result in the subject's not believing *p*.[108]

Cohen states the objection as follows:

> Imagine that unbeknown to us, our cognitive processes (e.g., perception, memory, inference) are not reliable owing to the machinations of the malevolent demon. It follows on a Reliabilist view that the beliefs generated by those processes are never justified. Is this a tenable result? I maintain that it is not ... [W]e would have

---

[106] Gibbons 2010 argues that because there is no explanation as to why epistemic and non-epistemic obligations differ in terms of whether they depend upon our perspectives or not, we should expect that either they both do or both do not. In Chapter 6, I discuss his view, which I have dubbed 'Unificationism,' the view that there are principled connections between epistemic and practical obligations. He is an internalist about both (in a sense) and I defend Externalism about both. We both agree, for example, that there are no false, justified judgments about what to do.

[107] See Cohen 1984 and Cohen and Lehrer 1983 for early discussions of the problem.

[108] Goldman 1979, p. 20.

every reason for holding our beliefs that we have in the actual world. Moreover since we actually have reason to believe that our cognitive processes are reliable, it follows that in the demon world we would have every reason to believe that our cognitive processes were in fact reliable … It strikes me as clearly false to deny that under these circumstances our beliefs could be justified. If we have every reason to believe e.g., perception, is a reliable process, the mere fact that unbeknown to us it is not reliable should not affect its justification-conferring status.[109]

We can state the argument this way:

1. Our deceived counterparts are no less justified in their beliefs than we are in ours.
2. The processes that produce our deceived counterparts' beliefs are wholly unreliable.
3. (Therefore) Justification does not require reliability.

Wedgwood observes that there is a general lesson here, which is that the demon could arrange things so that one of your counterparts meets none of the external conditions that matter to justification.[110] Intuitively, we want to say that you and your counterparts are equally justified in your beliefs, so we have the makings of an intuitively powerful argument for the supervenience of justification upon the internal.

While you might expect externalists to reject (1), externalists often modify their views to try to accommodate the intuition that underwrites (1). Goldman, for example, modified R and defended Normal Worlds Reliabilism:

R_{NW}: S's belief that p is justified only if the processes that produced S's belief are reliable in normal worlds (i.e., worlds in which our general beliefs about the actual world are true).[111]

Note the crucial difference between R and R_{NW}. According to R, your beliefs are justified only if the processes that produce them are reliable in the world in which your beliefs were produced. According to R_{NW}, justification requires only that the processes that produce your beliefs would be reliable in a normal world. Since perception is reliable in normal worlds, R_{NW} tells us that our counterparts' beliefs are justified even if their beliefs are produced in worlds with Cartesian demons.

There are two problems with Goldman's response to the new evil demon objection. First, since clairvoyance is unreliable in normal worlds,

---

[109] Cohen 1984, p. 281.   [110] Wedgwood 2002a.
[111] Goldman 1986, p. 107.

R_{NW} implies that clairvoyance cannot confer justification in any world. It seems wrong to say that it would be impossible for clairvoyance to generate knowledge much in the way that perception does.[112] Second, it seems R_{NW} implies that we cannot coherently question the justification of those beliefs that fill out our conception of what a normal world is like. Since a normal world is a world in which our general beliefs about the actual world are true, it would trivially be true that these general beliefs are justified. Yet, it seems to be no trivial matter whether these beliefs are justified.[113]

Goldman abandoned Normal Worlds Reliabilism and tried to accommodate the internalist's intuition by distinguishing 'weak' from 'strong' justification:

SJ: S's belief that p is strongly justified only if the processes that produced S's belief are reliable in the kind of environment in which S's belief was formed.

WJ: S's belief that p is weakly justified if and only if S is blameless for believing p but believes p on the basis of a process that is unreliable in the circumstances in which S's belief is produced.[114]

On this proposal, there is a sense in which our beliefs are justified and a sense in which our counterparts' beliefs are justified. BonJour did not think that drawing this distinction would allow Goldman to accommodate the relevant intuition and said, "The question is whether this really accommodates the intuition … which seems to be that the demon world people are at least as justified in their beliefs as we are in ours."[115] As he sees it, it would not be enough to show that there is some sense in which your deceived counterparts are justified unless you could show that they are as justified as we are. On Goldman's account, no belief could be both weakly and strongly justified, and so Goldman cannot account for BonJour's intuition.

We could modify WJ:

WJ*: S's belief that p is weakly justified if and only if S is blameless for believing p.

With this modification, we can say that your beliefs are both strongly justified and weakly* justified. We can say that your deceived counterparts' beliefs are weakly* justified. Thus, we can accommodate BonJour's intuition that there is a sense in which your beliefs and your counterparts'

---

[112] N. Lemos 2007, p. 96.   [113] Peacocke 2004, p. 133.
[114] Goldman 1988, p. 59.   [115] BonJour 2002, p. 248

beliefs are equally justified. The problem with this modification is that it fails to capture the intuition that there is *more* going for your systematically deceived counterparts' beliefs than just that they are blamelessly held.[116] Unfortunately, neither WJ* nor SJ captures this.

Sosa maintains that a justified belief is arrived at through the exercise of one or more intellectual virtues where these are understood as reliable cognitive faculties.[117] He and Comesaña tried to solve the new evil demon problem by distinguishing between two ways we might use the notion of an intellectual virtue in appraising someone's beliefs.[118] We can say that someone's belief is 'apt-justified' only if the belief is acquired through the exercise of an intellectual virtue that is reliable in the circumstances in which that belief is formed. A belief is 'adroit-justified' only if the belief is acquired in an intellectually virtuous way where this is a matter of acquiring beliefs in a way that would be reliable if only the subject did not suffer the misfortune of being in the inhospitable epistemic environment. We cannot say that our deceived counterparts' beliefs are apt-justified, but we can say that they are adroit-justified. Sosa thinks adroit-justification is largely a matter of the coherence of the attitudes of the subject being evaluated. Since our deceived counterparts' beliefs are no less coherent than our own, we can say that there is a sense in which justification requires reliability (this is apt-justification) and a sense in which our deceived counterparts are no less justified than we are (this is adroit-justification). An advantage of this approach is that it does not say that the deceived are justified in their beliefs just in the sense that their beliefs are blamelessly held.

Comesaña and Sosa suggest that we can accommodate the intuitions that underwrite the new evil demon argument by saying that your beliefs are 'justified' because the processes that produced them were reliable in the circumstances in which they were deployed (i.e., they are apt-justified) while your deceived counterparts' beliefs are 'justified' because the processes that produced them would have been reliable in appropriate circumstances even if those are not the circumstances that your counterparts find themselves in (i.e., they are adroit-justified). Context determines which of these notions we are talking about.

Goldman objected to this proposal on the grounds that ordinary folk are not disposed to appraise beliefs relative to different circumstances in the way Comesaña and Sosa suggest.[119] If this is right, their proposal does

---

[116] Audi 1993, p. 28.   [117] Sosa 1991.
[118] Comesaña 2002 and Sosa 2003, pp. 159–61.   [119] Goldman 1993, p. 281.

not accommodate folk intuition. I think Goldman's skepticism is warranted. Consider Norman. Suppose Norman knows *p* because he has a vision and his visions reliably indicate the truth of what they represent. Norman's belief is not adroit-justified because the visions that Norman has do not reliably lead to truth here. Now, consider Norman's epistemic counterpart, a subject that is systematically deceived by a Cartesian demon who induces in Norman's counterpart visions that are subjectively indistinguishable from Norman's visions. Intuitively, Norman's counterpart is just as justified as Norman is in believing what he does. His counterpart's beliefs, however, are neither adroit-justified nor apt-justified. Thus, I doubt that the distinction between apt- and adroit-justification can do justice to the intuitions that underwrite the new evil demon argument.

Majors and Sawyer defend Home Worlds Reliabilism, which says that justification requires reliability in 'home worlds' (i.e., sets of environments relative to which the natures of your intentional contents are individuated):

> R_{HW}: S's belief that *p* is justified only if the processes that produced S's beliefs are reliable in S's home world.[120]

Thanks to Burge's efforts, it is now widely believed that features of the external environment are among the features that determine the contents of our intentional states.[121] In setting up the new evil demon thought experiment, we were supposed to imagine an individual who is mentally just like us living in an environment that is radically different from our own. Because this subject was systematically deceived, she was prevented from causally interacting with her environment in the ways that we do. If being mentally just like us requires causally interacting with environments like ours in the ways that we do, nobody deceived by a demon from birth will be mentally just like us.

Comesaña raises the worry that an appeal to anti-individualism would just push around the bump in the rug because the new evil demon problem reemerges in the form of switching cases.[122] Anti-individualists should say that it is possible for someone who was raised in an environment like yours to fall into the demon's clutches at thirty. She would be deceived for a time without acquiring new concepts. Her beliefs will be unreliably formed (in some sense of 'reliable'), but it seems intuitive to many people that this subject is just as justified in her beliefs as you are

---

[120] Majors and Sawyer 2005, p. 272.   [121] Burge 1979.
[122] Comesaña 2002, p. 264.

in yours. The home worlds reliabilist can say that Comesaña's objection is unwarranted and that their view delivers the right verdict about justification in switching cases. If we want to say that the switched subject's beliefs are just as justified after the switch, the home worlds reliabilist can deliver this verdict. If the subject had been forming her beliefs in the kind of epistemically hospitable environment in which she acquired the concepts that constitute her thought contents, her beliefs would have largely turned out to be correct.

I think the real problem with the view is that it handles Comesaña's worry in this way. If the home worlds reliabilist tries to accommodate internalist intuitions this way, they will abandon the local reliability requirement for justification. The strongest argument for Externalism seems to be the argument from the truth-connection. The guiding thought behind this argument is that nothing could justify your beliefs unless it filled an important epistemic need. It has to establish the kind of connection between your beliefs and the truth that makes your belief better than a lucky guess by making it likely that your beliefs are correct. It is hard to see how anything you have in the demon scenario could meet that need. If the argument from the truth-connection is the fundamental rationale for Externalism, reliabilists should retain something like a local reliability requirement and say that the demon robs you of justification by deceiving you.

There are two further objections to consider. For the sake of completeness, the home worlds reliabilist should say something about the justificatory status of beliefs held by those who are systematically deceived. Even if the contents of their beliefs differ from ours, we can ask whether these subjects are justified in believing what they believe when they take experience at face value. We know the home world reliabilist will say that *if* these subjects have justified beliefs, there must be something they get right reliably. If their beliefs are about matters external to them, however, it is hard to imagine what these beliefs possibly could be. Internalists will say that if these subjects reason well and form beliefs by taking experience at face value, there is something they are justified in believing even if there is nothing that they get right reliably. The home worlds reliabilist cannot accommodate the internalist intuition.

Here is a second objection. Suppose philosophers discovered that some kind of error theory is true. The folk believe in things like rectangular, colored tiles, but philosophers learn that none of the tiles are colored. Should we say that in light of this hard-earned philosophical discovery folk beliefs about the colors of the tiles they see are never justified? I think every reliabilist view implies that these beliefs about color would be unjustified since the error theory implies that these subjects' beliefs are not reliably correct. This seems to clash with the basic intuition that underwrites the new evil demon argument. If your counterpart falls into the demon's clutches, takes her experience at face value, and judges falsely that the book she is holding is rectangular on the basis of hallucination and you judge that the book you see is green, it would be odd to say that your counterpart's judgment about shape is better justified than your judgment about color. Both of you form your beliefs on the basis of experience, and your experiences typically produce knowledge when they concern the perceptible qualities of the objects you see (excepting, of course, the case where you attribute colors to objects).

Rather than modify the reliability requirement and run the risk of losing the support of the argument from the truth-conducive nature of justification, externalists can accommodate the intuition that your systematically deceived counterparts are just as justified as you are by saying that your counterparts are just as *personally* justified in their beliefs as you are. Your counterparts are *personally* justified because they pursue their epistemic ends rationally and responsibly. You do not count as less rational or responsible just because you get things right more often than they do. The externalists should deny that your beliefs and your counterparts' beliefs are equally *doxastically* justified as that depends upon whether you do equally well in meeting your epistemic obligations. At the very least, they can say that it does not follow from the fact that you and your counterparts are equally justified that your beliefs are equally well justified.

To motivate this response, it helps to think about what successful justifications must do. To justify something, you have to defend it from critical evaluation. That which cannot call for a defense cannot call for a justification and that which can be defended is justified. The thesis that justifications are defenses is a thesis about pleas, not properties or statuses. Audi suggests that there is a way of linking claims about pleas to claims about properties or statuses. He says that if something has the property or properties that would constitute a successful justification if cited, it must also have the property of being justified.[123] If we combine the thesis that justifications are defenses with Audi's process-property integration thesis, the result is that something is justified if it has the properties that we could cite in successfully defending it.

---

[123] Audi 1993, p. 305.

If justifications are defenses, a person is justified when they deserve to be excused for what they have done or for what they believe. Suppose the agent Φ'd impermissibly. It might be possible to defend the agent if, say, you can show that the agent deserves to be excused (e.g., she did not know that Φ-ing was impermissible because of some mistaken belief). If she can be excused, she can be defended from criticism. Thus, she can be justified even if she commits some wrong without sufficient justification for doing so. If, however, our agent commits a wrong without sufficient reason, her Φ-ing cannot be defended from criticism, because we criticize actions and attitudes for violating norms. If her Φ-ing cannot be defended, it cannot be justified. Thus, doxastic justification requires more than an excuse and there has to be more to doxastic justification than just personal justification.

Kvanvig and Menzel argue that personal and doxastic justification amount to the same thing.[124] If they are right, I cannot try to accommodate the intuition that underwrites the new evil demon argument by saying that our deceived counterparts are justified while also saying that their beliefs are not justified. They argue that personal justification can be identified with doxastic justification by first offering an account of the truth-conditions of justification ascriptions:

> PJ: 'S is justified in believing p' is true iff S has the property of being an x such that x's believing of p is justified.
>
> DJ: 'S's belief that p is justified' is true iff S's believing of p has the property of being justified.

They observe that if the right-hand side of PJ is true, the right-hand side of DJ cannot be false since it follows from the assumption that S is the individual such that S's believing of p is justified that S's believing of p is justified. If they are right and 'S is justified in believing p' is equivalent to 'S's belief that p is justified,' you cannot say that doxastic justification is an externalist notion if you concede that personal justification is an internalist notion.

If their argument were cogent, it would undermine my strategy for accommodating the intuition that underwrites the new evil demon objection in an externalist framework. I think their argument proves too much. Their argument, if it shows us anything about the logic of justification ascriptions, should show that 'S is F in Φ-ing' is logically equivalent to 'S's Φ-ing is F'. Suppose someone has to choose between two competing

124 See Kvanvig and Menzel 1990.

prima facie duties and makes a reasonable mistake about which of these duties is more stringent. If she fails to do what she has stronger reason to do we still might say that although she made the wrong decision, she is beyond criticism. Nevertheless, it should not follow that her decision is beyond criticism. The problem with their argument is that PJ does not capture the thought that ascriptions of personal justification tell us something about the qualities of the person.

I have not yet shown that doxastic justification is an externalist notion, only argued that this possibility is not ruled out if we concede that personal justification is an internalist notion. Internalists either need to show that doxastic justification reduces to personal justification or show that our systematically deceived counterparts' beliefs are just as justified as our beliefs are by showing that the deceived subjects meet their epistemic obligations just as often as we do. To do this, internalists should tell us what our epistemic obligations are and explain why they cannot include any obligation to refrain from believing what you do not know, what is not true, what is based on non-veridical experience, or to refrain from believing when your evidence is as bad as the evidence you would have if you were systematically deceived. Until they do that, externalists should not worry about the intuitions elicited by the new evil demon thought experiment.

1.5 CONCLUSION

None of the arguments considered here is all that compelling. In the next chapter, we shall consider whether considerations having to do with epistemic value might help us decide whether to think of justification as an internalist notion.

CHAPTER 2

Epistemic value

2.1 INTRODUCTION

It might be better to know the way to San Jose than to just justifiably believe that you should head west on 85, but it is nevertheless better to believe with justification than without it. Not only is it better to believe with justification, it is always good from the epistemic point of view to have justification. In this chapter, I want to see if considerations having to do with epistemic value might help us determine whether justification depends upon anything but conditions internal to us.

Intuitions about epistemic value might play one of two roles in deciding between competing accounts of justification. The first is rather modest. You should hope for a theory of justification that can be brought into reflective equilibrium with your settled judgments and firmly held intuitions. It is a mark against a theory if it clashes with your intuitions whether they concern epistemic value or not. According to Feldman, something of epistemic value is realized whenever you follow your evidence even when following the evidence does not lead you to the truth.[1] If this value provides or indicates a justification, we can show that justification supervenes upon relations between your evidence your beliefs and is independent from any further condition that does not so supervene.

Intuitions about value might also play a more ambitious role in a theory of justification. You have the right to believe whatever you believe with justification. Just as Ethical Consequentialism turns to value theory to explain what makes right acts right, Epistemic Consequentialism (EC) provides an account of epistemic rightness or justification in terms of some prior account of the epistemically good. Justified beliefs, EC says, are beliefs that promote epistemic value. An attractive feature of this approach is that it provides a neat explanation of intuitions about

---

[1] Feldman 2000.

the value of justification. If epistemic goodness makes for rightness, it is easy to see why it is always better to have justified beliefs than unjustified beliefs. According to Moore, "The only possible reason that can justify any action is that by it the greatest possible amount of what is good absolutely should be realized."[2] Perhaps the only possible reason that can justify any belief is that it would realize the greatest possible amount of what is epistemically good.

While I think considerations of epistemic value should play some role in constructing theories of justification, they cannot settle the Internalism–Externalism debate. At best, evaluative considerations can help us fill in some of the details of a theory of justification (e.g., to accommodate intuitions about value, we might say that epistemic responsibility is required for justification). The intuitions that seem to favor Internalism can be accommodated by externalist accounts that incorporate internalist elements. It might seem that consequentialist arguments would support Externalism since it seems quite plausible that external conditions will partially determine whether anything of epistemic value results from believing what you do. Even if this is so, I think the internalists have nothing to fear from such arguments. I shall argue that we should be epistemic non-consequentialists.

2.2 EVIDENTIALISM AND EPISTEMIC VALUE

In this section, I want to look at Feldman's value-driven argument for Evidentialism. He thinks something of epistemic value is realized when you form beliefs that fit the evidence and maintains that this value justifies your beliefs whatever the external conditions and consequences happen to be. On his evidentialist view, epistemic wrongs (EW) and rights (ER) are determined by relations between your beliefs and the evidence, not further relations between your beliefs and the external world:

EW: It is wrong always, everywhere, and for anyone to believe without sufficient evidence.

ER: It is right always, everywhere, and for anyone to believe with sufficient evidence.[3]

---

[2] G. E. Moore 1993, p. 153

[3] This claim is trivial if 'sufficient' is understood as the amount of evidence that ensures that you have the right to believe. It is non-trivial if 'sufficient' is read in some other way. Let's say that a subject has sufficient evidence if the subject has knowledge-level evidence (i.e., she would not fail to have knowledge because of a lack of evidence or because of defeating evidence).

Not all evidentialists are internalists, but Feldman thinks that you and your epistemic counterparts have precisely the same evidence. While I shall argue in the next chapter that it is possible for epistemic counterparts to have different bodies of evidence, I think he is right that there is a value that is realized in virtue of conditions common to you and your epistemic counterparts. He is also right that it is wrong to believe without sufficient evidence. The problem with his view is ER. In later chapters, I shall argue that it is false. Here, I shall argue that it is unmotivated. Since he needs to establish ER to complete his argument for Internalism, his argument for Internalism fails.

Feldman claims, quite plausibly, that, "following one's evidence is the proper way to achieve something of epistemic value."[4] Expanding on this, he says:

> While true beliefs may have considerable instrumental value, a person who irrationally believes a lot of truths is not doing well epistemically. In contrast, a person who forms a lot of rational but false beliefs is doing well epistemically ... Consider a person who is contemplating a particular proposition. To carry out the role of being a believer in a good way, in a way that maximizes epistemic value, the person must adopt a rational attitude towards a proposition ... To achieve epistemic value one must, in each case, follow one's evidence.

We can reconstruct his argument for ER as follows:

1. If you form the belief supported by sufficient evidence, you form the epistemically rational attitude towards a proposition.
2. If you form the epistemically rational attitude towards a proposition, you maximize something of epistemic value.
3. In maximizing something of epistemic value, it is not wrong for you to believe in the way you do.
4. (Therefore) It is never wrong (i.e., always right) to form the belief supported by sufficient evidence.

I think (1) might be true if we think of evidence in the terms that he does. Even if we grant (1), there are two problems with his argument. First, the value of rational belief might be one epistemic value among many, so (2) might be false even if (3) is true. Second, the value of rational belief might call for a response without calling for you to form the belief that fits the evidence, in which case (3) might be false even if (2) is true.

Something of value is realized whenever you believe or act rationally and responsibly, but just as the value of rational and responsible action

---

[4] Feldman 2000, p. 682.

is not the only value in the practical domain, the value of rational belief might not be the only epistemic value. Feldman either has to defend Epistemic Value Monism and show that the value of rational belief is the only epistemic value there is or he faces the selection problem, the problem of explaining why the value of rational belief matters to justification when other values do not.

Feldman might be right that someone who forms lots of irrationally held true beliefs it not doing well epistemically, but that is consistent with the claim that someone is doing better epistemically if, say, they have knowledge or true, rational beliefs than if they have rational, false beliefs.[5] Thus, he has not ruled out Epistemic Value Pluralism. Nor should he try. It would be odd to say that it matters how you pursue your epistemic ends if achieving your epistemic ends has no value at all. As Aristotle observed, "Where there are ends apart from the actions, it is the nature of the products to be better than the activities."[6] Since the goal of doxastic deliberation is to believe correctly, not just establish some proper fit between belief and evidence, Feldman should acknowledge that rationally held true belief has a value over and above that of rational, false belief.

Since Epistemic Value Monism seems unsustainable, Feldman has to deal with the selection problem and explain why the value of rational belief matters to justification when other values do not. He might say that intuitions about error show that any value realized by conditions external to us does not matter to justification, but we have already seen that these intuitions should not be taken to show that justification does not depend upon these external conditions. Instead, he could try to show that the value of rational belief calls for belief whereas the other epistemic values call for some other sort of response. I shall argue below that this cannot solve the selection problem because the value of rational belief does not call for us to believe. At the very least, it does *not* provide overriding

---

[5] There is a difference between so-and-so doing well epistemically and so-and-so making things better epistemically. It might be that Feldman's idea is that rational belief is the only value that matters to an individual's epistemic well-being, not that rational belief is the only value that matters when it comes to determining the total epistemic value contained in a world. As someone nearly convinced of hedonism, I certainly cannot fault Feldman for being attracted to a view on which the value atoms that contribute to well-being are constituted by something internal to us. (Value atoms are states of affairs that are basically good [i.e., their values are not determined by the values of their parts and these atoms determine all the value there is]. See Bradley 2009, p. 6.) In explaining why we should reject EC, I will explain why Internalism about the atoms of epistemic value that determine an individual's epistemic well-being does not support Internalism about the justification of belief.

[6] Aristotle 2009, p. 3.

reason to believe when there are further reasons not to believe. This should be clear once we see why (3) is unmotivated.

Let's consider (3). We can see why (3) is problematic when we consider how Feldman might respond to the following argument against ER:

5. If you believe on sufficient evidence that you should Φ, you rationally believe you should Φ.
6. If you rationally believe this proposition, you maximize something of epistemic value.
7. If maximizing something of epistemic value justified believing you should Φ, it would justify Φ-ing in accordance with your belief.
8. You can have sufficient evidence to believe you should Φ even if you are obligated to refrain from Φ-ing.
9. (Therefore) It does not follow from the fact that you have sufficient evidence to believe that you should Φ that you justifiably believe you should Φ.

I shall later argue that you cannot be obligated to refrain from Φ-ing if you justifiably believe you should Φ and also that the deontic status of your actions does not supervene upon your evidence. If these views are correct, Feldman is wrong that the factors that determine whether it is permissible for you to believe something supervene upon your evidence. Rather than defend the premises in my argument for (9), I want to see what Feldman can say in response. He has to deny (9), so he has to reject one of the premises in my argument.

Feldman rejects (7).[7] In this passage, he explains why he accepts (8):

With regard to ethical justification, it is clear that there are cases in which what is moderately subjectively justified differs from what is objectively justified. Such cases occur when a person has reasonable but incorrect beliefs about what action is morally best. One may have reasonable but incorrect beliefs about what the consequences of an action will be or about the values of correctly identified consequences. In such cases, one may have a good reason to believe that an action is best when it actually is not best. Thus, there can be actions that are subjectively justified, but are not objectively justified.[8]

Here he explains why he thinks subjects with the same evidence have the same epistemic obligations even if their practical obligations differ:

[A]ll subjectively justified beliefs are also objectively justified. Whenever one is subjectively justified in believing *p*, then one is objectively justified in believing

---

[7] He did so in Feldman 1988a. In conversation, he suggested that he might now reject (8).
[8] Feldman 1988a, p. 415.

that one's reasons for believing *p* are good ones. But then the evidence for this [second-order] belief together with the reasons for thinking that those are good reasons constitute an objectively good reason for believing *p*. Hence … moderate subjective justification implies objective justification.[9]

Feldman's argument against (7) rests on the thought that reasons to believe that your reasons for belief are good are themselves good reasons to believe, but they are not thereby reasons to act on your beliefs.[10] Does this show that (7) is false?

No. Even if reasons to believe that you have reasons to believe *p* are reasons to believe *p*, (7) could still be true. Feldman accepts (8), so he accepts that you can have sufficient evidence to believe you ought to Φ even if you are obligated to refrain from Φ-ing. So, for example, he might say that the fact that this box contains a lovely gift is a reason to give it to a friend but that you have overriding reason not to give it to your friend if it contains a bomb (even if you know nothing about the bomb). We can say something similar for beliefs, such as the belief that you have sufficient reason to give your friend the present. Feldman says that this belief is false because the reasons you are aware of do not override the reasons not to give your friend the package. So, why not say that something similar can happen in the epistemic case? Even if reasons to believe are reasons to believe, the crucial question is whether there are further reasons that do not supervene upon your evidence *not* to believe that are analogous to the reasons that Feldman thinks you have not to give your friend the package. Since Feldman's argument gives us no reason to reject this possibility and this is the view you would accept if you accepted (7) and (8), Feldman's argument gives us no reason to reject (7).

To deal with this problem Feldman has to show that the external facts you are non-culpably ignorant of can constitute a decisive case against Φ-ing without constituting a decisive case against judging that you should Φ. Myself, I think that the reasons that bear on whether to Φ bear on whether to intend to Φ and that the reasons that speak against intending to Φ and against Φ-ing would bear on whether to judge that you should Φ. The reader might have her own reasons for rejecting this view, but if you reject this view, you should see that Feldman's intuitive motivation for (3) is problematic.

---

[9] Feldman 1988a, p. 416.
[10] For an argument against Feldman's claim that evidence of evidence is evidence, see Fitelson in press.

The only reason Feldman provides for accepting (3) and thinking that external facts the subject is non-culpably ignorant of have no bearing on epistemic justification is that something of epistemic value is realized whenever certain internal facts obtain (i.e., that the subject follows the evidence and forms a rational belief). This intuition seems right, but it does not show what Feldman needs it to. Focus on the moral case. If you give your friend a present without knowing that the package containing your present contains a bomb, your action still has some sort of value. Your action was rational, there might have been a *pro tanto* reason to give your friend the package, and your action might have had moral worth, but Feldman recognizes that whatever value your action had, it did not justify giving your friend the bomb that killed him. So, while he thinks that the value that is realized by rational action and morally worthy action does not justify action when there are reasons you are unaware of not to act, he thinks that the value that is realized by rational belief justifies believing even if there are reasons you are unaware of not to hold this belief. Naturally, we want to know why the value of rationality justifies in the epistemic case when it does not justify in the practical case. Until we have an answer to that question, we have reason to doubt (3).

I want to close this section by briefly explaining why I doubt that the value of rational belief is the only value that matters to justification. We have already seen that the rational is not the mark of the permissible. If this is correct, it tells us something about the normativity of rationality.[11] If rationality is normative, it is not because the rational determines what is permissible or required. If rationality is normative, it is only so in a very weak sense (e.g., perhaps there is some *pro tanto* reason not to act or believe in irrational ways). If this is all that the normativity of rationality comes to, then the value of rational belief or action either does not call for us to act or believe in ways that would be rational or provides only defeasible reasons to do so.

Rational belief might have a kind of epistemic value, but the proper response to that value might not be to form rational beliefs. While every value calls for a response, they do not call for the same response. Some values call for promotion and thereby give us defeasible reason to promote

---

[11] Broome 1999 suggested that rational requirements could be understood as wide-scope requirements on combinations of attitudes that one 'ought' or 'ought not' have, which suggests that there are reasons to refrain from certain combinations of irrational attitudes and reasons to maintain rational combinations of attitudes. He does not think, however, that there are reasons to satisfy these rational requirements. For discussion of whether there are reasons to satisfy the requirements of rationality, see Kolodny 2005 and Way 2009.

them. Others should be honored, respected, or admired and give us defeasible reasons to honor, respect, and admire things that have that value.[12] If the value of rational belief called for promotion, it would give us a *pro tanto* reason to form rational beliefs much in the way that the value of pleasure gives us a *pro tanto* reason to perform acts that are pleasurable. This rings false. Failing to form beliefs that would be rational to form is not like failing to perform acts of beneficence. If so, they do not give us defeasible reasons to believe.

I think that when you follow the evidence and rationally come to believe *p*, the value of this belief is analogous to the value an action has when it is done responsibly and from a sense of duty. That is to say, the value is analogous to moral worth. When you act responsibly and from a sense of duty, your actions have moral worth. They are a credit to you. If you form beliefs by following the evidence, your beliefs have epistemic worth and so they are a credit to you. If something has moral or epistemic worth, it is worthy of admiration and respect because it is the result of responsible agency. If this is right, the value of rational belief could be a genuine epistemic value even if it did not provide sufficient justification for your beliefs. It is not the value of moral worth that determines what we are permitted to do since actions can have moral worth even if they were a breach of duty. Similarly, the value of epistemic worth does not tell us what to believe. At most, we should not form beliefs that lack epistemic worth. If this is correct, there might be a value-driven argument for EW, but not for ER. Since Feldman cannot establish that justification supervenes upon your evidence until he establishes that ER is true, his argument for Internalism is inconclusive.

2.3 EPISTEMIC CONSEQUENTIALISM

In this section, I want to see if it is possible to argue for Externalism on consequentialist grounds. We will focus on the epistemic analogues of Act- and Rule-Consequentialism, Epistemic Belief-Consequentialism and Epistemic Rule-Consequentialism:

EBC: There is sufficient justification for you to believe *p* if there is no alternative to believing *p* that would result in a greater amount of epistemic value.

ERC: There is sufficient justification for you to believe *p* if the amount of epistemic value that results from conforming to some set of rules

---

[12] For discussion, see Baron 1995 and Swanton 2003.

that permits believing *p* is at least as good as the amount of epistemic value that would result from conforming to a set of rules that prohibits believing *p*.

Given some plausible assumptions about the bearers of epistemic value (e.g., that true belief has intrinsic value), some external conditions will be among those that determine whether your beliefs promote something of epistemic value. So, there seem to be prima facie plausible arguments from ERC and EBC to Externalism. The question I want to consider is whether EC is a viable approach to epistemic justification.

2.3.1 *Epistemic Rule-Consequentialism versus Pluralist Epistemic Non-Consequentialism*

In *Epistemology and Cognition*, Goldman says that your beliefs are justified if formed in conformity with the right rules:

> I approach justification in terms of a rule framework. This is warranted by purely semantic connotations. Calling a belief justified implies that it is a proper doxastic attitude, one to which the cognizer has an epistemic right or entitlement. These notions have a strong deontic flavor … They are naturally captured in the language of "permission" and "prohibition", which readily invite the rule formulation.[13]

He also says that justification depends upon the reliability of the processes that produce your beliefs.[14] His account is modeled on Rule-Consequentialism in ethics. ERC tells you how to distinguish genuine epistemic rules (i.e., J-rules) from spurious ones. The J-rules, he says, reliably lead to truth. Spurious rules are spurious because little epistemic good comes of following them.

   To defend ERC, Goldman has to address two kinds of critic. The first objects to the very idea of providing a value-theoretic justification for the J-rules. Non-consequentialists might say that J-rules stand on their own feet and do not need any value-theoretic justification. The second kind of critic agrees with Goldman that justification should be understood in terms of the promotion of epistemic value, but denies that we need a

---

[13] Goldman 1986, p. 59.
[14] This is subject to an important proviso. Goldman holds that features of your cognitive state can undermine your justification. While it makes sense to make such provisos, you might wonder if the addition of this qualification makes sense from a consequentialist perspective. I suspect that Goldman never intended to defend a pure form of EC. My goal is to see whether anyone could build on Goldman's suggestions and defend a pure version of ERC and use it to defend Externalism, not to attack Goldman's Reliabilism.

plurality of J-rules. Specifically, she would say that nothing could justify following a rule on those occasions where doing so stands in the way of maximizing epistemic value.

Do J-rules need any justification? Some say that the search for a value-theoretic justification is misguided and defend as an alternative Pluralist Epistemic Non-Consequentialism (PENC). This view is modeled on Ross' pluralist account of right action.[15] PENC states that there is a plurality of J-rules and each rule identifies some *pro tanto* reason for belief. Beliefs formed in accordance with these rules are justified if nothing defeats the justification provided by *pro tanto* reasons associated with the J-rules. As Pollock might have put it, ERC and PENC are both consistent with Belief Internalism. ERC is a version of Norm Externalism, but PENC is not.

Since the difference between these views has to do with the justification of J-rules, not their formulation, ERC and PENC might agree that these are J-rules:

PER: If it perceptually seems to you as if some available object *a* is *F* and this seeming causes or sustains in the normal way your belief that *a* is *F*, your belief that *a* is *F* is prima facie justified.

MEM: If you seem to remember that *p* and this causes or sustains in the normal way your belief that *p* is true, your belief that *p* is true is prima facie justified.

INT: If it introspectively seems to you that *p* and this causes or sustains in the normal way your belief that *p* is true, your belief that *p* is true is prima facie justified.[16]

In fact, ERC and PENC might agree on all of the J-rules. If so, ERC would seem to enjoy an important explanatory advantage over PENC. Whereas PENC offers an unconnected heap of J-rules, ERC offers a unifying explanation as to why these rules confer justification and others do not. Epistemic non-consequentialists should either try to show that ERC recognizes the wrong rules or try to show that there is something wrong with the consequentialist justification of J-rules.

Those who defend PENC have objected to ERC on the grounds that the J-rules it recognizes would confer justification even if they did not reliably lead to the truth. This, they say, is what intuitions about cases of deception show. Subjects that form beliefs that fit experience and apparent memory seem justified in their beliefs even if these apparent memories

---

[15] Graham 2010 and Nelson 2002.
[16] Graham 2010 offers these as examples of J-rules.

and experiences are produced by a Cartesian demon bent on deceiving them at every turn. Not only is the reliability of our J-rules a contingent feature of these rules, they say we can know *a priori* that rules such as MEM and PER are J-rules. We know *a priori*, for example, that these rules will confer justification whether they reliably lead to truth or not. Thus, knowing that these rules are J-rules does not depend upon any empirical knowledge of the circumstances under which they were followed. ERC cannot explain the modal or epistemic status of J-rules, so we have good reason to prefer PENC to ERC.[17]

This objection has no more force than the new evil demon objection we considered earlier. While it might be necessarily true that *you* are justified in forming beliefs in response to (apparent) perceptual experiences, it does not follow that your *beliefs* are justified by these experiences. So, even if we know *a priori* that experiences provide personal justification, this does not show that we can know *a priori* that PER is a J-rule. J-rules tell us whether there is sufficient justification for belief, not whether a person would be justified in her beliefs.[18]

At this point the epistemic rule-consequentialists should go on the offensive. PENC postulates a heap of unconnected epistemic rules and denies that there is a unifying explanation that could help us see why these rules in particular are J-rules.[19] The problem with PENC is not Pluralism, per se. There is a sound rationale for Ethical Pluralism. The trouble is that the rationale for Ethical Pluralism does not support Pluralism about J-rules. Recall Ross' reasons for rejecting Monism in ethics:

> [T]he theory of 'ideal utilitarianism' ... seems to simplify unduly our relations to our fellows. It says, in effect, that the only morally significant relation in which my neighbors stand to me is that of being possible beneficiaries by my actions. They do stand in this relation to me, and this relation is morally significant. But they may also stand to me in the relation of a promisee to a promiser, of friend to friend, of fellow countryman to fellow countryman, and the like; and each of these relations is the foundation of a *prima facie* duty.[20]

Examples should help illustrate Ross' point. Suppose that you could feed your child or an equally hungry stranger, but there is not enough food

---

[17] Graham 2010 and Nelson 2002 argue that the modal and epistemic statuses of J-rules create problems for ERC.

[18] How can we know *a priori* that experience is sufficient for personal justification? Perhaps because we know *a priori* that it would make sense to form beliefs in response to these experiences given the aim of believing only what is true.

[19] For a discussion of this objection to Ross' Pluralism, see McNaughton 1996.

[20] Ross 1930, p. 19.

for both. If we can identify a morally significant relation between you and your child that does not hold between you and the stranger, we can explain why it would be right to help your child first (e.g., you created your child without her consent thereby putting her in need of assistance and this comes with special responsibilities).[21] If, however, sixteen hungry strangers came along, it might be wrong to feed your child rather than the strangers. Notice that you stand in the same morally significant relations to your child in these two cases and the strangers in these two cases. In the first case, the relation between you and your child determines what your obligation is. In the second, the relation between you and those you have no prior relation to determines what your obligation is. Thus, there is no single morally significant relation that determines in every case what your obligation is, so Monism is false.

Ross' rationale for Ethical Pluralism does not support Epistemic Pluralism. Perceptual experience presumably justifies belief when it does because it puts you in the right relation to truth (whatever that relation is). If experience does not put you in this relation to truth, it is not as if memory or testimony can justify belief by putting you in the right relation to something other than truth. If you push the analogy between Pluralism in ethics and epistemology, you should expect that there would be a plurality of epistemically significant relations that could justify belief, not just the right relation to truth (whatever that relation is). Yet, this is not what we find. In ethics, there is nothing further that right-making relations have in common apart from the fact that they can make right acts right. In epistemology, there is a single thing that all justified beliefs share in common by virtue of which they are justified, which is that they stand in the right relation to truth (whatever that relation is).

There is a further reason to think Ross would rightly reject PENC. He thought that there had to be a plurality of right-making relations because you can rationally regret doing what you know is right. In the case of conflicting moral reasons, the reasons you judge to be defeated typically continue to exert some force:

If, as almost all moralists except Kant are agreed, and as most plain men think, it is sometimes right to tell a lie or to break a promise, it must be maintained that there is a difference between prima facie duty and actual or absolute duty.

---

[21] If you think having children does not call for a justification, you might have some other story to tell about why the morally significant relations between you and your children are not like the morally significant relations between you and those who would benefit from your assistance. The force of the example does not depend upon recognizing that it is prima facie wrong to have children by virtue of the lifetime of hardship you cause them to suffer.

When we think ourselves justified in breaking ... a promise in order to relieve someone's distress, we do not for a moment cease to recognize a prima facie duty to keep our promise, and this leads us to feel, not indeed shame or repentance, but certainly compunction for behaving as we do; we recognize, further, that it is our duty to make up somehow to the promisee for the breaking of the promise.[22]

A mark of genuine pluralism is the moral residue that rationalizes the regret you feel in acting rightly while acting against a defeated reason.[23] To see why this phenomenon supports Pluralism, consider two cases. In the first, there is a conflict between the demands of beneficence and fidelity. In the second, you are offered the choice between taking five dollars and taking ten. If you take the ten, there is nothing to regret because whatever good there is in the neglected option is wholly contained in the option you picked. In the first case, however, whether you decide to help or decide to refrain, there is something to regret. You either regret having had to break a confidence or you regret that you missed the opportunity to help another. The regret is an indication that there is some good contained in the neglected option that is not contained in the option you picked.

PENC denies that there is some unifying reason that explains why J-rules have their status. If there is no unifying rationale for these rules, then the reasons associated with these rules would be grounded in a plurality of deontically relevant features of belief. Suppose two reasons came into conflict (e.g., experience suggests *p* and memory suggests you should not trust your lying eyes). When these perceptual and memorial reasons came into conflict, we should regret that we could not believe in all of the ways these reasons would have us believe because something of value is contained in the defeated reason that we acted against. As Williams observed, this is not what happens when we face conflicting epistemic reasons.[24] If we believe on one of these reasons, we take the neglected reasons to be misleading. They lose their rational force and there is nothing to regret. In believing on one reason, we take that reason to be genuine because we take it to show that what we believe is true. Once we take ourselves to see that a proposition is true, belief in the proposition's negation seems to have nothing going for it. Perhaps Adler puts it best:

What it is best to do is that act which is better than all the alternatives on the available reasons. But what one can or should believe is only what is genuinely

[22] Ross 1930, p. 28.   [23] For helpful discussion, see Stocker 1990.
[24] Williams 1965, p. 107.

worthy of belief, not what is currently better than the alternatives (think here of the difference between poker, where the best hand wins, and rummy, where only the right or proper hand can win).[25]

None of the objections to ERC points to any serious defect in the view. In fact, ERC compares quite favorably to one of its main non-consequentialist rivals.

2.3.2 *The case for Epistemic Non-Consequentialism*

Although ERC might compare favorably to some of its rivals, it would be a mistake to defend a consequentialist approach to epistemic justification. In this section, I shall argue that we ought to reject EC in all of its forms.

According to ERC, the total epistemic value that would result from following a rule (or a system of rules that includes this rule) determines whether it is a J-rule. ERC does not tell us which rules are J-rules because it does not tell us how to compare the values of the possible outcomes of following epistemic rules. To do that, Goldman offers us this account of epistemic value:

> Veritism: True beliefs are intrinsically epistemically good, false beliefs are intrinsically epistemically bad, and these are the only values that matter to inquiry.[26]

In addition, we need to know the absolute value of true and false belief. Goldman suggests that true and false beliefs have the same absolute value, which means that the total value that results from forming no beliefs is equal to that of forming an equal number of true and false beliefs.[27] With these three assumptions in place, we can determine which rules are J-rules.

One apparent advantage ERC has over EBC is that EBC seems to clash with intuition. For example, some have suggested that EBC undermines the distinction between truth and justification, classifying all true beliefs as justified and all false beliefs as unjustified.[28] The idea is simple enough. Every true belief has intrinsic value, so if we evaluate beliefs directly, it seems to be justified. Every false belief has intrinsic disvalue, so if we evaluate beliefs directly, it seems to be unjustified. ERC does not undermine the distinction between justification and truth because it evaluates beliefs indirectly by looking at the consequences of following rules that

---

[25] Adler 2002b, p. 4.   [26] See Goldman and Olsson 2009, p. 24.
[27] Goldman 1999b, p. 89.   [28] Maitzen 1995.

permit forming these beliefs. If the result of following some rule is sufficiently good, ERC seems to say that your belief is justified even if nothing
good comes from forming that belief. ERC can maintain the distinction between justified and true belief because of its two-level structure.
Considerations having to do with value determine which rules are J-rules
and the rules, not the values, determine which beliefs are justified. The
relation between the good and the right is indirect.

ERC might do a better job accommodating intuition than EBC, but I
do not think it makes good theoretical sense. Consider Rawls' example:

> In a game of baseball if a batter were to ask "Can I have four strikes?" it would
> be assumed that he was asking what the rule was; and if, when told what the rule
> was, he were to say that he meant that on this occasion he thought it would be
> best on the whole for him to have four strikes rather than three, this would be
> most kindly taken as a joke.[29]

Suppose that some value (e.g., the enjoyment of the spectators) determined whether some rule would be recognized as a rule of baseball. The
rulebook determines whether an umpire's call is correct. The correctness
of the call does not depend upon whether the call promotes the value that
was used to select the rules. ERC is supposed to say that it is possible to
justifiably believe *p* without believing something true much in the way
that it is possible to make the correct call even if spectators would have
enjoyed the game more if the umpire made a different call. There is an
important difference between the two cases. Even if someone follows the
J-rules in forming her beliefs and believes a false proposition, there is still
a perfectly good sense in which her belief is mistaken. Compare this to
the umpire's call. Even if the call upsets the fans, the call is correct if the
umpire calls the batter out after correctly calling a third strike.

The problem is that rule-consequentialists say that a suboptimal action
is not mistaken in any sense so long as it conforms to the relevant rules.
The value-theoretic considerations are screened off and have no bearing
on whether the agent acted correctly or not. If we model ERC on Rule-
Consequentialism in ethics, the result should be a view on which beliefs
formed in conformity to the J-rules are not mistaken in any sense. This
is a mistake. It is essential to the state of belief that a belief is mistaken
iff it is false. Someone could say in response that there is a sense in which
false beliefs formed in accordance with J-rules are 'mistaken' and another
sense in which they are not, but this misses the point. There is *no* sense

---

[29] Rawls 1955, p. 26.

in which the umpire's call is mistaken. If the analogy holds up, there is no sense in which beliefs formed in accordance with the J-rules will be mistaken. The problem arises for ERC because of its two-level structure. While it seems ERC needs this two-level structure to maintain the distinction between justification and truth, it is precisely because it has this structure that it conflicts with the platitude that beliefs are correct iff they are true.

There is another problem with ERC, which has to do with the way that epistemic rule-consequentialists conceive of the relation between the right and the good. It is a familiar fact about practical reasoning that if there is equally good reason to pursue any of the available options you cannot act wrongly in picking between them. It is a familiar fact about theoretical reasoning that if there is equally good evidence for believing p and $\neg p$ there is a conclusive reason to refrain from believing both propositions. Unless we modify the view, ERC implies that it is permissible to believe p when you have equally good evidence for p and for $\neg p$.

To see this, suppose the total epistemic value that would result from following R1 is the same as the value that would result from following R2. Because ERC is a consequentialist view, it cannot say that R1 and R2 differ in their deontic properties. Thus, ERC implies that it is permissible to form beliefs in accordance with R1 iff it is permissible to form beliefs in accordance with R2.[30] Goldman says that there are no positive epistemic duties, and I think he is right.[31] On his view, J-rules tell us what we are permitted to believe. Suppose R1 forbids forming beliefs about the external world. Suppose R2 permits forming beliefs about the external world and you know that following it would lead to an equal number of true and false beliefs. If there are no positive epistemic duties, you are permitted to form beliefs in accordance with R1. If so, ERC implies that you are permitted to follow R2. (If you form an equal number of true and false beliefs about some subject matter, you are just as well off as you would be forming no beliefs at all about this subject matter given the value theory introduced earlier.) Of course, if you were to follow R2 knowing that there is an equal chance of forming a true belief or a false one, you would know that your evidence for believing p is just as good as your evidence for believing $\neg p$. ERC implies that the beliefs formed in accordance with R2 would be justified. Since you should reject any theory that implies that you can justifiably believe p when your evidence supports p and $\neg p$

---

[30] If these rules justify forming incompatible beliefs, ERC might tell you not to follow both rules. Assume that these rules do not tell you to form incompatible beliefs.

[31] Goldman 1986, p. 77.

equally well, you should reject any theory that says that you can justifiably believe p if you follow a rule that you know is as likely to lead to truth as it is to falsity.[32]

My initial objection to ERC rested on the assumption that there are no positive epistemic obligations and that the absolute values of true belief and of false belief are the same. We can modify these assumptions, but the underlying problems remain. Consider the first assumption, that there are no positive epistemic duties. Consequentialists are not terribly keen on the distinction between doing and allowing, so you might think that ERC ought to recognize positive epistemic obligations.[33] If you are obligated to maximize epistemic value and there is a rule you could follow in forming beliefs about the external world that would result in more true beliefs than false, ERC would say that neither R1 nor R2 is a J-rule.

This response does not get to the root of the problem. Consider R3, a rule that says that you should believe that the number of Fs is odd if you know the number of Fs is finite but too large to count. If your obligation is to follow the rules that would maximize epistemic value, this rule seems to fit the bill. Since you cannot justifiably believe that the number of ravens is odd, we know R3 is not a genuine epistemic rule. As such, recognizing positive epistemic obligations will not solve the problem ERC faces.

A different strategy would be to modify the value theory. We could say that the absolute value of false belief is greater than that of true belief. If so, no rule that leads you to form an equal number of true and false beliefs could be a J-rule since there will always be an alternative rule that would prohibit forming these beliefs and lead you to bring about better overall epistemic outcomes.

Unfortunately, modifying the value theory will not save ERC. Consider R4, a rule that says that you may believe that the number of Fs is not divisible by three without remainder if the number of Fs is known to be finite and too large to count. ERC with its modified value theory cannot tell us whether R4 is a J-rule until it tells us something about the magnitude of the difference in absolute value of true and false belief. Intuitively, R4 does not confer justification, so we need a value theory that tells as

---

[32] See DePaul 2004 for a discussion of this problem.
[33] If ERC posits positive epistemic obligations, I would add this to the list of problems with ERC. It is hard to see how we could justify the epistemic analogue of the doing/allowing distinction (the believing/refraining distinction?) on value-theoretic grounds, so I suspect that this is a problem for ERC. It also seems that the problem generalizes to all forms of EC, so we have the beginnings of another argument against EC here.

much. The value theory has to say that the difference in the magnitude of the absolute value of true and false belief is great enough that you are better off believing nothing than believing in accordance with R4.

If we adjust the value theory to give us the result we want, when can we stop? Consider R5. It tells us that if the number of Fs is finite but too large to count, we should believe that the number is composite. Intuitively, you cannot justifiably believe that the number of crows is composite. So, ERC with its modified value theory has to say that the difference in the positive and negative value of true and false belief is great enough to warrant saying this. In turn, this means that the only genuine J-rules would be rules that led to better outcomes than a rule that permits believing that the number of crows is composite. Think about how unlikely it is that the number of crows is prime. If beliefs based on perceptual experience are justified, ERC has to say that this is only because the ratio of true to false beliefs that result from forming beliefs in response to perceptual experience is greater than the ratio of true to false beliefs that result from following R5. If, as seems plausible from the armchair, taking apparent perceptual experience at face value does not lead to the truth more often than following R5, it seems that the value theory ERC needs to explain why R5 not being a genuine J-rule commits us to a kind of skeptical view on which our perceptual beliefs are not justified.

We can use lottery cases to drive the point home. R6 permits you to believe a ticket to be a loser on purely statistical grounds. Intuitively, R6 does not confer justification, not even if it leads to truth more often than rules that permit you to take experience at face value. Yet, as a number of commentators have noted, it seems intuitively right to believe what you seem to see and wrong to believe that a lottery ticket is a loser even if the statistical odds are such that you have a better chance of being right forming beliefs about lottery tickets.[34] This point has been contested, but notice that it is commonly held that you could not know that a ticket will lose without insider information. You cannot justifiably believe what you know you cannot know. If so, this does spell trouble for ERC. ERC can only say that R6 fails to confer justification and say that PER confers justification if perceptual experience is more reliable than lottery losses.

There is one final objection to ERC to consider, one inspired by Maitzen's objection to EC. It might seem that the evaluative consequences of ERC and EBC differ because ERC evaluates beliefs indirectly and EBC evaluates them individually to see if each belief would maximize

---

[34] See Nelkin 2000 for discussion.

epistemic value. Maitzen says that this is a mistake. These views cannot deliver different verdicts because ERC says (roughly) that the rules that justify belief are the rules that lead to the best epistemic outcomes and the rule that leads to the best epistemic outcome is the rule EBC identifies as the fundamental epistemic rule. Thus, ERC and EBC are extensionally equivalent and we should reject both views:

> If the nominal aim is the reason for having, or pursuing, justification, then it ought to follow that beliefs are justified insofar as they serve the nominal aim and unjustified insofar as they do not. But this consequence gives rise to an obvious problem. If justification is essentially a matter of serving the nominal aim [i.e., to maximize true belief and minimize false belief], then it seems we would evaluate no true belief as unjustified and no false belief as justified ... The reason is straightforward. If one seeks, above all else, to maximize the number of true (and minimize the number of false) beliefs in one's (presumably large) stock of beliefs, then adding one more true belief surely counts as serving that goal, while adding a false belief surely counts as disserving it.[35]

The upshot is supposed to be that because EBC undermines the distinction between justification and truth, so does ERC.

Maitzen's objection to ERC is a version of Lyons' collapse objection to Rule-Consequentialism.[36] Since it is controversial whether Rule-Consequentialism collapses into Act-Consequentialism, it is controversial whether ERC would undermine the distinction between justification and truth if EBC did.[37] Rather than get bogged down in a discussion of the coherence of Indirect Consequentialism, I shall argue that Maitzen's objection rests on a mistake. Once we see what it is, we can see why we should reject EC.

Veritism says false beliefs have some negative epistemic value, true beliefs have some positive epistemic value, and these are the values that matter to justification. Consequentialism says that the deontic status of an action or an attitude depends upon whether the total value realized when the action is performed or the attitude is formed is at least as great as the total value that could be realized without the action or attitude.[38] If it is, it is justified. If it is not, it is not. The crucial point is that consequentialists endorse the 'totalizing assumption,' the assumption that total intrinsic value determines deontic status. There is a straightforward rationale for the totalizing assumption. To reject this assumption is to say that it is right to prefer an acknowledged lesser good to a greater one.

---

[35] Maitzen 1995, p. 870.   [36] Lyons 1965.
[37] See Hooker 2000, pp. 93–9.   [38] Carlson 1995, p. 10.

To see why this matters, suppose Coop believes, say, that Audrey's intentions are good. Veritism says that *part* of the total value realized by the formation of this belief is determined by this belief's truth-value because it says that true beliefs are intrinsically valuable and false beliefs are intrinsically disvaluable. The *total* value that results will also include the intrinsic value contained in the consequences, and the deontic status will depend upon how the total value of believing that Audrey's intentions are good compares to the total value of not forming this belief. Justification collapses into truth only if it is necessarily the case that whenever you form a true belief, the total resulting epistemic value is greater than the value that would have resulted if you did not form that belief. This is not always the case.

True beliefs and false beliefs have both intrinsic and instrumental epistemic value.[39] Beliefs come with causal consequences and opportunity costs. This is why EBC does *not* imply that your beliefs are justified iff they are true. If, as a consequence of believing p, you come to believe a number of falsehoods you would not have believed otherwise, it could be that it would be better not to believe p than to believe p even if we suppose that p is true. EBC would thus say that this is a case of true, unjustified belief. If, as a consequence of believing correctly that p, you fail to believe a number of truths you would have seen were true otherwise, we have another case of true, unjustified belief. If, say, you were to believe q and q happened to be false, you might, as a consequence of believing this falsehood, believe a number of truths that you would not have believed otherwise or avoid believing a greater number of falsehoods that you would have believed otherwise. EBC would say that this is a case of false, justified belief.

Not only does EBC look at the effects of belief formation within a life, it looks at the effects of belief formation across lives. Consequentialists notoriously ignore the separateness of persons in ethics.[40] I do not see why they would respect the separateness of persons in epistemology. The world might be causally structured in such a way that every time Coop believes something true, five others believe something false. Better, the consequentialist says, for Coop to believe nothing. If so, Coop's obligation is to refrain from believing even if his belief is correct.

Once we see why EBC does not undermine the distinction between justification and truth, we see why Maitzen was right to reject ERC and EBC. You might know that Coop knows p even if you know that Coop's

---

[39] Selim Berker reminded me that this point was due to Firth 1981.
[40] Rawls 1971.

coming to believe p brought about some epistemically disastrous outcomes. Still, knowing that Coop knows p, you know that Coop's belief is justified in spite of these outcomes. Since EBC has to say that Coop's belief is not justified, EBC has to say that knowledge is not enough for justification. Worse, EBC cannot do justice to our anti-consequentialist approach to epistemic evaluation. As Berker puts it, EBC cannot respect the separateness of propositions.[41] To do that, EBC would have to reject the totalizing assumption.

The problem that arises for EBC does not arise because EBC evaluates beliefs directly. The problem that arises for EBC arises because it accepts the totalizing assumption. Since this assumption is an essential to Consequentialism, the argument against EBC should apply with equal force to all forms of EC. Thus, it does not matter in the end whether ERC is extensionally equivalent to EBC or not. If it is, counterexamples to EBC are counterexamples to ERC. If not, modified counterexamples would undermine the view. The objection applies with equal force to subjective forms of EC as well. Consider the view that says that your epistemic obligation is to maximize expected epistemic value. Since you can know Coop knows p even if he knows that believing p would not maximize expected epistemic value (e.g., Coop knows that, as a consequence of believing p, five others will form false beliefs that they would not have formed otherwise), the objections to EBC apply to this view as well.[42]

In this section, I have argued that EC does not provide a sound basis for a theory of justification. The objections to EC are directed towards EC, not Reliabilism. It might be that Reliabilism is a sound view, but the case for such a view cannot be made on value-theoretic grounds alone. While there is something good about believing with justification, it would be a mistake to try to derive a theory of the epistemic right from a theory of the epistemic good.

---

[41] Selim Berker, "Epistemic Teleology and the Separateness of Propositions" (unpublished manuscript).

[42] I mentioned the possibility that Feldman's 1988a view might be that justification is determined by epistemic well-being and that the value atoms that determine your epistemic well-being supervene upon your internal conditions. Arguably, the view would not be a form of Internalism because whether you successfully maximize epistemic well-being depends upon what alternatives were available to you and how much value these alternatives contain. These facts about alternatives do not supervene upon your internal conditions even if value atoms that supervene upon your internal conditions determine the total value of each alternative. Moreover, justification cannot be a function of epistemic well-being because the view that takes the justified belief to be a belief that contributes to epistemic well-being will accept the totalizing assumption and would thus clash with our anti-consequentialist approach to epistemic evaluation.

2.4 THE REMAINING VALUE PROBLEM

Discussions of epistemic value have focused primarily on the value of knowledge. The reader is probably familiar with the Meno Problem, the problem of explaining why knowledge is more valuable than true belief.[43] Could it be that knowledge is more valuable than mere true belief because it is a more stable basis for action? Perhaps, but this is the wrong kind of value twice over. We want to find some non-instrumental value to explain why knowledge is epistemically better than mere true belief. A more promising line of explanation starts with the observation that knowledge requires justification. If justification is always valuable from the epistemic point of view, we are well on our way to solving the Meno Problem.

We know that the discussion does not end here. Some will say that knowledge is more valuable than any status that falls short of it, in which case appealing to the value of justification might solve the Meno Problem while giving rise to another.[44] Ideally, my account of the value of justification will not undermine any otherwise plausible claims about the value of knowledge, but my primary concern here is the value of justification.

Some would take issue with my suggestion that justification is invariably and non-instrumentally valuable. If asked why we value justification, the obvious answer is that justification is connected to truth and truth or true belief is something we value. If this is what the value of justification consists in, that it puts us in the right relation to truth, it seems that the account of justification's value on offer is an instrumentalist account that would undermine any attempt to appeal to the value of justification to deal with the Meno Problem.

We can put the worry this way. Suppose the value of knowledge, V_K, is greater than the value of true belief, V_{TB}. We can only appeal to the value of justified belief, V_{JB}, to explain why V_K is greater than V_{TB} if V_{JB} is not itself contained in V_{TB}. It might seem that V_{JB} is not contained in V_{TB} since it is better to believe with justification than without it and since not all true beliefs are justified. While it does seem intuitive to say that it is better to believe with justification, some will press for an explanation of this claim. The obvious explanation as to why it is better to believe with justification than without it tries to explain what V_{JB} is in terms of justification's connection to truth and the value of the truth-connection, V_{JTC}. Now, I face a dilemma. If there is *more* to V_{JB} than just V_{JTC}, what is it?

---

[43] See Kvanvig 2003; Pritchard 2007; Riggs 2008; and Zagzebski 2003 for an introduction.
[44] Pritchard 2007, 2010.

If there is not, is seems that V_{JB} is only instrumentally valuable since it seems that V_{JTC} is only instrumentally valuable.

BonJour seems to think that V_{JB} is nothing over and above V_{JTC}:

> Why is such justification something to be sought and valued? Once the question is posed this way, the following answer seems obviously correct … We want our beliefs to correctly and accurately depict the world … The basic role of justification is that of a means to truth … We cannot, in most cases at least, bring it about directly that our beliefs are true, but we can presumably bring it about directly … that they are epistemically justified. And, if our standards of epistemic justification are appropriately chosen, bringing it about that our beliefs are epistemically justified will tend to bring it about … that they are true … It is only if we have some reason for thinking that epistemic justification constitutes a path to truth that we as cognitive beings have any motive for preferring epistemically justified beliefs to epistemically unjustified ones. Epistemic justification is therefore in the final analysis only an instrumental value, not an intrinsic one.[45]

If he is right that $V_{JB} = V_{JTC}$, we face a problem structurally similar to the swamping problem.[46] Unless V_{JTC} is a non-instrumental value, we cannot explain how V_{JB} could be a non-instrumental value. If V_{JTC} is merely instrumentally valuable, false beliefs will not have some positive value by virtue of having V_{JTC}. If the only value Fs ever have is instrumental value then on those occasions where nothing of intrinsic value is realized, F has no value at all. To borrow an example, if a terrible shot of espresso is made using the finest equipment, this shot is not better for this reason than a shot you could get at the gas station. If V_{JTC} is merely instrumentally valuable, then true beliefs should not have some additional value by virtue of possessing V_{JTC}, a value that unjustified true beliefs lack. If the only value the Fs ever have is instrumental value, when something of intrinsic value is realized, the presence of an F does not increase the total value. If a fantastic shot of espresso is made using the poorest equipment, it is not less valuable than a qualitatively indistinguishable shot of espresso made using the finest equipment.[47] So, if $V_{JB} = V_{JTC}$, it seems we cannot explain $V_K > V_{TB}$ in terms of V_{JB}. Thus, we are under some pressure to explain how it could be that $V_{JB} > V_{JTC}$ in order to properly explain how it is that $V_K > V_{TB}$ in terms of V_{JB} and yet we are also under some pressure to concede that $V_{JB} = V_{TB}$ on the grounds that $V_{JTC} = V_{TB}$.

---

[45] BonJour 1985, p. 8.

[46] The swamping problem arises for reliabilist views of knowledge in that it seems intuitively that it is better to know than just to truly believe a proposition but it is not better to attain something of value by reliable means than by unreliable means. For discussion, see Zagzebski 1996.

[47] See Zagzebski 2003, p. 13.

We can state BonJour's argument against the claim that justification is always valuable as follows:

1. The value of justification derives entirely from its connection to truth (i.e., $V_{JB} = V_{JTC}$).
2. When a justified belief is false, that belief has no additional value by virtue of being justified.
3. Some false beliefs have no epistemic value whatever.
4. (Therefore) It is not always good to believe with justification.

One response would be to reject (2) on the grounds that no false beliefs are ever justified. Even if (1) is true and the justified belief derives its value entirely from its connection to truth, we have a way of resisting the argument.[48] Few are willing to go this route, but I shall argue that there are no false, justified beliefs in later chapters. Even if we go this route, a problem remains. Do true beliefs have the same value whether or not they are justified? If so, it is not better to believe with justification than without it. If it is not, why is it not?

In responding to BonJour's argument, I think it is helpful to think about the notion of epistemic worth. Suppose that the conditions that justify a subject's belief thereby justify her reasoning from that belief. In justifying the belief, these conditions justify her treating what she believes as a reason for further beliefs and for actions rationalized by those beliefs. If the agent was properly motivated by a concern for the good, her action could have had moral worth even if she did not live up to her obligations. (An excusable wrong can have moral worth.) To be suitably motivated in acting, the agent had to have exercised due care in reasoning about what to do. If she exercised due care, it would have been epistemically rational for her to believe that she was acting rightly. If the value that attached to rational belief managed to justify belief, it would justify acting on the belief. Since nothing justifies the agent's actions, however, this value did *not* provide sufficient justification for what she did or what she believed.

---

[48] Just to foreshadow a little, my ultimate view is that justification involves cognitive success that manifests your ability to identify and respond to reasons. When success is from ability, some authors say that these successes have a value not wholly contained in what you bring about because success from ability is an achievement. See Greco 2010 and Sosa 2007 for a discussion and defense of this idea. If this is correct, it could help explain our intuitions about the value of justification (e.g., why it is better to believe with justification). I have two problems with this view. I do not think achievements are intrinsically or finally valuable. If what you achieve, you achieve after all sentient life is gone from the universe, it does not make your life or the world better by virtue of being an achievement. Also, I do not think success from ability is always an achievement. See Pritchard 2010 for a discussion of the problem of easy achievements. If I am wrong on these points, my view is easier to defend than I think it is.

The upshot is that the value that attaches to rational belief is necessary for moral worth and sufficient for epistemic worth, but it is not sufficient for moral or epistemic permissibility.

If this is correct, the value of reasonable belief is an essential component of moral worth and epistemic worth. The value of epistemic worth does not provide a justification for action or belief. Still, it seems valuable in its own way even on those occasions when the subject does not meet her various obligations. If this is right, the value of epistemic worth is not purely instrumental even though this value is connected to the pursuit of further ends. Consider BonJour's suggestion that V_{JB} is really nothing over and above V_{JTC}. Remember that V_{JTC} was defined in such a way that no justified beliefs lack it (i.e., you have it only if you satisfy *all* of the conditions necessary for doxastic justification). If a belief stands in the connection to truth necessary for the belief to be justified, it has V_{JTC}. While BonJour seems to think that this means that V_{JTC} is purely instrumental and that this shows that V_{JB} is also purely instrumental, the examples of moral worth and epistemic worth show this is a mistake. If what I have suggested is correct, no belief can stand in the proper relation to truth to count as justified unless it is responsibly held and has epistemic worth. Epistemic worth is not merely instrumentally valuable, so neither is V_{JB} or V_{JTC}.

In explaining why he thought V_{JTC} is purely instrumental, BonJour explained why you seek and value justification in instrumentalist terms. He said that you seek and value justification as a means to truth. He is right. However, it is one thing to say that the aspect of justification you should care about when trying to settle the question as to whether p is whether the considerations you have in mind correctly settle the question, and quite another to say that this is the only aspect of justification you should ever care about. When you settle to your satisfaction the question as to whether p only to later discover that $-p$, you might not value the justification you had because you can see that it misled you. Contrast this case with the case in which you settle to your satisfaction the question as whether p only later to be told that while technically you were correct, it was unreasonable for you to conclude that p was true given the evidence you had. On the instrumentalist picture, what concern would that be to you? Your belief turned out to be true. If the instrumentalist picture is right, it should be of no consequence at all. This does not ring true. In trying to settle the question as to whether p, you might settle it to your satisfaction without shifting your focus from whether p to whether you would live up to your responsibilities if you believed on the information available that *p*. Still, if you discover later that your beliefs lacked epistemic worth, you care. You care about whether you pursued the truth responsibly and reasonably *because* you care about the truth. So, even if there is nothing more to V_{JB} than V_{JTC}, it does not follow that V_{JB} is a purely instrumental value. V_{JTC} might be both an instrumental and non-instrumental value. There might be many aspects of the truth-connection necessary for justification and the subjective dimension connected to epistemic worth is certainly part of it. If V_{JTC} accrues only to beliefs that have epistemic worth, we can explain why V_{JB} is not swamped by V_{TB}. Not every true belief has epistemic worth and not every belief with epistemic worth is true. Both truth and epistemic worth confer value upon a belief, and so can explain $V_K > V_{TB}$ by appeal to a non-instrumental value contained in all justified beliefs.

One problem remains. In explaining why it is always good to believe with justification, I have not explained why it is always better to believe with justification than without it. Epistemic worth is necessary for justified belief, but it is not sufficient. Thus, to explain why it is better to believe with justification than without it, I have to show that there is more to the value of justified belief than just epistemic worth. My suggestion is one that non-consequentialists often offer. It is better to believe with justification because it is better to meet your obligations. If you believe with justification, you have met your epistemic obligations. If you do not, you have not. It is not better to believe with justification because some independent notion of better and worse determines what your obligation is. We have rejected EC. Intuitions about what is better or best often reflect prior judgments about what would be right or required by duty.[49] As such, they do not provide an independent guide to determining what our duty might be.

2.5 CONCLUSION

Here is where things stand. I explained why it is always good to believe with justification in terms of epistemic worth, which I claim is a non-epistemic value required for both personal and doxastic justification. Epistemic worth is an internalist notion. While my account of the value of justification is compatible with internalist views, it is not incompatible

---

[49] See Foot 1985 and Gardner 2005.

with any externalist view that allows that justification can have an internal dimension. As for the second guiding intuition, I maintain that it is always better to believe with justification precisely because it is better to live up to your obligations. Since value-theoretic considerations alone cannot tell us what your epistemic obligations are, we take a turn away from considerations having to do with epistemic value.

CHAPTER 3

Reasons for belief (I)

3.1 INTRODUCTION

In this chapter, I shall argue that some externalist views enjoy an important advantage over their internalist rivals. Once we understand what reasons for belief are and which reasons you have, we can see that the justification of your beliefs does depend to some extent upon matters external to you. Your evidence consists of facts or true propositions.[1] Not all the facts, obviously, but it includes some facts that are inaccessible to your epistemic counterparts. This is because your basic or ultimate evidence includes any fact that you believe if your belief is non-inferentially justified. Given some mild anti-skeptical assumptions, this includes much of what you see, not just what you seem to see or what you know via introspection.

This view is at odds with a commonly accepted internalist approach to evidence:

Evidential Internalism: Necessarily, you and your epistemic counterparts (i.e., your non-factive mental duplicates) have the same bodies of evidence.[2]

This internalist thesis is mistaken. Once we see why, we shall see that a commonly accepted internalist approach to justification is also mistaken:

Supervenience Internalism: Necessarily, you and your epistemic counterparts are justificationally the same.[3]

---

[1] Collins 1997; Dancy 2000; Hyman 1999; Maher 1996; Unger 1975; and Williamson 2000a also defend this view.
[2] Audi 2001; Conee and Feldman 2004; Greco 2000; Moser 1991; Silins 2005; and Steup 2001.
[3] Audi 2001; Bird 2007; Cohen 1984; Conee and Feldman 2004; Langsam 2008; Madison 2010; Pollock and Cruz 1999; and Wedgwood 2002a. With the exception of a handful of disjunctivists, accessibilists and mentalists accept Evidential and Supervenience Internalism.

According to Supervenience Internalism, you and your epistemic counterparts are justificationally the same. This means that the same beliefs would be justified for you, these beliefs would be justified just as well, the same reasons for believing would apply to you, and you would believe for the very same reasons. If you and your epistemic counterparts can have different bodies of evidence, you and your counterparts would be justificationally different. Since you and your epistemic counterparts can have different bodies of evidence, your beliefs might be backed by better evidence than theirs. Both Evidential and Supervenience Internalism deny this, but I shall argue that their only grounds for doing so would be a kind of skepticism that most of them disavow.[4]

It might seem difficult to know how we should go about testing competing accounts of evidence because the notion of evidence is so slippery, but there are some general points that are relatively uncontroversial that should help us get a fix on the notion. First, your evidence is said to be what you have to go on when trying to determine whether something is so.[5] Because of this, your access to the evidence should not be more epistemically problematic than your access to the facts you hope to uncover (e.g., Coop might learn what Ben is up to if he digs through his trash, but Coop would not typically have to dig through his own trash to see what he is up to). Second, there is some general agreement about the roles that evidence plays in inference and explanation. It would be a mark against a theory if, for instance, it denied that evidence plays the role we take it to in inference to best explanation. Third, just as a theory of knowledge should fit with our understanding of what knowledge ascriptions do, a theory of evidence should fit with our understanding of what evidence ascriptions do. Linguistic evidence might provide only defeasible support for a view, but defeasible support is support. Fourth, we do have intuitions about what your evidence rules out and what is consistent with your evidence. Better to accommodate our intuitions, *ceteris paribus*, than for theories to clash with them. The externalist account of evidence defended here does a better job accommodating these points than its rivals.

---

[4] Remember that many internalists cite the intuition that your systematically deceived counterparts are justified in their beliefs as a reason to reject Externalism. Thus, the anti-skeptical assumptions that I shall argue cause trouble for their view are among the assumptions they rely on in arguing for their view.

[5] Kelly 2008 and Silins 2005.

3.2 AN ARGUMENT AGAINST EVIDENTIAL INTERNALISM

If your evidence consists of those facts that you believe with non-inferential justification, this should constitute a refutation of Evidential Internalism:

1. My evidence includes the proposition that I have hands.
2. My evidence includes the proposition that I have hands only if I have hands.
3. Since hands are objects met in space, my evidence can include the proposition that I have hands only if facts about my evidence do not strongly supervene upon facts about my non-factive mental states.
4. (Therefore) Facts about my evidence do not strongly supervene upon facts about my non-factive mental states.

My account of evidence incorporates three features. First, evidence consists of propositions. I defend a strong reading of this claim, but the weaker thesis suffices for arguing against Evidential Internalism:

Strong Propositionalism: All evidence consists of propositions.[6]
Weak Propositionalism: Some evidence consists of propositions.

Second, only true propositions constitute evidence:

Factivity$_E$: If p is a justifying reason for belief, p is true.

I shall assume that pieces of evidence are justifying reasons for belief. The first two theses tell us what evidence is, but not what evidence you have. The third feature of my account is a claim about the possession of evidence (immediate knowledge suffices for evidence, IKSE):

IKSE: If you know p non-inferentially, p is part of your evidence.

Why think what you know non-inferentially is part of your evidence? If it is not, it is either because (i) what you know or the belief that constitutes knowledge is not the sort of thing that could be evidence or (ii) knowledge does not give you the right to treat something as a reason for belief. The former is wrong. Evidence either consists of mental states such as belief or propositions believed. The latter is wrong. What you know you

---

[6] Dougherty 2011; Hyman 2006; Kvanvig 2007; Littlejohn 2008; Millar 1991; Schroeder 2008; Swain 1979; and Williamson 2000a. There are passages where it seems that Feldman endorses this view. He says, for example, that your evidence is what you "actively believe." See Conee and Feldman 2004, pp. 226–8. He now sides with those who say that pieces of evidence are mental states. See Conee and Feldman 2011.

justifiably believe and what you justifiably believe you can rightly treat as a reason for further beliefs. So, whatever evidence turns out to be, something in the neighborhood of IKSE is correct.

Considered individually, these three claims (i.e., Weak Propositionalism, Factivity$_E$, and IKSE) are quite plausible. If, however, Liberal Foundationalism is true and you have non-inferential knowledge of the external world, these three claims show that Evidential and Supervenience Internalism are mistaken.

3.3 WHAT ARE REASONS FOR BELIEF?

Here we shall focus on two competing accounts of evidence. According to the first, evidence consists of propositions. According to the second, evidence never consists of propositions. If this second view is to serve the purposes of Evidential Internalism, this second view has to say that your evidence consists of items that strongly supervene upon your non-factive mental states. The natural view to adopt would be this:

> Psychologism: Justifying reasons consist of non-factive mental states or mental events.[7]

Psychologism says that certain mental states constitute evidence, not just that your mental states provide you with evidence. Notice that while Psychologism is the natural view for some internalists to take, Psychologism does not commit you to Evidential or Supervenience Internalism. Someone who believes that justifying reasons are non-factive mental states can say that certain external conditions have to obtain for these states to constitute reasons for belief. Your experiences, for example, might constitute justifying reasons, but only because your experiences reliably indicate that certain propositions are true. On this view, reasons would be internal states and external conditions would be the enabling conditions by virtue of which that which constitutes your reason can be a reason. (By way of analogy, coins are nothing but hunks of metal, but only the hunks that come from the mint are coins.) I would not defend this view, but it is an option to consider. With these preliminary points out of the way, let's see what case can be made for Psychologism.

---

[7] Brueckner 2009; Cohen 1984; Conee and Feldman 2011; Davidson 2001, p. 310; Langsam 2002; Moser 1991; Pollock 1974; Pollock and Gillies 2000; and Turri 2009.

3.3.1 *The subtraction argument*

Our first argument for Psychologism is the subtraction argument:

What is it that justifies a belief? ... For example, consider the case of a person who believes there is a sheep in the field because he sees a dog that looks very much like a sheep – so much like a sheep that anyone would be justified in taking it to be a sheep until he examined it quite closely. One is apt to say that it is the fact that the dog looks like a sheep that justifies the person in thinking that there is a sheep in the field. But this is misleading. What is important in deciding whether the person is justified in his belief is not the fact itself but rather the person's belief that it is a fact. After all, if the person did not believe that the dog looked like a sheep, then his belief that there was a sheep in the field would not be justified, although it would of course still be a fact that the dog looked like a sheep. Thus we must say that what justifies a belief is always another belief.[8]

The subtraction argument is so-called because it employs a subtraction test: if you subtract the subject's belief, the fact or proposition believed could not justify anything. Thus, the reasons that justify belief are the subject's mental states.[9]

The subtraction test is too crude. Think about the distinction between reasons and enabling conditions. If you subtract the subject's reasons, she will be left without any justifying reasons. If you subtract the enabling conditions, she will be left without any justifying reasons. The subtraction test tells us that if you subtract something and you thereby lose the reasons, what you subtracted was the reason and so the subtraction test would undermine the distinction between reasons and enablers. Nevertheless, this seems like a perfectly good distinction. If Coop is in distress, Audrey might have a reason to help, but not if everything she tried would only make things worse. Suppose, however, that Audrey can help. That Coop is in distress would be a reason for her to help. That she would not make things worse if she tried is not itself a reason for her to act.[10] Since the distinction between reasons and enablers is sound, the subtraction argument is not.

3.3.2 *The logical relations argument*

A second argument might help determine whether the subject's mental states are reasons or enablers. Davidson argued that "nothing can count as a reason for holding a belief except another belief" on these grounds:

---

[8] Pollock 1974, p. 25. See also Pollock and Gillies 2000.
[9] Similar arguments can be found in a number of places. See Huemer 2007a, for example.
[10] Dancy 2004, p. 38.

1. Nothing can be a reason for belief unless it stands in a logical relation to that belief.
2. Unlike beliefs, sensations do not stand in any logical relation to belief.
3. (Therefore) Nothing could be a reason for belief except another belief.[11]

How does his logical relations argument fare? In one respect, it is an improvement over the subtraction argument because it identifies a feature that is useful for distinguishing reasons from enablers. In one respect, it is not. If anything, the argument shows why we ought to reject Psychologism.

Davidson thought that sensations could not constitute reasons because he thought that they did not stand in any logical relations.[12] While he was right that sensations do not stand in any logical relations, neither do beliefs. Mental states entail nothing and are entailed by nothing. If Laura firmly believes that ostriches are not birds on the grounds that they cannot fly, what does her firmly held belief entail? It does not entail the disjunctive proposition that either ostriches are not birds or sharks are fish. It does not entail that she needs to read more about ostriches. What Laura believes can stand in logical relations, but what she believes is a proposition, not a mental state. It is true that we can say that Laura's belief is inconsistent with the facts, but this only shows that 'belief' is subject to a state/content ambiguity, not that we have some reason to accept (2).

If Davidson is right about (1), the logical relations argument is, as Williamson saw, an argument *against* Psychologism:

4. Any piece of evidence can rule out a hypothesis by being inconsistent with it.
5. Only propositions can be inconsistent with a hypothesis.
6. (Therefore) Only propositions can be evidence.[13]

Why did Davidson miss this? I doubt that he thought that a mental state could literally entail something or that he forgot about the state/content ambiguity. My guess is that Davidson's goal was to show that only states with contents can *rationalize* further beliefs (i.e., figure in rationalizing explanations as to why these beliefs are formed). Perhaps he

---

[11] Davidson 2001, p. 141.
[12] Critics (e.g., Brewer 1999 and McDowell 1997) objected to Davidson's argument on the grounds that Davidson was wrong to deny that experience has representational content. For a helpful overview, see Ginsborg 2006.
[13] Williamson 2000a, p. 196.

thought this because he thought that only contentful states could provide the subject with reasons by making the subject cognizant of these reasons. (States without representational content cannot make you cognizant of anything even if you can be cognizant of them.) If you are keeping score, we have an inconclusive argument for Psychologism and an argument for Psychologism that refutes Psychologism and supports Strong Propositionalism.

3.3.3 *The causal argument*

Our third argument for Psychologism is the causal argument:

1. Reasons are causes.
2. Propositions are not causes.
3. (Therefore) Reasons are not propositions.
4. Reasons are either propositions or the subject's mental states.
5. (Therefore) Reasons are the subject's mental states.[14]

As with the previous argument, this argument tries to identify a feature that distinguishes reasons from enabling conditions. Because of the popularity of causal accounts of the basing relation, I suspect that this argument is largely responsible for the popularity of Psychologism.[15] We have seen that if your beliefs are justified, it is not enough that you happen to have good reasons for your beliefs; you have to believe for good reasons. In other words, doxastic justification requires that you base your beliefs on good reasons. If the basing relation involves a causal connection, you might think that (1) is correct, but I think this is unwarranted.

A thorough evaluation of the argument requires us to address some difficult metaphysical issues. While (2) seems initially plausible, remember we are working under the assumption that facts are true propositions. Thus, (2) is true only if there is no fact causation. Since much of our ordinary talk suggests that facts can be causes (e.g., "The fact that Ben was so drunk caused him to fall down the stairs" or "The rope's being so weak caused it to break when Audrey pulled it"), there had better be strong reasons not to take such talk at face value and reject (2).

---

[14] Swain 1981 and Turri in press argue that certain kinds of reasons are mental states by appeal to the thesis that causes have causal powers. Swain distinguishes causal reasons from justifying reasons, insisting that the latter are propositions. Turri seems to want to follow Dancy 2000 in insisting that justifying reasons and motivating reasons belong to the same ontological category.

[15] For defenses of a causal requirement on the basing relation, see Audi 1993 and Korcz 2000.

One suggestion is that propositions cannot be causes because they are not spatiotemporal objects and only such objects have causal powers.[16] If the thesis that causes have causal powers is correct, propositions could not be causes, but this thesis is controversial. In the course of explaining why he rejects the suggestion that "when an explosion causes a fire, the explosion emits force, pushes things around, acts as the elbow in the ribs," Bennett observes:

> When an explosion causes a fire, what happens is that the molecules bump into other molecules, increasing their velocity to the point where they react rapidly with the ambient gases, etc. The idea that the pushing is done not by the molecules but by the explosion is just the afterglow of ignorance about what an explosion is.[17]

Typically, those who think facts cannot be causes would say that events are, but Bennett is right that events do not have causal powers. If causes have to have causal powers, events could not be causes for the same reasons facts cannot be. Thus, the motivation for (2) rests on a highly contentious assumption about the ontology of causation. Worse, the thesis that causes have causal powers combined with (1) implies that Psychologism is false. States do not have causal powers. Whatever can exercise its causal powers has to be the subject of change. Since states are not coarse-grained particulars, they are not subjects of change.[18] If all causes have causal powers, it seems only substances could be causes.[19] If Psychologism is right about anything, it rightly rejects the idea that substances are reasons. No metaphysician should try to explain how it could be that Amy is my reason for shaving every morning or Agnes is my reason for spending so much time in the park.

Perhaps the real motivation for (2) is not that causes have causal powers but that causes are immanent. While this suggestion is more plausible, it is controversial whether this intuition could do the work it must as it is unclear whether states are immanent, much less the only immanent items to play the role of causally operative reasons. Some believe that facts or fact-like entities are immanent, for example.[20] If so, (2) or (4) might be mistaken. Rather than try to do the metaphysics better left to certified

---

[16] Turri in press.   [17] Bennett 1988, p. 23.

[18] For a helpful discussion of states, see Steward 1997.

[19] Truth doesn't make a noise. I agree with Turri that facts and true propositions are powerless. If not truths, what can make a noise? Bells can. States of bells and events involving bells, however, cannot.

[20] See Mellor 1988 for a defense of the view that facts can stand in spatiotemporal relations. See Menzies 1989 for a defense of the view that situations are the fundamental causal relata.

metaphysicians, I shall argue that we can see that the causal argument for Psychologism fails even if we grant (2) and (4).

Remember that there are three ways of reading (1):

1a. The reasons why the subject believes what she does are causes.
1b. The agent's reasons for believing what she does are causes.
1c. The reasons that bear on whether to believe what the agent believes are causes.

Since this is a debate about the ontology of normative reasons, the causal argument for Psychologism has to establish (1c). It does so indirectly. First, the psychologists argue that explanatory or motivating reasons are causes.[21] Second, they argue that (1c) follows from (1a) or (1b) because it is possible to act and believe for good reasons. Now, if we were feeling generous, we might grant (1a). Explanatory reasons or the reasons why someone acts need not be motivating reasons, the reasons in light of which they acted. Since (1a) does not entail (1b), we can accept (1a) and remain agnostic as to whether (1b) is true. And, if we can accept (1a) while denying that the reasons for which someone acted are psychological states, we can, say, turn the tables on the psychologists. Since it must be possible that the reasons we act for are good reasons, neither motivating nor normative reasons are psychological states. Thus, the psychologists have to show that (1b) is true. Typically, psychologists say that Davidson showed that motivating reasons are psychological states. In the next chapter, I shall explain why arguments for (1b) typically undermine the psychologists' suggestion that (1b) and (1c) are both true. Here, I shall explain why Davidson's arguments do not support (1b) and so cannot support (1c).

The argument that Davidson was supposed to provide for (1b) is found in "Actions, Reasons, and Causes," which opens with these remarks:

What is the relation between a reason and an action when the reason explains the action by giving the agent's reason for doing what he did? We may call such explanations *rationalizations*, and say that the reason *rationalizes* the action. In this paper I want to defend the ancient – and commonsense – position that rationalization is a species of causal explanation.[22]

His aim was to show that the force of the 'because' that figures in a rationalization (e.g., "Audrey went outside because she believed Donna

---

[21] The distinction between explanatory and motivating reasons is often neglected. The reason why Audrey stays home might be that she is so shy. Audrey's reason for staying home might be that there will be so many strangers at the party. For a helpful discussion of the difference, see Alvarez 2010.

[22] Davidson 1980, p. 3.

was waiting for her") is the same as the force of the 'because' that figures in sentential causal explanations (e.g., "Coop went through the front door because he was pushed").

Davidson's argument is contained in this passage:

Noting that non-teleological causal explanations do not display the element of justification provided by reasons, some philosophers have concluded that the concept of cause that applies elsewhere cannot apply to the relation between reasons and actions, and that the pattern of justification provides, in the case of reasons, the required explanation. But suppose we grant that reasons alone justify actions in the course of explaining them; it does not follow that the explanation is not also … causal … How about the other claim: that justifying is a kind of explaining, so that the ordinary notion of a cause need not be brought in? Here it is necessary to decide what is being included under justification. It could be taken to cover only … that the agent have certain beliefs and attitudes in the light of which the action is reasonable. But then something essential has certainly been left out, for a person can have a reason for an action, and perform the action, and yet this reason not be the reason why he did it. Central to the relation between a reason and an action it explains is the idea that the agent performed the action *because* he had the reason.[23]

His point was that if we want to understand the difference between (i) simply having reasons that could potentially justify an action but do not move you to act and (ii) acting for those reasons, we have to say that agents act because they have certain reasons. To say that she acted because she had these reasons is to say more than just that she simply had these reasons or had them in mind, for these reasons could be explanatorily idle (e.g., I might desire to amuse my roommate and annoy my neighbors and believe that tap dancing in my boots to Tupac would be a way of fulfilling both desires. If I start dancing, I might do so in order to amuse my roommate and not to annoy the neighbors or might do so in order to annoy my neighbors). To distinguish cases where reasons are idle from cases in which the reasons are operative, we need to posit some causal difference between the agent's desires and actions to decide which reasons are operative. Thus, we cannot understand how rationalizing explanations work unless the force of the 'because' in a rationalizing explanation is the same as in a causal explanation.

Suppose Davidson is right and rationalizations are causal explanations. What does this tell us about the relation between reasons and causes? Nothing. I realize that many people believe that it shows that reasons are causes, but this simply does not follow. Since it does not show that

---

[23] Davidson 1980, p. 9.

motivating reasons are the causes of the agent's action or attitudes, it cannot support the crucial premise in the causal argument for Psychologism. To see this, remember that if the argument for Psychologism has any hope of success, we have to assume that facts are not causes. If facts are not causes, then causes belong to a different ontological category than the *explanantes* that figure in rationalizing explanations.[24] This is so even if rationalizing explanations are causal explanations because facts are *explanantes* and we have stipulated that facts are not causes.

The Davidsonian thesis that rationalizing explanations are causal explanations is consistent with one of two views. The first identifies motivating reasons with the subject's mental states and states that motivating reasons are causes rather than the *explanantes* of successful causal/ rationalizing explanations. The second identifies motivating reasons with the *explanantes* of successful causal/rationalizing explanations and distinguishes them from the agent's mental states/the causal antecedents of the agent's actions. Both of these options are consistent with the conclusion of Davidson's argument, but the second is incompatible with (1b) and incompatible with Psychologism. Thus, even if Davidson's arguments succeed, they do not support (1b) or Psychologism.

3.3.4 The explanatory argument

Having run out of arguments for Psychologism, I want to turn to the arguments for Propositionalism, starting with the explanatory argument:

1. Your evidence is the sort of thing that can be explained.
2. What we explain is propositional.
3. (Therefore) Evidence is propositional.[25]

Your evidence is the sort of thing that can be explained. We cannot ask someone to explain a state (e.g., the solidity of this liquid, the shape of this rock), a substance (e.g., Agnes), or an event (e.g., World War II), but we can ask someone to explain why something is true. So, your evidence has to be the kind of thing that can be true. We might explain that Agnes is in the kitchen because it is time for breakfast or that the liquid is solid because it is so cold, but, as Williamson notes, we cannot "simply *explain Albania*, for 'Albania because ...' is ill-formed."[26]

---

[24] This point is not lost on Davidson. He maintained that the relata of the causation relation were events and the relata of the causal explanation relation were facts. See Davidson 1980, p. 153.
[25] Williamson 2000a, p. 194. For helpful discussion of this argument, see Dougherty 2011.
[26] Williamson 2000a, p. 194.

Neta raises the possibility that the grammatical evidence might be misleading.[27] If, he asks, we speak of photographs, bloody gloves, and bruises as being evidence, what stops the psychologists from saying that the grammar of 'because' is an unreliable guide to the metaphysics of explanation? Conee and Feldman develop this worry and explain why they would reject (2):

As we see it, explaining the occurrence of World War II is not explaining any proposition. It is explaining a gigantic complex spatiotemporal occurrence that included thousands of battles and millions of people. The occurrence of the one huge event, WWII, that is the combination of all of these things, can be explained by giving an argument the conclusion of which reads "and so WWII occurred." The last two words do express the proposition that WWII occurred. That proposition is the conclusion of the explanatory reasoning. What is explained, though, is not the proposition, but the occurrence of the war that the proposition asserts to have occurred. Concluding that sort of explanatory argument is not identical to explaining the proposition in it that is the conclusion. It is explaining the worldly phenomenon that the proposition reports or represents.[28]

Their criticism of (2) is unconvincing. First, it is easy to square the intuition that to explain the occurrence of World War II is to explain something worldly with Strong Propositionalism because facts are true propositions and facts are worldly enough. Second, to explain the occurrence of World War II is not to explain an event, but why an event occurred, and that is to explain a fact.

One reason to be skeptical of the idea that events figure in explanations either as *explanans* or *explanandum* is that events are complex particulars that can be picked out by means of a variety of descriptions.[29] The truth or falsity of singular causal claims (e.g., "The shot caused Coop to fall to the ground in agony") depends upon whether the events described stand in a suitable causal relation, not on how these events are described. The truth or falsity of sentential explanations, however, depends (in part) upon the way we describe things. Thus, the truth or falsity of an explanatory statement does not depend solely upon whether events stand in various natural relations to each another, but also upon the features of these events and the ways these features are related. Suppose Coop drank the contents of the bottle and this caused him to vomit. The wine in the bottle was poisoned. It was also from Burgundy. When Coop drank the

[27] Neta 2008, p. 96.   [28] Conee and Feldman 2011, p. 322.
[29] See Ruben 1990, p. 162.

wine he drank the poison and drank a Burgundy. We have one event under three descriptions. So, if drinking the wine caused him to vomit, drinking the poison caused him to vomit, and drinking a Burgundy caused him to vomit. If the reason why he vomited is that he drank the poison, it does not follow that the reason why he vomited was that he drank a Burgundy.

I think we can build on Williamson's argument for Strong Propositionalism to show that Factivity$_E$ is true and that only true propositions constitute evidence:

4. If you know that p is part of your evidence, you know that p is either a brute fact or p can be explained by something further.
5. If p is a brute fact, p is true.
6. If p can be explained by something further, there is a reason why p is true, in which case p is true.
7. (Therefore) If you know that p is part of your evidence, you know that p is true.

Once you know that p is part of your evidence, you do not need to know anything further to know that p is either a brute fact or explained by further facts. It follows from the fact that p is a brute fact that p is a fact. It follows from the fact that there is some q that would make 'p because q' true that p is true. Either way, if you know that p is part of your evidence, p must be true.

The argument shows that you cannot know that p is part of your evidence unless you are in a position to know that p is true. It does not follow immediately from (7) that p must be true to be part of your evidence. Still, (7) does support Factivity$_E$. If you accept (7) and deny Factivity$_E$, you have to say that the truth of p is necessary for knowing that p is part of your evidence without it being necessary for p to be part of your evidence. You would have to explain this surprising fact. Why is it that you cannot know that p is part of your evidence when p happens to be false if p can nevertheless be part of your evidence when p is false? Surely you could believe p to be part of your evidence even if $\sim p$. If p could be part of your evidence even if $\sim p$, I see no reason to think that you could not justifiably believe p to be part of your evidence simply because $\sim p$. Your belief that p is part of your evidence would not be Gettiered whenever you believed p to be part of your evidence and p happened to be false. It seems the only plausible explanation as to why (7) is true is that Factivity$_E$ is true. You cannot know that p is part of your evidence when $\sim p$ because falsehoods do not constitute evidence.

A second argument for Factivity$_E$ focuses on the role normative reasons play in explaining the normative properties of our beliefs and actions:

8. If p is part of your evidence, p is a justifying reason that bears on whether to believe the obvious consequences of p and whether to perform actions that would be favorable if p.
9. Nothing could be a justifying reason for belief or action unless it explained some normative features of those beliefs and actions.
10. If p is part of your evidence, p explains some normative feature of beliefs that concern the obvious consequences of p and actions that would be favorable if p.
11. Falsehoods explain nothing.[30]
12. (Therefore) If p is part of your evidence, p is true.

If p is part of your evidence, p explains something about the normative properties of beliefs. If these beliefs are beliefs in the obvious consequences of p, p explains why there is something that supports them. If the beliefs would involve denying the obvious consequences of p, p would explain why there is something that counts against them. If p plays these explanatory roles, p must be true since false propositions cannot explain anything.

3.3.5 *The linguistic evidence*

In this section, I want to discuss some linguistic evidence that supports Factivity$_E$. Unger once argued for the disturbing conclusion that nothing you ever do, think, or feel is rational.[31] He thought that nothing could be rational because he thought that you could never have reasons for doing, thinking, or feeling anything. He thought that we could not have any knowledge and that there was an important connection between knowledge and reasons:

Known Reasons: If p is your reason for Φ-ing, you know p.

What was his evidence for Known Reasons? Consider:

1. I'm going to the store for the reason that I'm out of coffee, but I don't know I'm out of coffee.
2. I believe I should go to the store for the reason that I'm out of coffee, but I don't know I'm out of coffee.

---

[30] This might be controversial. I defend this assumption below.
[31] See Unger 1975.

These both seem contradictory and so this seems to be some evidence for Known Reasons. Some say that this is not good evidence since these claims could be true even though they sound contradictory:

3. I'm out of coffee, but I don't know that I am.

This is just a Moorean absurdity. It seems contradictory (in some sense), but the proposition it expresses could be true. This is evidenced by the fact that it is felicitous if restated in the third person:

3'. Audrey is out of coffee, but she does not know she is.

So, you might think, the appearance of contradiction is incredibly weak evidence for Known Reasons.

But this is too quick. On the hypothesis that (1) and (2) are defective for the same reason (3) is, (1) and (2) should be felicitous if restated in the third person:

1'. Audrey is going to the store for the reason that she's out of coffee, but she doesn't know that she's out of coffee.
2'. Audrey believes she should go to the store for the reason that she's out of coffee, but she doesn't know she's out of coffee.

Yet, these are defective. The natural explanation as to why they are defective is that they are contradictory. So, we do have some evidence for Known Reasons and Factivity$_E$. If p is Audrey's reason for Φ-ing only if she knows p, only facts constitute her reasons.

It would be much easier for me to show that Factivity$_E$ is true if I could argue from Known Reasons, but I am not entirely convinced that Known Reasons is correct. Known Reasons predicts that this could be a successful challenge to (1):

1c. Audrey believed that she was out of coffee, but her belief was not justified. There was a ton of misleading evidence that we planted in the hopes of tricking her into thinking that she had coffee. She knew of the evidence, but she completely ignored it. So, her reason for going wasn't that she was out of coffee.

The considerations offered might show that Audrey's belief was not justifiably held and did not satisfy the conditions necessary for knowledge, but they do not threaten (1). A natural explanation of this would be that we sometimes use 'knows' to pick out something like a true belief even if we know the belief does not constitute knowledge.[32] Think about

---

[32] Goldman 2002, p. 183.

unfaithful lovers who say others 'know' of their affair knowing full well that nobody has solid evidence that they are having this affair. The behavior of 'knows' in such contexts is not reliable evidence for claims about the relation between knowledge and reasons.

There is further evidence for Factivity$_E$ worth considering. Consider this exchange:

HARRY: Do they have solid evidence against Leo?
GORDON: They think they do. Here's the evidence they have: that he was the last one to see the victim alive, that he lied about his whereabouts on the night of the crime, that his fingerprints were on the murder weapon, and that he wrote a letter containing details the police think only the killer could have known.
HARRY: But didn't you say that he wasn't the last person to see him alive and his fingerprints couldn't have been on the weapon?
GORDON: That's right. He also didn't lie about his whereabouts and wasn't the last one to see him alive.

Gordon seems to contradict himself. In stating the facts as he takes them to be, he contradicts his claims about what evidence the prosecution has. If evidence ascriptions were non-factive, Gordon's remarks should be perfectly coherent. Saying that someone has p as part of her evidence and denying p would be akin to saying that someone believed something false.

These remarks also seem defective:

HARRY: Do they have solid evidence against Leo?
GORDON: People seem to think they do. Here's the evidence they have: that he was the last one to see the victim alive, that he lied about his whereabouts on the night of the crime, that his fingerprints were on the murder weapon, and that he wrote a letter containing details the police think only the killer could have known. That being said, I don't know if he's the last one who saw the victim alive and I don't know if he lied.

Gordon's concession strikes me as odd in just the way that Moorean absurd assertions do (e.g., "Dogs bark, but I do not know that they do"). If his remarks are absurd in this way, this must be because in ascribing evidence to the prosecution he is committing himself to the truth of the propositions that constitute their evidence. If evidence ascriptions were non-factive in the way that belief ascriptions are, Gordon's remarks would be no more problematic than conceding that he does not know if the prosecution's case is strong having just asserted that *they* think it is. With Factivity$_E$, it is easy to see why Gordon's remarks are defective. Without it, it seems his remarks should be in perfectly good order.

We find additional evidence for Factivity$_E$ when we look at the link between evidence and epistemic modality. A standard view concerning epistemic possibility is that something is epistemically impossible if it is obviously inconsistent with something you know.[33] Dougherty and Rysiew have recently argued that what is epistemically possible depends upon your evidence.[34] (Because the relation between knowledge and evidence is a vexed issue, it is not clear whether their view is an alternative to the knowledge account of epistemic possibility or a refinement of it.[35]) On their view, if *p* is inconsistent with your evidence, *p* is not epistemically possible. It seems plausible to me that a hypothesis is not epistemically possible for you if your ultimate evidence rules it out. Notice that if *p* is not epistemically possible, ~*p* must be true.[36] If what is epistemically possible depends upon your evidence, Factivity$_E$ provides a nice explanation as to how 'must' could still be factive on this view. If your evidence consists of truths, anything logically incompatible with your evidence must be false. If, however, evidence did not consist of true propositions, we would either have to say that the hypotheses that your evidence rules out are nevertheless epistemically possible or deny that 'must' is factive. Neither option seems at all palatable.

3.3.6 The argument from the unity of reasons

I want to consider one final argument for Factivity$_E$, the argument from the unity of reasons:

1. Reasons for action are facts.
2. According to Psychologism, if reasons for action are facts, normative reasons for belief belong to a different ontological category from reasons for action.
3. (Therefore) Psychologism implies that reasons for belief belong to a different ontological category from reasons for action.

---

[33] See DeRose 1991 and Hawthorne 2004.
[34] See Dougherty and Rysiew 2009.
[35] Littlejohn in press argues that there is very little that distinguishes these two views of epistemic possibility.
[36] If you say that the umbrella must be in the closet it seems you tell us something about your reasons for thinking that the umbrella is in the closet. If you say (just) that the umbrella is in the closet, however, it does not seem that you tell us anything about your reasons. Even if this is so, this is consistent with the claim that 'must' is factive. For a defense of the factivity of 'must', see von Fintel and Gillies 2007.

4. Reasons for belief and for action belong to the same ontological category.
5. (Therefore) Psychologism is mistaken because reasons for belief are facts.

The key premises are (1) and (4). Since reasons for belief and for action have to play explanatory roles, (1) must be true. In later chapters I shall argue that your obligations depend, in part, upon facts about the circumstances in which you act. Since 'ought' implies 'reason,' the reasons that determine what to do will often have to be things external to you. If reasons for action are external to you, Psychologism has to say that these reasons could never be reasons for belief.

What should we say about (4)? Psychologists cannot plausibly reject (4) if they concede that (1) is true. There is little that distinguishes the arguments for (1) from the arguments against Psychologism. Moreover, it seems rather obvious that the very same thing can be a reason for belief and for action. If Audrey is hiding from Ben the very same thing could be both a reason for Ben to believe that Audrey is hiding behind the curtain and a reason for Audrey to try to run from the house (e.g., that Ben can see her feet). If anything can be a reason for both belief and for action, (4) must be true.

3.3.7 *False evidence?*

Factivity$_E$ has recently come in for heavy criticism. Comesaña and Kantin argue that Factivity$_E$ is incompatible with an intuitively plausible justification-closure principle.[37] Conee and Feldman, Goldman, and Rizzieri argue that cases of mistaken belief cause trouble for Factivity$_E$.[38] These objections assume that what you justifiably believe is a justifying reason:

Justified Basis: If you justifiably believe p, p is a justifying reason of yours that can justify further beliefs.

Once we see why Rizzieri's example fails, it is easy to see why you cannot argue from Justified Basis against Factivity$_E$.

Rizzieri asks us to consider this example:

---

[37] Comesaña and Kantin 2010.
[38] See Conee and Feldman 2008; Goldman 2009b; and Rizzieri 2011. For further defenses of the idea that falsehoods can constitute evidence, see Alex Arnold, "A Knowledge-Centric Argument against E = K" (unpublished manuscript), and Neil Mehta, "Evidence for False Evidence" (unpublished manuscript).

I believe that nobody can enter my office (O for now) because I believe that I have just locked the door (LD for now). Let us stipulate that I have inferred (O) from (LD). I pushed the lock in and gave it a quick twist to the left, which usually does the trick; however, my lock is damaged and does not work. Hence, (LD) is false.[39]

He says:

[If Factivity$_E$] is correct then (LD) cannot serve as an evidential ground for (O) … The first difficulty is that it is very plausible that (LD) does partially constitute my evidence for (O). After all, I am justified in believing (LD), (LD) supports (O), and an explicit inference from (LD) is my most immediate basis or ground for (O).[40]

He adds that it is difficult to deny that LD is evidence for O because LD renders O more probable than it would have been otherwise.[41] This example poses no threat to Factivity$_E$. Once we see why, it is hard to imagine what a counterexample to Factivity$_E$ would look like.

If the case is a counterexample to Factivity$_E$, we have to assume (1):

1. That I have just locked my door is evidence that nobody can enter my office.

Let's suppose that if p is evidence for q, the probability of q has to be higher when p is part of your evidence than it would have been otherwise. Given this assumption, (1) entails:

2. Because I just locked my door, it is more probable than it would have been otherwise that nobody could get into my office.

The problem is that (2) entails:

3. I just locked my door.

The case is a potential counterexample to Factivity$_E$ only if (1) is true and (3) is false, but the argument just sketched shows that (1) entails (3). The objection to Factivity$_E$ fails.[42]

My response to Rizzieri's objection assumes that evidence for q raises q's evidential probability and that 'because' is factive. Some have objected

[39] Rizzieri 2011, p. 236. O and LD are *propositions believed*, not the subject's *beliefs*. The objection is directed against Factivity$_E$, not Strong Propositionalism.

[40] Rizzieri 2011, p. 237. His target is Williamson's thesis that your evidence consists of all and only what you know. He objects to E = K because it implies Factivity$_E$, as do the other authors discussed in this section, so I have modified their remarks to highlight this fact.

[41] Rizzieri 2011, p. 237.

[42] It might be possible for p to be evidence for q even if the probability of q on the total evidence is not increased by the addition of p. This worry is easily addressed.

to both claims, but I think the defense of Factivity$_E$ holds up.[43] Let's suppose that while evidence for q would typically raise q's evidential probability, this is not invariably the case. Even if it is not, there has to be some necessary condition on evidential support for p to be evidence for q, otherwise everything and anything would be evidence for q. This condition might be highly disjunctive, but whatever that condition is, let us say that C is that condition. Thus, unless 'p is evidence for q' entails 'q satisfies C', p is not evidence for q. If the example discussed is a counterexample to Factivity$_E$ we have to assume that for the relevant p and q:

   (i) p is evidence for q.

We saw that (i) entails (ii) and (iii):

  (ii) Because of p, q satisfies C.
 (iii) p is true.

If (iii) is true, the example is not a potential counterexample to Factivity$_E$ because the counterexample needs to be one in which a falsehood is evidence for q.

   In arguing that (2) entails (3), I assumed that 'because' is factive. The evidence suggests that it is:

4. The crops died because there was a drought. Not only that, there was a drought.
5. He knows that conservatives overreached. Indeed, the conservatives did overreach.
6. Yes, I have a friend who has voted for a Republican. I have exactly one such friend. He is listed in my acknowledgments.

You cannot reinforce entailments. If you try, you end up with redundant conjunctions (e.g., (5)). You can, however, reinforce pragmatically imparted information (e.g., in (6)).[44] It seems to me that (4) is a redundant conjunction, in which case the relation between 'p because q' and 'p and q' is stronger than pragmatic implication. It seems to be an entailment.

   For further evidence of the factivity of 'because', consider:

7. Although nobody was on the bridge, the bolt snapped because there were so many people on the bridge.

This seems to be a contradiction. This would not be surprising if (8) and (9) were equivalent:

---

[43] I am grateful to Christopher Cloos and Trent Dougherty for discussion.
[44] See Sadock 1978 and Stanley 2008.

8. The bolt snapped because there were so many people on the bridge.
9. There were too many people on the bridge. That's why the bolt snapped.

It does seem that (8) and (9) are equivalent since it seems contradictory to assert (8) and (~9) or to assert (~8) and (9). It also seems you cannot reinforce (8) with (9) or vice versa. If these are equivalent, (7) is a contradiction, in which case 'p because q' is true only if p and q are true. The assumptions I need to show that the alleged counterexamples to Factivity$_E$ fail seem to hold up rather well.

3.4 HAVING EVIDENCE

Our focus has been on the constitution of evidence. We know now that evidence consists of true propositions, but not which true propositions belong to your evidence. I shall argue that your non-derivative, foundational, or ultimate evidence includes anything that you know non-inferentially. If Liberal Foundationalism is true and the scope of non-inferential knowledge includes facts about the external world, we have our argument against Evidential and Supervenience Internalism.

Earlier I outlined an argument against Evidential Internalism:

1. My evidence includes the proposition that I have hands.
2. My evidence includes the proposition that I have hands only if I have hands.
3. Since hands are objects met in space, my evidence can include the proposition that I have hands if facts about my evidence do not strongly supervene upon facts about my non-factive mental states.
4. (Therefore) Facts about my evidence do not strongly supervene upon facts about my non-factive mental states.

With the arguments for Factivity$_E$ and Strong Propositionalism in place, we now see why (1) and (2) are true. In this section, I shall argue that your evidence includes propositions about the external world (i.e., e-propositions). There might be limits on which e-propositions constitute evidence. It might be that your evidence does not include the proposition that you have hands. If I can show that one e-proposition could belong to your evidence, the refutation of Evidential Internalism is complete.

According to Williamson, your evidence consists of what you know:

E = K: Your evidence includes p iff you know p.[45]

---

[45] Williamson 2000a.

Given the mildly anti-skeptical assumption that I know I have hands, there is a straightforward argument for (1). The problem with arguing from E = K is that it seems that knowledge is neither necessary nor sufficient for evidence. According to E = K, knowledge suffices for evidence and evidence suffices for knowledge:

ESK: If your evidence includes p, you know p.
KSE: If you know p, your evidence includes p.

Against ESK, I shall argue that there can be cases of evidence without knowledge. As for KSE, it is not obvious that all of what you know belongs to your evidence.

E = K needs revision because ESK is too restrictive. On his drive through fake-barn country, Coop sees what he correctly takes to be a barn. Because there are so many barn facades in the area, he does not know that what he sees is a barn. Because he happens upon the one actual barn in the area, he believes correctly and quite reasonably that the building he sees is a barn. According to ESK, Coop's evidence cannot include the proposition that the building he sees is a barn. According to KSE, Coop's evidence would have included this proposition if only the fakes he never sees had not been constructed. Intuitively, Coop has the same evidence in both the original fake-barn case and the case of no fakes. Ideally, we would want to explain Coop's ignorance in terms of factors external to his evidence. We should let Coop's evidence include e-propositions he comes to believe by taking his veridical experience at face value even if he does not know that they are true for purely Gettierish reasons. In a perfectly good sense, something shows him that some fact is true and he can correctly judge that this fact is true without engaging in any sort of inference.

E = K might also need revision because KSE might be too permissive. You know the details of the study and know that the reason scientists believe that only female foxes like to eat berries is that they observed hundreds of very hungry foxes and saw that only the females would eat berries. The male foxes preferred chicken and root vegetables. You look out the window and see a fox in your yard eating berries from the bushes and judge:

1. There is a female fox in the yard.

Knowing that female foxes are vixens, you deduce:

2. There is a vixen in the yard.

You remember that (2) entails (1), so you think to yourself (correctly) that (-2) is inconsistent with what you know iff (-1) is inconsistent with what you know. You then note that if E = K is correct, you can know that (1) is true only if (-2) is inconsistent with your evidence. Intuitively, it seems that (-2) is consistent with your evidence prior to believing (1) and is consistent with your evidence after believing (1). After all, your grounds for believing (1) are inductive grounds. The problem is that E = K can only accommodate the intuition that (-2) is consistent with your evidence if we say that (1) is never part of your evidence. This would compel us to say that you do not know that (1) is so. Remember that it is part of the story that (1) is supported by strong inductive grounds. You can make those grounds as strong as you like and it seems intuitive to say that the negations of the deductive consequences of what you believe on such grounds are logically consistent with your evidence.

I do not know what Williamson would say in response to my objection to ESK, but I think I know what he should say in response to my objection to KSE. Following Conee and Feldman, he should distinguish your *ultimate* evidence from your *intermediate* evidence.[46] Your ultimate evidence is evidence that you do not need evidence for in order for it to be part of your evidence. The propositions that constitute intermediate evidence are evidence in that they can provide you with reasons for forming further beliefs, but only if your beliefs concerning these propositions are inferentially justified. He can accommodate the intuition that the negations of the conclusions of inductive inference are compatible with your evidence by saying that the negations of the conclusions of inductive inference are compatible with your ultimate evidence. He can accommodate the intuitions underwriting my objection to KSE by saying that your intermediate evidence will include those propositions that you know inferentially.

Conee and Feldman would object to any view that combines Factivity$_E$ with the further view that your ultimate evidence can include e-propositions because they defend Evidential Internalism. In this passage, they tell us what they take ultimate evidence to be:

Some philosophers have argued that only believed propositions can be part of the evidence one has. Our view differs radically from this one. We hold that experiences can be evidence, and beliefs are only derivatively evidence. Examples intuitively support that we have experiences as evidence. Your evidence for the proposition that it is warm where you are typically includes your feeling

---

[46] Conee and Feldman 2008, p. 87 n. 5.

of warmth ... It is not just other propositions that you believe that contribute to your justification. The experience itself contributes. Experience is our point of interaction with the world – conscious awareness is how we gain whatever evidence we have. Furthermore, all ultimate evidence is experiential. Believing a proposition, all by itself, is not evidence for its truth. Something at the interface of your mind and the world – your experiences – serves to justify belief in a proposition ... What we are calling your "ultimate evidence" does this without needing any justification in order to provide it.[47]

I do not think Conee and Feldman can square their circle. In terms of its function, they say that your ultimate evidence is evidence you have where you do not need any further evidence for it to belong to your evidence. Thus, they accept:

> Basicality: p is part of your ultimate evidence iff p is a justifying reason of yours where you do not need any additional evidence for p to have this status.

In terms of its substance, they say that ultimate evidence is experiential. We know now that all evidence is propositional, so we know that if they want to maintain the connection between ultimate evidence and experience they have to defend one of these two theses:

> Narrow Experientialism: If p is part of your ultimate evidence, p is the content of some introspective state that represents your experience, not some contingent proposition about the external world.
> Broad Experientialism: If p is part of your ultimate evidence, p is either the content of some introspective state or the content of one of your perceptual experiences.

Neither of these theses suits their purposes.

Suppose you see that p is true. You seem to see that p and your experience is veridical. Intuitively, you can treat p as a reason for forming a belief without needing any further evidence to do so. In this case p is both an e-proposition (because it is part of the content of your experience) and part of your ultimate evidence (because it is evidence you have without needing to have any evidence for p). This is consistent with Broad Experientialism, but inconsistent with Evidential Internalism. If p is an e-proposition and part of your evidence, you have evidence that your epistemic counterparts might not have. You could have an epistemic counterpart who falsely believed p even though it seemed to them that p given their experiences.

---

[47] Conee and Feldman 2008, p. 88.

To save Evidential Internalism, Conee and Feldman have to reject Broad Experientialism. If they opt for Narrow Experientialism, they can avoid saying that what you see when your experience is veridical is part of your evidence and still retain Basicality and Evidential Internalism. Unfortunately, this combination of views leads to external-world skepticism.

To see why, consider Pryor's 'cognitive scientist's discovery argument'.[48] If the traditional foundationalist view is correct and all of our foundational beliefs are beliefs that concern our own mental states, someone could know that, say, there is a tree before her only if she based that belief on a belief that she is having a 'treeish experience'. Cognitive scientists might discover that we simply do not have these beliefs about our present conscious mental life and that we form our beliefs about the external world just by taking experience at face value. If we do that, we endorse the e-propositions that are part of the content of our experience without treating anything else as a reason for believing these e-propositions. It seems that subjects like us or very similar to us could come to know that they are standing in front of a tree without forming any belief about the character of their experience. Thus, Traditional Foundationalism is mistaken in thinking that we can have knowledge of an external world only on the basis of self-knowledge. Thus, if Narrow Experientialism was true and our basic beliefs are limited to beliefs about our own experiences, we would know nothing of the external world. Since we do have knowledge of the external world, we have to reject Narrow Experientialism.

We can sum up the case against Evidential Internalism as follows. Basicality states that your ultimate evidence consists of facts you can treat as reasons without needing any further evidence to do so. What you know non-inferentially is ideally suited for this role. What is known non-inferentially is a fact, so it is the right sort of thing to be evidence. What you know non-inferentially you justifiably believe, so it is the sort of thing you can rightly rely on in trying to determine what is true. So, if the liberal foundationalists are right that the scope of non-inferential knowledge includes some e-propositions, Evidential Internalism is sunk. It denies that it is possible for your evidence to include these e-propositions.

---

[48] Pryor 2000, p. 539. Feldman 2004 endorses Pryor's argument, but does not discuss whether Liberal Foundationalism supports Evidential Externalism.

3.5 ACCESS AND EVIDENCE

In this section, I want to address some of the more powerful objections to Evidential Externalism. While there are good reasons for revising some externalist views, they give us no reason to reject Evidential Externalism altogether.

The first objection to Evidential Externalism is that it conflicts with an important platitude about the kind of access you have to your ultimate evidence:

> Unproblematic Access: You have unproblematic access to your evidence.

Silins suggests that if you have unproblematic access to your evidence, you have armchair access to your evidence:

> Armchair Access: If p is part of your evidence, you can know that p is part of your evidence from the armchair alone.

Appealing to Armchair Access, he objects to E = K on the following grounds:

1. You know that E = K is true from the armchair.
2. You know p on the basis of observation.
3. (Therefore) p is part of your evidence.
4. If p is part of your evidence, you could know that p is part of your evidence from the armchair alone.
5. (Therefore) You know that p is part of your evidence from the armchair alone.
6. You know from the armchair that if you know that p is part of your evidence from the armchair alone, you can know p from the armchair alone.
7. (Therefore) You can know p from the armchair alone. [49]

It would be absurd to suggest that anything we can know via observation could have been known from the armchair alone, so we need to somehow block the argument for (7).

While I have already expressed some doubts about E = K, I cannot simply deny E = K and thereby dispense with Silins' objection. His objection applies with equal force to any non-skeptical view that incorporates IKSE and Factivity$_E$. You get the same troubling result if you replace (3) with:

---

[49] Silins 2005, p. 381.

3′. You know IKSE and Factivity$_E$ from the armchair.

I shall argue that the best way to deal with this objection is to deny Armchair Access.

To see why we should reject Armchair Access, notice that we can generate skeptical problems from the assumption of Armchair Access. Just as Silins suggests (plausibly) that if E = K is true, we should be able to know that it is from the armchair, I shall assume the same holds for Armchair Access:

8. You can know from the armchair that your evidence is limited to propositions that you can know from the armchair belong to your evidence.
9. If p is part of your evidence, p is true.
10. If you know non-inferentially that p is true, p is part of your evidence.
11. (Therefore) If your evidence includes the proposition that you have hands, you know from armchair that you have hands.
12. But, it is absurd to think you could know from the armchair that you have hands.
13. (Therefore) Your evidence cannot include the proposition that you have hands.
14. If your evidence cannot include the proposition that you have hands, you are either fooled into thinking that you have hands when in reality you are handless or the fact that you have hands is not something anyone can know non-inferentially.
15. (Therefore) You are either fooled into thinking that you have hands or you cannot know non-inferentially that you have hands.
16. (Therefore) If you have hands, you cannot know non-inferentially that you do.
17. (Therefore) If you do not have hands, you cannot know non-inferentially that you do.
18. (Therefore) You cannot know non-inferentially that you have hands whether you happen to have hands or not.

Armchair Access leads to external-world skepticism.

Since my argument assumed IKSE and Factivity$_E$, it might seem that it would be easy to dispense with my objection by denying IKSE or Factivity$_E$. Let me say two things in response. First, it would be odd to think that these two theses are responsible for generating any untoward skeptical results since they seem to suggest that we have copious amounts of evidence whereas Armchair Access suggests that our body of evidence is quite limited. Surely skeptical pressures come from saying that we have little evidence, not lots of it. Second, we can generate the same skeptical result arguing from weaker assumptions than I employed above:

19. If you know from the armchair that p could be part of your evidence only if you had empirical justification to believe p, then you cannot know from the armchair that p is part of your evidence.
20. You know from the armchair that if the proposition that you have hands is part of your evidence, you would have to have empirical justification to believe that you have hands.
21. You know that you cannot know from the armchair that you have empirical justification to believe that you have hands.
22. You know that you cannot know from the armchair that the proposition that you have hands is part of your evidence.
23. Your evidence cannot include the proposition that you have hands.
24. If you could know non-inferentially that you have hands, your evidence could include the proposition that you have hands.
25. (Therefore) You know you cannot know non-inferentially that you have hands.

Remember that armchair knowledge is knowledge that does not depend constitutively upon experience and the justification it provides. So, (19) and (21) should be true if Armchair Access is. As for (20), the thought is that you cannot properly treat e-propositions as reasons for further belief unless they received some sort of support from experience. This seems to be something you could know upon reflection alone. So, it is a good candidate for armchair knowledge.

   If you recall Pryor's argument for Liberal Foundationalism, he argued that it is contingent on whether the scope of non-inferential knowledge includes contingent worldly propositions. The argument just sketched shows that if Armchair Access is true, no such proposition could be part of anyone's evidence regardless of whether they were wired in such a way that their beliefs about such contingent worldly propositions were based on propositions about the subject's own mental life or were instead beliefs in the propositions that are part of the content of experience. If the lesson you took from his argument is that any argument that purports to show that we cannot have non-inferential knowledge of contingent worldly propositions would show that we cannot have knowledge of such propositions, the argument just sketched shows that Armchair Access commits us to the skeptical conclusion that you cannot know you have hands.

If Armchair Access gives us any reason to reject Evidential Externalism, we have to assume that the intuition that supports Unproblematic Access supports Armchair Access. If it does, then we would have to say that facts that you know about the external world non-inferentially do not belong to our evidence because we have only epistemically problematic access to these facts. While there is something strange to the suggestion that your evidence consists of facts you have only problematic access to, there is equally something strange to the suggestion that you can know p non-inferentially even if your access to the fact that p is epistemically problematic. If it were problematic, it seems you could not justifiably believe p without further evidence for p. But, if you could not justifiably believe p without further evidence, your belief in p would not constitute non-inferential knowledge. Thus, it seems that Unproblematic Access cannot support Armchair Access for the simple reason that you have unproblematic access to what you know non-inferentially including e-propositions that you know on the basis of observation.

Perhaps Unproblematic Access supports something weaker than Armchair Access:

> Modified Armchair Access: If p is part of your evidence, it is possible for you to know that p is part of your evidence without needing any empirical justification for believing that p is part of your evidence beyond the justification needed for p to be part of your evidence.

Unlike Armchair Access, Modified Armchair Access does not imply that anything you cannot know from the armchair is epistemically problematic. Thus, Modified Armchair Access does not conflict with a view that incorporates IKSE and Factivity$_E$. It does, however, cause trouble for E = K:

26. You know on the basis of observation that p is true.
27. (Therefore) p is part of your evidence.
28. You know that p is part of your evidence without further empirical investigation.
29. You know from the armchair that if p is part of your evidence, you know p.
30. You know that if you know p, your belief in p is not Gettiered.
31. You know from the armchair that if p is part of your evidence, your belief in p is not Gettiered.
32. (Therefore) You know without further empirical investigation that your belief in p is not Gettiered.

If this were so, fake-barn detection would be impossibly easy. Since you cannot know that your beliefs concerning e-propositions are not Gettiered without drawing on more empirical evidence than the evidence that supports your belief, I think Unproblematic Access gives us some reason to think E = K is mistaken. It gives us no reason, however, to reject views that incorporate Factivity$_E$ and IKSE because these claims are consistent with the further claim that you can have the same evidence whether you are in fake-barn country or real-barn country. Since Unproblematic Access seems to be compatible with Evidential Externalism, intuitions about the kind of access we have to our evidence do not support Evidential Internalism.

3.6 EVIDENCE AND EPISTEMIC RATIONALITY

I want to close this chapter by considering one of the standard arguments for Evidential Internalism. The crucial premise in the argument is the plausible suggestion that rationality is an internalist notion:

> Rationality Internalism: The conditions that determine whether your beliefs are rationally held strongly supervene upon your non-factive mental states.

The epistemically rational believer respects her evidence. If so, should rationality internalists be evidential internalists? Suppose Harry and Cooper are in precisely the same mental states and that they both believe that Leo is the killer. Harry saw Leo kill his victim. Cooper was hallucinating. Suppose some version of Evidential Externalism is correct (e.g., one that incorporates Factivity$_E$ and IKSE). Harry's evidence includes everything that Coop's evidence includes, but it includes more besides. Now, if Cooper knew that his evidence included only the evidence someone would have in the bad case (i.e., the case in which his beliefs are mistaken or based on hallucinations), he ought to be significantly less confident in his beliefs than Harry is. Perhaps if he knew he had less evidence than Harry, he ought to suspend judgment. If he knew that his evidence included just the evidence someone had in the bad case and did not adjust his attitudes accordingly, he would not be as reasonable or rational as Harry is. But, if Factivity$_E$ and IKSE are true, he is not in a position to know that he has less evidence than Harry does. Indeed, it seems he could not be rational unless he was ignorant of the fact that he had less evidence. But, then we have to say that he is rational because he fails to know what his evidence is. So, how can we say that epistemic rationality consists in respecting the evidence?

Williamson has offered two responses to this kind of argument for Evidential Internalism. First, he says that the demands of rationality are not luminous.[50] He might be right, but if this is going to undercut the argument, we have to say that Coop does not know what rationality demands simply because his experience is non-veridical. That seems rather counterintuitive. Moreover, saying that Coop does not know what the demands of rationality are seems to suggest that Rationality Internalism might be false, not that Rationality Internalism does not support Evidential Internalism. Since Rationality Internalism seems rather intuitive, I would prefer a different line of response.

Williamson's second response is to say that subjects in the bad case might have less evidence for their worldly beliefs than subjects in the good case do even if both have sufficient evidence to justifiably believe what they do.[51] If they both have good enough evidence for their beliefs, perhaps both subjects are rational in their beliefs even if they have different bodies of evidence.

I agree that someone can have less evidence than someone in the good case and still have sufficient evidence for her beliefs. What worries me about this response is that while he is right that evidential externalists can say that subjects in the bad case are rational, it is not entirely clear that they can also say that subjects in the good case are just as rational. Suppose subjects in the good and bad case are equally confident in believing what they do on the basis of their experiences. It seems subjects in the good case ought to be more confident since they have more evidence. Yet, these subjects are equally confident in these cases. So, some subject is either too confident or not confident enough. So, some subject is not perfectly rational. So, the objection continues, evidential externalists have to deny Rationality Internalism.[52]

There are two things to say in response to the argument from Rationality Internalism. First, for reasons discussed earlier, it is a mistake to say that the rational is the mark of the justified. Thus, two subjects can be equally rational in how they respond to the reasons that apply to them even if different reasons apply to them and the right response to these reasons differs. In the case of excusable wrongdoing, for example, the agent counts as being equally rational and responsible as the agent who acts rightly even though she acts against an undefeated reason. (If the reason had been defeated, this would have been a wrongful act that was justified by

---

[50] Williamson 2000b, p. 624.   [51] Williamson 2000a, p. 197.
[52] Silins 2005, p. 387. See also Conee and Feldman 2008 and Schiffer 2009.

overriding reasons.) Thus, the platitude that the rational believer respects the evidence should not be taken to show that every failure to respond correctly to the evidence is an indication of irrationality. Now, what if we bite the bullet and say that if subjects in the case of hallucination and perception are equally confident, one of these subjects is not as confident as she should be? If they ought to have different degrees of confidence, there is an undefeated reason for them to adjust their degrees of confidence accordingly. It does not follow that one of these subjects is less than perfectly rational because failing to respond to the reasons that apply to them is not a failure of rationality, per se.

Harry and Cooper are equally confident in their perceptual beliefs. On the bullet-biting response, both are sufficiently confident to believe on the basis of their respective experiences, but at most one of these subjects ought to be as confident as they are. So, one of them ought either to be more confident or less so. In the next chapter I shall argue that you should not believe on the basis of non-veridical experience. Thus, at most, one of these subjects' experiential beliefs is justified. If a subject ought not believe *p* but he believes *p*, he ought to be less confident in *p*. He should lower his level of confidence below whatever threshold he must to avoid having the false belief. Clearly, Cooper is too confident because he believes Leo is the killer, but he should not be so confident because his belief is based on a non-veridical experience. It does not follow that he is less than fully rational, mind you, but he ought to be less confident. Rationality seems to be more a matter of responding in ways that would be right if what seemed to be your reasons were your reasons and less a matter of responding correctly to all the reasons that apply to you.

3.7 CONCLUSION

We should reject Evidential and Supervenience Internalism on the grounds that you can have better evidence than your epistemic counterparts. Given the plausible anti-skeptical assumption that you have non-inferential knowledge of e-propositions, your evidence can include e-propositions that cannot belong to your systematically deceived counterparts' evidence. In the next chapter, I shall argue that the version of Evidential Externalism defended here causes serious problems for orthodox internalist and externalist views.

CHAPTER 4

Reasons for belief (II)

4.1 INTRODUCTION

In the previous chapter, I argued that evidence consists of facts, not your attitudes or false propositions you rationally accept. Your ultimate evidence includes whatever true propositions you believe with non-inferential justification. Given the mildly anti-skeptical assumption that this includes propositions about the external world, it is possible for you to have better evidence than your epistemic counterparts. Internalists about justification might respond to these arguments with indifference. These external epistemic reasons, they might say, are epistemically idle.[1] They are not your reasons for believing anything about the external world and they cannot make you better off than your systematically deceived counterparts. While you and your epistemic counterparts might have different bodies of evidence, your beliefs will be justified to the same degree and this is what really matters. They might admit that Evidential Internalism and Supervenience Internalism are not strictly speaking true, but say that overall justificatory status still supervenes upon your internal conditions.

One of my aims in this chapter is to show that this deflationary response is mistaken. Once we see that our reasons are better than the reasons we would have if we were systematically deceived, we will see that we are better positioned to meet our epistemic obligations than our systematically deceived epistemic counterparts are. They are not just systematically deceived about the external world. They are deceived about the reasons they have and what epistemic duty requires of them.

Another aim of this chapter is to refine my account of evidence. E = K is simple and elegant in precisely the way that the view that emerged from the previous chapter is not:

---

[1] Conee and Feldman 2008 press this charge against McDowell 1995, 1998 and Williamson 2000a.

E = IJTB: Your ultimate evidence includes *p* iff *p* is true and your belief that *p* is true is non-inferentially justified.

Williamson raises the worry that this sort of view is "a rather unnatural hybrid [because] the truth-condition is an *ad hoc* afterthought, not an organic consequence."[2] I agree. To show that the truth-condition is not some ad hoc afterthought, I shall argue that the truth-condition is redundant. Your ultimate evidence is what you believe with non-inferential justification. Your total evidence (i.e., your ultimate and intermediate evidence) consists of what you justifiably believe:

E = J: Your evidence includes *p* iff you justifiably believe *p*.

The truth-condition is redundant because there are no false, justified beliefs:

Factivity$_J$: You cannot justifiably believe *p* unless *p* is true.

Factivity$_J$ is a consequence of two theses concerning the ontology of reasons for belief and action:

Factivity$_E$: If *p* is a justifying reason of yours to believe, *p* is true.
Factivity$_P$: If *p* is a justifying reason of yours to act, *p* is true.

The motivation for Factivity$_J$ is the simple thought that if you justifiably believe something, what you believe can justify further beliefs or justify actions that your justified beliefs rationalize. When your beliefs do not fit the facts, they are not fit for deliberation and this is why they cannot be justifiably held.

4.2 THE MYTH OF THE FALSE, JUSTIFIED BELIEF

You can derive Factivity$_J$ from Factivity$_E$ given three assumptions about doxastic justification:

Proper Basis: If you justifiably believe *p*, you have some justifying reason for this belief and your belief is based on it.
Same Basis: If you justifiably believe *p* on the basis of some reason, *q*, any epistemic counterpart of yours that justifiably believes *p* on the basis of some reason will believe it on the basis of *q*.
J-Closure: If you justifiably believe *p*, you have sufficient justification to believe at least one of *p*'s obvious logical consequences and could

---

[2] Williamson 2009, p. 311.

come justifiably to believe this proposition if you form this belief by means of competent deduction.

These assumptions are reasonably uncontroversial, but it might be a good idea to offer a brief word in support of each of them.

According to Proper Basis, you have a justifying reason to believe whatever you justifiably believe and this reason is the reason for which you believe what you do. If Proper Basis were false, it would be possible to (i) justifiably believe something without having any reason whatever to believe it or (ii) to justifiably believe something you need good reasons to believe without believing for good reasons. On its face, (i) seems rather implausible. It sounds contradictory to say that although Audrey has no reason to believe the market will recover, she justifiably believes that it will or to say that there is no justification for Audrey's belief that there will be an uptick in consumer confidence, but she nevertheless justifiably believes there will be.

Once you accept (i) it is hard to reject (ii). As Pollock and Cruz note:

One could have a good reason at one's disposal but never make the connection. Suppose, for instance, that you are giving a mathematical proof. At a certain point you get stuck. You want to derive a particular intermediate conclusion, but you cannot see how to do it. In despair, you just write it down and think to yourself, "That's got to be true." In fact, the conclusion follows from two earlier lines by modus ponens, but you have overlooked that. Surely, you are not justified in believing the conclusion, despite the fact that you have impeccable reasons for it at your disposal. What is lacking is that you do not believe the conclusion on the basis of those reasons.[3]

It makes little sense to say that you cannot justifiably accept the proof's conclusion without justifiably believing the proof's premises if it does not matter whether belief in the premises is what convinces you of the conclusion. If the premises do not persuade you to accept the conclusion, how could you be better off for having them?

Let's look at Same Basis. Audrey thinks the conservatives will do badly in the upcoming elections. Her reason for thinking so is that the conservatives overreached in the recent budget negotiations. According to Same Basis, Audrey's epistemic counterparts will believe what Audrey believes for the same reasons that Audrey does if their beliefs are based on any reasons at all. If Audrey's reason for believing that the conservatives will do poorly in the upcoming elections is not that the liberal base is energized,

---

[3] Pollock and Cruz 1999, p. 35. For further defense of the view that doxastic justification is a matter of propositional justification plus proper basing, see Kvanvig and Menzel 1990.

her epistemic counterparts will not believe the conservatives will do poorly in the upcoming elections on the basis that the liberal base is energized. If some subject is Audrey's epistemic counterpart, she is Audrey's non-factive mental duplicate and the causal relations between their mental states are the same as the causal relations between Audrey's mental states. On standard accounts of the basing relation, causal relations among your mental states determine which reasons (if any) move you to believe or act. If we hold these relations fixed, the reasons for which epistemic counter-parts believe what they do will not vary.

Finally, let's look at J-Closure. J-Closure is far weaker than standard formulations of closure principles since they say you that you have suf-ficient justification to believe the known logical consequences of what you justifiably believe. While I think these stronger principles are correct, these principles invite distracting objections. Maybe you cannot justifi-ably believe that the animal in the cage is not a cleverly disguised mule even if you justifiably believe that it is a zebra. Even if you thought there were counterexamples to unrestricted closure principles for justification, J-Closure is restricted. J-Closure requires something incredibly modest, which is that for any proposition you justifiably believe you have suffi-cient justification to believe *one* of its obvious logical consequences. Can you justifiably believe you have hands without having sufficient justifi-cation to believe the disjunctive proposition that either you have hands or Custer died at Little Big Horn? Not if you have a modicum of logical ability.

With these three assumptions in place, let's turn to the derivation. Start with the case of non-inferentially justified belief. Suppose you believe p and that your belief is justified non-inferentially. According to Proper Basis, you have some justifying reason for this belief and your belief is based on this reason. If your belief is based on p itself, Factivity$_E$ says that p must be true.[4] Thus, there are no non-inferentially justified, false beliefs.

---

[4] Millar 2000 argues quite persuasively that there can be cases of non-inferentially justified belief where the content of the belief and the reason on which it is based differ. You might know non-inferentially, for instance, that the building you see through the window is a barn on the basis of perceptual experiences that would have been veridical if you had seen a barn facade rather than a barn. If veridicality conditions tell us what the content of an experience is, it seems possible to know that some building is a barn directly even if experience does not represent anything as being a barn. If such cases are possible, the argument against the possibility of false, justified belief based on non-entailing inferential reasons should cover cases where what you know non-inferentially is not itself the content of any experience.

Suppose you believe p and this belief is inferentially justified. According to Proper Basis, you have some justifying reason for that belief, q, where q is your basis for believing p. According to Factivity$_E$, q is true. If we suppose that q entails p, p must be true, too. Thus, there are no inferentially justified, false beliefs based on entailing evidence.[5] To complete the derivation, suppose you justifiably believe p on the basis of q where q does not entail p. According to J-Closure, if you justifiably believe p you could justifiably believe at least one obvious logical consequence of p. Suppose you know that r is an obvious logical consequence of p and you competently deduce r from p. Across modal space, your epistemic counterparts follow suit. In some possible world one of your counterparts justifiably concludes that r is the case on the basis of p. According to Proper Basis, p is one of your counterpart's justifying reasons. According to Factivity$_E$, your counterpart is in a p-world. If you justifiably believe r, Proper Basis implies that you have a justifying reason. According to Same Basis, your justifying reason is what your counterpart's justifying reason is. Thus, your justifying reason for believing r is p. According to Factivity$_E$, you are in a p-world. This completes the argument. You cannot justifiably believe any false propositions whether your belief is non-inferentially justified, justified by entailing evidence, or justified by non-entailing evidence.

Williamson also defends Factivity$_E$, but he rejects Factivity$_J$. He endorses closure principles for knowledge stronger than J-Closure and thinks knowledge requires justified belief.[6] He also seems to like the idea that justification depends upon whether the subject fits her beliefs to the evidence, basing what she believes on what she knows. If he accepts J-Closure and Proper Basis, he can block the derivation only by denying Same Basis. In discussing cases of perceptual illusion, he does say that we have less evidence than we do in the case of perceptual knowledge:

In unfavorable circumstances, one fails to gain perceptual knowledge, perhaps because things are not the way they appear to be. One does not know that things are that way, and E=K excludes the proposition that they are as evidence. Nevertheless, one still has perceptual evidence, even if the propositions it supports are false. True propositions can make a false proposition probable, as when someone is skillfully framed for a crime of which she is innocent. If perceptual evidence in the case of illusions consists of true propositions, what are they? The

---

[5] This might seem trivial, but it is not. Remember that some believe that falsehoods can constitute evidence. On these views, it is possible to have entailing evidence (in some sense) for false propositions.

[6] For his discussion of closure principles for knowledge, see Williamson 2000a, p. 117. For his argument that knowledge requires justification, see Williamson 2007, p. 111.

obvious answer is: the proposition that things appear to be that way. The mountain appears to be that shape.[7]

I cannot tell if he denies Same Basis, but there are good reasons for him not to do so.[8] First, if he denies Same Basis it seems he has to say that two subjects can believe for different reasons even if there is no difference in their non-factive mental states, the causal relations between them, and the facts that they have in mind. If psychology, causal relations between psychological states, and causal relations between these states and the facts do not determine which reasons (if any) you believe for, what could? Second, the pressure to deny Same Basis seems to stem from the thought that your reasons for believing p in the good case (i.e., the case where you know p) are better than your reasons in the bad case (i.e., the case where you believe p without knowing that p is true). In the case of perception, I think this is the right thing to say. In cases of inductive inference, this leads to some serious problems. In cases of inductive inference, you should be able to knowingly infer that all Fs are Gs if you have observed a sufficiently large representative sample of Fs. If knowledge that the generalization holds requires having reasons to believe that all Fs are Gs that are better than the reasons anyone could have if they falsely believed that all Fs are Gs, it would be impossible to know that all the Fs are Gs without entailing evidence for the generalization that the Fs are Gs. Thus, inductive inference could not generate knowledge.

Given that he defends Factivity$_E$, you might wonder why he rejects Factivity$_J$. He says:

One's evidence justifies belief in the hypothesis if and only if one's knowledge justifies that belief. Knowledge figures in the account primarily as what justifies, not as what gets justified. Knowledge can justify a belief which is not itself knowledge, for the justification relation is not deductive.[9]

He is right that the justification relation is not deductive. You can justifiably believe something without entailing reasons for your belief. The argument for Factivity$_J$ does not assume that you can only justifiably believe on the basis of entailing evidence or show that you need such

---

[7] Williamson 2000a, p. 197.
[8] In responding to critics, Williamson says that a proposition about how something looks "does more work" in the bad case than it does in the good. In the good case, such a proposition is part of your evidence, but it is made redundant by other propositions you know. If Williamson accepts Proper Basis, the evidence that shoulders a justificatory burden has to be the basis for holding a belief. It might be that he rejects Proper Basis, however, in which case the arguments for Proper Basis constitute arguments against his view. See Williamson 2009, p. 283.
[9] Williamson 2000a, p. 9.

evidence for justification. Instead, the idea was that justification depends upon two kinds of reasons. Justification depends positively upon the quality of the reasons that support your beliefs and negatively upon reasons not to believe. Because beliefs are supposed to provide support for further beliefs, there is a reason not to believe *p* if that belief cannot lend support to further beliefs. Since false beliefs cannot provide reasons for belief, they cannot lend support to further beliefs, so there is a reason not to believe falsehoods. This reason defeats the support your evidence provides even if the fact that your belief is mistaken is one you are non-culpably ignorant of.[10]

4.3 PRACTICAL REASONS AND EPISTEMIC JUSTIFICATION

In this section, I want to offer a second argument for Factivity$_J$, one that appeals to the idea that justifying reasons for action consist of facts. Just as we can derive Factivity$_J$ from Factivity$_E$, Factivity$_J$ can be derived from Factivity$_P$. My suggestion is that because of belief's role in practical deliberation, we not only see why much of practical rationality can be understood in terms of epistemically rational beliefs about what to do, we can see that epistemic permissibility can depend constitutively upon whether beliefs are fit for service in practical deliberation.[11]

The argument proceeds as follows:

1. The belief that *p* is true can only contribute a reason to practical deliberation if *p* is true. If, however, *p* is false, the belief that *p* is true will pass off a counterfeit reason as if it were genuine.
2. If the belief that *p* is true would merely pass off a counterfeit reason as one that is genuine, there is no normative reason to include that belief in practical deliberation that bears on whether to Φ.
3. There is, however, a normative reason to exclude the belief that *p* from practical and theoretical deliberation, if the belief would pass off a counterfeit reason as if it were genuine.
4. If there are reasons not to believe or to act, the belief or act can be justified only if there are equally strong reasons to believe or act.

---

[10] I appreciate that a commonly held view is that reasons for or against Φ-ing can only bear on whether to Φ if they are available to the subject. I address this concern below.
[11] For discussion and defense of the view that it is practically rational to Φ whenever it is epistemically rational to believe that there is sufficient practical reason to Φ, see Foley 2001 and Gibbons 2009.

5. (Therefore) Only true beliefs can be justifiably included in practical deliberation.

6. A belief cannot be justified if it cannot justifiably be included in the process of practical deliberation.

7. (Therefore) Only true beliefs can be justified.

The first premise is a consequence of Factivity$_P$. When your beliefs figure in deliberation about whether to Φ, say, because you take what you believe to count in favor or against Φ-ing, what you believe cannot be a reason to Φ or refrain from Φ-ing if what you believe is false. As we have seen, falsehoods do not constitute justifying reasons.

According to (2), there are no normative reasons to reason from p if p is not itself a reason. This seems intuitively correct. You have reason to get others to treat counterfeit reasons as if they were genuine whenever you have a reason to deceive them, but do you have any reason to treat counterfeit reasons as if they were genuine when you are deliberating about what to do? If there are such reasons, there should be counterexamples to (2). Potential counterexamples would likely have this structure. Someone offers you a large sum of money to sincerely assert that the number of stars is odd. You do not believe that the number is odd, so you cannot now get the money. You can, however, take a pill or hire a hypnotist to induce the belief. Once the belief is in place, you can sincerely assert that the number is odd. So, do you now have a reason to include a false belief in practical deliberation?

I think not. First, whatever reason the money gives you is a reason to cause yourself to have a belief, not a reason to believe. Since it is the wrong kind of reason to believe the number of stars is odd, it is not clear that it could be the right kind of reason to include this belief in deliberation. After all, the reasons that bear on whether to include the belief in practical deliberation seem to be connected to whether these beliefs provide reasons and whether these reasons bear on what to do. The reason in question does neither of these things.[12]

---

[12] See Hieronymi 2005 for a helpful discussion of how to distinguish the right from the wrong kinds of reasons. Even if the money gave you the right kind of reason, it would be easy to rewrite my argument for Factivity$_J$. I could argue for the conditional claim that you cannot justifiably believe falsehoods unless you have practical reason to manipulate yourself so as to form false beliefs. Since those who deny Factivity$_J$ do not do so because they think practical incentives to act can give you reason to manipulate yourself into believing falsehoods that will thereby result in epistemically justified beliefs, denying (2) on these sorts of grounds would not make for a very satisfying response.

According to (3), there is a normative reason to exclude non-reasons from reasoning. In other words, there is a reason not to treat counterfeit reasons as reasons when deliberating about whether to Φ. If (3) is mistaken and there are no such reasons, treating non-reasons as if they are genuine reasons would be all the reason you needed to properly do so. Remember, 'ought' implies 'reason.' If there is no reason not to Φ, it is not be the case that you ought not Φ. In other words, Φ-ing is permissible. In other words, treating something as a reason would not be the sort of thing that called for a justification. The problem with this is that we are required to justify treating certain considerations as reasons for action. We criticize people for reasoning from beliefs they have no reason to hold (e.g., we criticize those who run up massive credit card debt because they believe the end of the world is near, not because this would be a bad idea if it were true, but precisely because the belief that the world will end is defective).

(4) seems to be a plausible claim about justification and conflicting reasons. There can be some reason to Φ even if there are stronger reasons not to Φ. When we ask if Φ-ing could be justified, we want to know if there are sufficiently good reasons for Φ-ing, not just if there is some reason to Φ. If all it took to justify an action was to show that there was some reason to do it, all sorts of horrible actions could be justified by the trivial reasons that count in favor of them. It would be excruciatingly painful to stick a fork into a live outlet, but it would be interesting to know what it is like to receive the strong shock you would if you did it. That hardly serves as a justification to stick a fork into an electrical outlet.

Someone might object to (6) on the grounds that they do not think there are epistemic norms governing practical reasoning. To address this worry, consider Hawthorne's example. He asks us to consider someone trying to decide whether to sell a ticket she has for tomorrow's lottery and reasons in this way:

Because this ticket is a loser, I will get nothing if I keep it. If I sell this ticket for a penny, I will get something for it. So, I should sell the ticket for a penny. (The agent accordingly sells the ticket for a penny and brings practical reasoning to its conclusion.)[13]

He thinks there is something wrong with the reasoning that leads the agent to sell the ticket for a penny. I think this intuition is one that is widely shared. The question is whether the wrong is *epistemic* or *practical*.

---

[13] Hawthorne 2004, p. 29.

Hawthorne thinks that this bit of practical reasoning is flawed for epistemic reasons. Specifically, the reasoning is flawed because the agent treats something as a reason she does not know to be true (i.e., that the ticket she holds will lose when the numbers are drawn). The lesson he draws from this is that there is an epistemic norm that governs practical reasoning – you should not treat p as a reason to act if you do not know that p is true. While I would quibble with Hawthorne about the proper formulation of this norm, I think he is right that the reasoning is defective. The hypothesis that the reasoning is improper for purely practical reasons cannot account for the intuition that the reasoning is defective. If there are no epistemic norms governing practical reasoning, it is not clear what could be wrong with the reasoning from a purely practical standpoint. We can describe the case as one in which selling the ticket maximizes expected and actual utility. Still, there is something wrong with the reasoning. So, the reason the reasoning is flawed is not that it leads the agent to act irrationally or leads the agent to bring about some bad outcome.

Someone could say that the epistemic credentials of our beliefs matter from the practical standpoint, but that concedes the very point at issue. It concedes that among the norms that govern practical reasoning there is a norm that enjoins you to keep epistemically defective beliefs out of deliberation. If there are such norms, we can ask whether such norms enjoin you to reason only from what you know, what you justifiably believe, what you have strong evidence to believe, what is true, etc. If there are such norms and I was right that the standards we use to determine whether a belief is fit to function in deliberation just are the standards we use to determine whether to hold the belief in the first place, we should accept (6). Once we accept (6), the argument is complete. If reasons for action consist of facts, justified beliefs fit the facts because justified beliefs are fit for figuring in practical deliberation.

4.4 EXTERNALISM AND EPISTEMOLOGICAL DISJUNCTIVISM

Even if the arguments for Factivity$_J$ are sound, they show only that justification is an externalist notion given some modest anti-skeptical assumptions. Some have argued that Factivity$_J$ is incompatible with the anti-skeptical assumptions I need to show that epistemic counterparts can differ in terms of what they justifiably believe. Cohen was the first to raise this kind of worry:

The strongest view one could take regarding the truth-connection is that taken by Descartes. The Cartesian view is that justification logically entails truth. To put it schematically: It is a conceptual truth that, if conditions C justify belief B for subject S, then C logically entails that B is true … The legacy of the Cartesian view is scepticism. Descartes demonstrated this in the first meditation that no such connection is forthcoming … Given any plausible specification of C for any S, it will always be logically consistent to suppose that not B. That is what the evil demon argument shows. Where, e.g., C comprises facts about sensory data, and where B is a belief about the truth of some empirical proposition, it is always logically possible that the evil demon has arranged for C to obtain where B is false.[14]

While there are infallibilist views that generate genuine skeptical worries, he has not shown that Factivity_J commits us to these infallibilist views.[15]

Let's look at three views. First, consider the view that you justifiably believe p iff you know p.[16] This view is committed to Factivity_J. Given the reasonable anti-skeptical assumption that we have knowledge of the external world, it implies that many of our beliefs about the external world are justified. Second, if justified beliefs were sensitive beliefs, there would be no false, justified beliefs.[17] You cannot generate any skeptical consequences from this view without first arguing that none of our beliefs are sensitive. Third, the view that you justifiably believe p iff p is true implies that there can be no false, justified beliefs. We both believe that unicorns do not exist and believe the conceptual truth that all unicorns are animals. If true beliefs are always justified, at least one of our beliefs is true.[18] The problem with Cohen's objection is the assumption that Factivity_J implies that justified beliefs are based on entailing reasons. Factivity_J is a consequence of each of the views just described, but none of these views implies that the justification of your beliefs depends upon whether you have entailing reasons for them.

Conee thinks that with some minor tweaking, Cohen's objection succeeds:

Suppose you have the belief that someone is speaking. You infer this from your justified belief that Mr. Jones is speaking. Thus, your external world belief that

---

[14] Cohen 1984, p. 281.

[15] We should distinguish the infallibilist view that you can only justifiably believe what is true from the infallibilist view that you can only justifiably believe when your justification/reason for that belief entails that the belief is true. See Cohen 1988. The latter view does lead to skepticism. I maintain that the former does not, although it would if it were combined with Accessibilism or Evidentialism.

[16] Sutton 2007.

[17] You sensitively believe p iff the following holds: you believe p and if it were not the case that p you would not believe it. Assume the subjunctive conditional is true. It follows that the following material conditional is true: if $-p$, then you do not believe p. Since you believe what you sensitively believe, p is true if sensitively believed. See Williamson 2000a, p. 148.

[18] Gemes 2009 discusses these examples. Tim Kraft drew my attention to Müller's 2003 discussion of the unicorn example.

someone is speaking is a belief for which you have an entailing justification, your justified belief that Jones is speaking. However, it is quite plausible that your belief that Jones is speaking must itself be justified in order to justify any other belief. In general, it is quite plausible that a belief can contribute epistemic justification only if the belief is justified. When we consider candidate justifications for entailing justifiers like the belief that Jones is speaking, it becomes plain that at some point there is always a proposition that is justified without being entailed by its justification. In the present instance, the non-entailing justifier may well be your justification for the belief that Jones is speaking. This belief may be justified by the experience of its seeming to you that you hear what you seem to recall to be the sound of Jones' voice. This experience does not necessitate that Jones, or anyone else, is speaking. But it may be all that you have, and all that you need, in favor of the belief that Jones is speaking. Exactly how this justification works is another matter … [I]n any plausible view, at some point in the justification of each external world belief that is justified, there is justification without entailment. When this further assumption is added to the assumption that the entailment account is correct, we have a valid argument for the conclusion that no external world belief is well enough justified to be known … The entailment claim is the argument's least plausible assumption. So, if the skeptical conclusion is to be avoided, then the entailment account of the truth connection is the best candidate for rejection.[19]

One strategy for dealing with Conee's objection is to say that we do have entailing reasons for our beliefs about the external world. I do think that we often have entailing evidence for beliefs about the external world as I think that much of our evidence consists of the e-propositions that are the contents of our veridical experiences. I do not, however, think that we need entailing reasons to justifiably believe what we do. On this point, Conee and McDowell would disagree and say that we do need these reasons. McDowell would argue that the only way for me to avoid external-world skepticism is to embrace a disjunctivist conception of experience on which experience embraces facts about the external world and thereby provides us with reflectively accessible factive reasons (i.e., reasons you can know you have upon reflection that entail that your beliefs about the external world are correct).[20] He insists that knowledge of an external world depends upon our having these reasons.[21] I disagree.

We need to make a brief detour to deal with issues having to do with the nature of experience and the reasons experience provides. I want to start by considering a tempting, popular, but flawed line of reasoning:

---

[19] Conee and Feldman 2004, p. 245.
[20] Brewer 1999 defends a similar view.
[21] Neta and Pritchard 2007 defend the idea that we could have factive reasons that are reflectively accessible. Also see Byrne and Logue 2008 for a helpful discussion of the epistemological significance of disjunctivism.

If there is a cat in the corner and it looks to you as if there is, you have good reason to believe there is a cat in the corner. Indeed, you might have good enough reason to believe this. Since it can look to you as if there is a cat there even if the nearest cat is miles away, experience can provide you with a sufficiently good reason for belief even if there is no cat. The reasons provided by veridical experience give you the right to believe. The same is true for the reasons provided by some subjectively indistinguishable hallucination. If so, the justificatory work is done by the elements common to hallucination and perception. These elements do their justificatory work just as well in cases of perception and hallucination. After all, you have the same evidence either way.[22]

For their part, evidential internalists say that there is nothing wrong with this sort of reasoning. On their view if two individuals have the same evidence, the same reasons bear on their beliefs and it is impossible for two individuals to have different evidence if they are non-factive mental duplicates. As they see it, the conditions that determine whether your experience is veridical or not do not determine the nature of your experience, they do not determine what evidence you have, and so these conditions have nothing to do with the proper description of your reasons for believing any of the worldly propositions you believe. So, they endorse:

> Same Reasons: Veridical experience and subjectively indistinguishable hallucination provide you with the same evidence for your worldly beliefs.[23]

McDowell agrees that this line of reasoning is defective. He thinks the mistake is in thinking that since it can look as if there is a cat in the corner when no cat is there, if it looks as if there is a cat there you have the same reason to believe there is, cat or no cat. The conditions that distinguish veridical experience from hallucination are essential to perceptual knowledge. Everyone agrees to that. Knowledge, he says, is a standing in the space of reasons.[24] So, the difference between perceptual knowledge and ignorance requires that there are different reasons to believe worldly propositions in the case of veridical perceptual experience and subjectively indistinguishable hallucination.[25] As he sees it, Same Reasons leads to skepticism. To avoid skepticism, he thinks we should accept:

---

[22] I believe Brueckner 2009; Conee and Feldman 2004; Huemer 2001; and Wedgwood 2002a would endorse this sort of argument.

[23] This is a popular view. Among others, Huemer 2006 and Silins 2005 defend Same Reasons.

[24] McDowell 1995, p. 877.

[25] Rödl 2007 also defends this view.

Better Reasons: The evidence veridical experience provides is better than the evidence provided by subjectively indistinguishable hallucination in the sense that veridical experience provides evidence that hallucination does not.

So far, he and I are in perfect agreement.

Even if Same Reasons leads to skepticism, Better Reasons might not save you from the skeptic. If your view is that the nature of the psychological states and events by virtue of which it looks to you as if such and such is the case are the same in the case of perception and hallucination, McDowell would say that your view leads right back to skepticism. On such a view, the qualities by virtue of which your reasons are thought to be better would be blankly external to you. For McDowell, this is *verboten*:

> The root idea is that one's epistemic standing … cannot intelligibly be constituted, even in part, by matters blankly external to how it is with one subjectively. For how could such matters be other than beyond one's ken? And how could matters beyond one's ken make any difference to one's epistemic standing? … But the disjunctive conception of appearances shows a way to detach this "internalist" intuition from the requirement of a non-question begging demonstration. When someone has a fact made manifest to him, the obtaining of this fact contributes to his epistemic standing on the question. But the obtaining of the fact is precisely not blankly external to his subjectivity, as it would be if the truth about that were exhausted by the highest common factor.[26]

The point on which McDowell and the evidential internalists agree is that nothing can confer any justificatory benefit upon you that others do not enjoy unless it corresponds to some mental difference that distinguishes you from them. For this reason we can classify McDowell's view as internalist, albeit an unorthodox version of Internalism that says that the justification of belief depends upon whether your beliefs about the external world are based on the factive mental states. Because he thinks that experience can embrace worldly facts, McDowell is happy to say that the veridicality of an experience can provide a justificatory benefit by virtue of which you enjoy a superior epistemic standing to those who form beliefs in response to hallucinations. The evidential internalists either deny that there are factive mental states of the kind McDowell thinks are distinctive of cases of perceptual knowledge or deny that such states can confer any benefit upon you.[27]

---

[26] McDowell 1998, p. 390.   [27] See Conee and Feldman 2008.

As the passage above indicates, McDowell thinks that the problems that arise for evidential internalists arise for anyone who rejects Disjunctivism:

Disjunctivism: An appearance can either be a mere appearance, as with hallucination, or a fact made perceptually manifest. The nature of the psychological states and events by virtue of which it looks to you as if *p* depends upon whether you are hallucinating or your experience is veridical.

His target includes all of the orthodox accounts of epistemic justification since these accounts deny that the veridicality of a particular experience is part of what determines whether beliefs formed in response to these experiences are justified.

McDowell's epistemological argument for Disjunctivism comes to this. Given the internalist intuition that epistemic standing cannot be constituted by factors blankly external to you or beyond your ken, Same Reasons leads to skepticism. Knowledge is an epistemic standing and Same Reasons asserts that the conditions essential to that standing are blankly external to you in the case of veridical experience. If you accept Better Reasons but deny Disjunctivism, you cannot avoid the skeptical consequences of Same Reasons because your view commits you to saying that the conditions essential to knowledge are beyond your ken even in cases of veridical experience. Thus, the only alternative to skepticism is a view that combines Better Reasons with Disjunctivism. So, on the plausible assumption that we have perceptual knowledge, we have to reject the traditional conception of experience. Moreover, we have to embrace the kind of Infallibilism I had hoped to avoid, one on which knowledge of an external world requires not just Better Reasons, but that there are reasons that supervene upon your mental states that entail that your perceptual beliefs are correct.

Those who take a dim view of McDowell's argument for Disjunctivism might say that McDowell tries to derive an implausible claim about the nature of experience from implausible claims about the justification of perceptual belief. Not only is he wrong to think that Same Reasons leads to skepticism and wrong to endorse Better Reasons, he is wrong to think Disjunctivism could explain how Better Reasons could be true. I also have reservations about his argument, but the problem with his argument is not that it assumes Better Reasons. Not only is Better Reasons true, so is this stronger thesis:

Good Enough: Only in the case of veridical perception do you have good enough reason for your worldly beliefs. If you believe on the basis of hallucination, you cannot believe with justification. You can believe with sufficient justification if your experience is veridical.

The questionable step in McDowell's argument is the step where he says that claims such as Better Reasons and Good Enough commit us to Disjunctivism.

4.4.1 *Preliminary objections*

Some object to McDowell's view on the grounds that it commits him to an infallibilist view that leads to skepticism.[28] If knowledge is a standing in the space of reasons and the difference between knowledge and ignorance cannot be blankly external to you or beyond your ken, the difference between knowledge and ignorance can never be due entirely to differences in the truth or falsity of two subjects' beliefs. In fact, the difference between knowledge and ignorance can never be due to anything that does not supervene upon a full description of the reasons you have for your beliefs. Thus, it seems that McDowell is committed to this thesis:

Different Basis: If you know p, you believe p on a different basis from anyone who believes p without knowing p.

Different Basis entails that if you know p, anyone in a $\sim p$-world believes for different reasons from you no matter how similar their epistemic predicament might otherwise be to yours. This means that if you know p, you believe on a basis that is incompatible with $\sim p$. This just is the infallibilist view:

Infallibilism: If you know p, your belief must be based on something incompatible with $\sim p$.

The argument from Infallibilism to inductive skepticism is straightforward. In cases of inductive inference, the basis for your belief is a basis you could have even if your belief is mistaken. If I believe correctly that the n+1st draw from my bag will be black on the basis of n observations of black draws and you believe incorrectly that the n+1st draw from your bag will be black on the basis of n observations of black draws, there is a perfectly good sense in which we believe what we do on the same basis. I get

---

[28] Comesaña 2005a.

things right, but you do not. According to Infallibilism, I cannot know unless everyone who believes on your basis knows. But, you did not know the next marble would be black. You pulled the first white ball.

To avoid this skeptical conclusion, we have to deny Different Basis and allow for the possibility of knowing *p* on the very same basis as someone who could have mistakenly believed that *p*. McDowell's critics might say that if you reject Different Basis, you have to reject Better Reasons and Good Enough. Unless Different Basis is true, your (allegedly) better reasons cannot make you epistemically better off because the conditions by virtue of which your reasons are better are blankly external to you or they are beyond your ken. If you deny Better Reasons, you also have to deny Good Enough. How could you have the same reasons as someone else and only one of you have reasons that are good enough? McDowell and his critics seem to agree that Better Reasons and Good Enough could be true only if Different Basis is true. McDowell thinks that this is why you should accept Disjunctivism and his critics think this is why his view leads to skepticism. I think this is a mistake.

Let us consider a second objection to McDowell's view. In explaining how it is possible to have knowledge of an external world, McDowell argues that we need Disjunctivism to explain how Better Reasons could be true. Nothing could be a reason that contributes to the justificatory standing of your belief unless that reason is part of your basis for believing. For reasons we have touched on, he thinks having such reasons requires having direct contact with the facts you come to know via perceptual experience. Conee argues that Disjunctivism could not explain how Better Reasons could be true because any such explanation would run afoul of this principle:

> Defeat: A subject's justification for a belief is not stronger than a second subject's justification for the same belief, if their respective justifications are prone to being equally well defeated by the same defeaters.[29]

If Defeat says that two reasons defeated by the same defeater cannot differ in strength, the principle is implausible. A full house is stronger than a pair even if four aces would beat both hands. On a more charitable reading, Defeat says that the justifications provided by two experiences would be equally strong if these justifications could be defeated by all of the same defeaters.

---

[29] Conee 2007, p. 19.

While Defeat is more plausible on this weaker reading, it is hardly self-evident. It is not obvious that the comparative strength of two reasons can be measured in terms of what can defeat them. Think about boxers. Nobody can defeat Harry in a boxing match. Apart from Harry, nobody can defeat Leo or Cooper. Leo and Cooper cannot box against each other because they share gloves. Cooper and Bobby cannot box each other because they share trunks. No one can box without both gloves and trunks. Suppose you have debts you can repay only if you come into some quick money. The only way to come into some quick money is to set up a boxing match. You have to bet on the boxer you send to the ring, but do not know who the opponent will be. You manage Leo and Cooper. You know the fight will not take place if you try to send Cooper up against Bobby, so there is stronger reason to send in Leo. The same boxers would defeat Leo and Coop, but you still have stronger reason to send Leo to fight. If reasons are like boxers, strength cannot be measured simply in terms of what could defeat what you have in your corner.

There is a more principled reason for thinking that Conee has no basis for rejecting Better Reasons. Remember that the reason he thinks that veridical perceptual experience and subjectively indistinguishable hallucination are liable to defeat by the same defeaters and thus provide equally good reasons for belief is that they are subjectively indistinguishable. Let's consider two theses about indiscriminability and justification:

Transitivity$_I$: $(x)(y)(z)[((Ixy \ \& \ Iyz) \rightarrow Ixz)]$.
Transitivity$_J$: $(x)(y)(z)[((Jxy \ \& \ Jyz) \rightarrow Jxz)]$.

According to Transitivity$_I$, token experiences a and c are indistinguishable for you if you cannot distinguish between experiences a and b and cannot distinguish b from c.[30] According to Transitivity$_J$, if a and b justify the same (i.e., justify the same beliefs to the same degree) and b and c justify the same, it follows that a and c justify the same.

Transitivity$_I$ is false.[31] Suppose a, b, and c are the experiences you would have if you looked at three similar paint chips individually under the same viewing conditions. If we had shown you the first chip or the second, you would not be able to discriminate a from b. If we had shown you the second chip or the third chip, you would not be able to discriminate b

---

[30] This should be restricted to a single method of discrimination, one that does not involve inferential reasoning.
[31] See Williamson 1990 for detailed discussion of the arguments against the transitivity of indiscriminability.

from *c*. Still, if we had shown you the first or the third chip, you might be able to discriminate *a* from *c* on the basis of introspection.

While Transitivity$_I$ is false, Transitivity$_J$ is true. If Transitivity$_J$ were false, there would have to be some proposition, *p*, such that the degrees to which *a* and *c* justified belief in *p* differed even though both *a* and *c* justified belief in *p* to the same degree that *b* does. This is impossible.

We can now see why Defeat does not cause any problems for McDowell's view. Conee's objection assumes:

1. $(x)(y)(Ixy \supset Jxy)$.

Consider this further assumption:

2. $(x)(y)(\sim Ixy \supset Jxy)$.

The reason (2) is plausible is that in discriminating between two things, you can know that they are distinct. If you can discriminate between *a* and *c*, you will have stronger reasons for believing that you are undergoing *a* while undergoing *a* than you will have for believing that you are undergoing some experience you can knowingly discriminate from *a* (e.g., *c*). If Transitivity$_I$ is false, we can coherently suppose that *a* is indiscriminable from *b*, *b* is indiscriminable from *c*, but you can discriminate between *a* and *c*. (1) entails that *a* and *b* justify the same beliefs to the same degree. It also entails that *b* and *c* justify the same beliefs to the same degree. It follows by Transitivity$_J$ that *a* and *c* justify the same beliefs to the same degree. But, if (2) is correct, this contradicts the further assumption that you can discriminate between experiences *a* and *c*. The most obvious way to avoid this contradiction is to deny (1). If (1) is false, Conee's Defeat principle is no threat to Better Reasons. Conee's objection to McDowell's view was that it implied that it is possible for indistinguishable states to provide reasons that differed in strength. His objection assumed that indistinguishable states can be defeated by precisely the same considerations and that states that can be defeated by precisely the same considerations cannot provide reasons that differ in strength. We know now that these assumptions cannot both be correct. Either the reasons provided by two indistinguishable states are not susceptible to being defeated by the same defeaters or the reasons provided by two states can be defeated by the same considerations even if these states provide different reasons.

There is a deeper problem with Conee's objection. It is tempting to think (as I think Conee and McDowell do) that Better Reasons and Good Enough could be true only if the reasons we have in the case of perceptual knowledge are stronger than the reasons we have in cases of hallucination. Although we do have stronger reasons in the case of veridical perception, it is important to remember that strength of epistemic position is not simply a function of the strength of your reasons for believing. It is also a function of reasons against or reasons to refrain from believing.

4.4.2 *The epistemological argument for Disjunctivism*

Conee's objection does not undermine Better Reasons or Good Enough and it does not show that Disjunctivism would be incapable of explaining how these claims are true. I would defend Better Reasons and Good Enough as follows. Given the anti-skeptical assumption that we have perceptual knowledge of an external world, Better Reasons follows from IKSE and Factivity$_E$. Good Enough follows from Factivity$_J$. McDowell would say that the arguments I have offered for Better Reasons and Good Enough do not go far enough because they tell us nothing about the nature of experience.

The motivation for McDowell's argument for Disjunctivism is the internalist thought that nothing could confer any epistemic benefit upon you if it is beyond your ken. And that seems quite right. If the vat operator induced in two subjects subjectively matching hallucinations of a cat and a cat happened to walk right to the spot where the first subject took a cat to be without this having any impact on the subject's experience, it is not as if the subject should get some justificatory boost because the subject's hallucinations are now veridical. This is just the picture that McDowell wants to avoid, and he is right to do so. In addressing Conee's objections, I had hoped to show that it is not impossible for two subjects in indistinguishable subjective states to have different reasons for their beliefs. Now, I want to show that we do not need Disjunctivism to understand how this is possible.

We can summarize McDowell's epistemological argument for Disjunctivism as follows:

1. If q is blankly external to your subjectivity, q is beyond your ken.
2. If q is beyond your ken, q cannot make a difference to your epistemic standing.
3. (Therefore) If q is blankly external to your subjectivity, q cannot make a difference to your epistemic standing.

As van Cleve suggests, the most natural interpretation of McDowell's talk of something being blankly external to your subjectivity is this: q is blankly external to your subjectivity iff a complete description of your psychological states entails neither *-q* nor *-p*. As for this talk of what is beyond your ken, we know that McDowell wants to show that perceptual knowledge is possible only if it puts us in direct contact with facts in the external world and so I think he would agree that if *q* is beyond your ken, you cannot know *q* non-inferentially. Thus, if *q* is something you do know non-inferentially, it is not beyond your ken. We can now rewrite McDowell's argument as follows:

1'. If a full description of your psychological states entails neither *q* nor *-q*, you cannot know whether *q* non-inferentially.
2'. If you cannot know whether *q* non-inferentially, *q* itself cannot make a difference to the justificatory status of your non-inferential beliefs.
3'. (Therefore) If a full description of your psychological states entails neither *q* nor *-q*, *q* itself cannot make a difference to the justificatory status of your beliefs.

With (3') in place, we can say that Better Reasons could only be true if Disjunctivism is true. And, if Better Reasons is false and you have the same reasons for the beliefs based on experience whether your experience is veridical or not, (2') tells us that your experience does not put you in a position to know non-inferentially anything about the external world.

There are various ways of trying to motivate the idea that whatever is beyond your ken cannot confer any epistemic benefit upon you and contribute to the justificatory status of your beliefs. Suppose Harry sees Bobby on the subway. He suspects that Bobby is up to no good, so he arrests him on some trumped-up charge and later discovers that Bobby had narcotics on him. The narcotics might have given Harry a reason to arrest Bobby, but the fact that Bobby had narcotics on him could not have motivated Harry to act because he was not cognizant of this fact. And it is tempting to say that it could not have justified his arrest. This might be because only that which motivates you to Φ can contribute to justifying Φ-ing and nothing can motivate you unless you are cognizant of it. It might be that nothing can justify unless you are cognizant of it and this point requires no explanation at all. Whichever way we go, we know that the reasons there were for Harry to act did not justify his conduct. We can make a similar point using epistemic examples, of course. Perhaps one of the lessons we should all take from BonJour's examples is that any reason there is to believe *p* can only justify if it partially explains why you believe *p* and is thus a reason you are cognizant of. Perhaps cases such as these convince McDowell that whatever is beyond your ken cannot confer any justificatory benefit upon you.

The problem with these examples is not that they do not show what they are supposed to, but that they do not give McDowell what he needs. Facts that you are not cognizant of do not motivate you to Φ and cannot contribute a justification for Φ-ing, but they can contribute something to justificatory status. Consider cases where an innocent person is convicted of a crime they did not commit and that the evidence that exonerates them surfaces decades after they were sentenced to imprisonment. It seems rather intuitive that something is owed to this person no matter how carefully the trial was conducted. It is not simply beneficent to apologize and offer some form of compensation. If, say, the people of France started providing Americans who were wrongly sentenced with generous stipends, the authorities in the United States would still be on the hook for what the American legal system did to these people and their families. In offering compensation, the American authorities would take a step towards making reparations and righting a past wrong. The support for this practice seems to be widespread and if this truly is a case in which there is a duty of reparation, it shows that the justificatory status of the initial sentencing and the decades of punishment depends in part upon facts that were obscure at the time of the sentencing and the punishment. There is widespread support for the practice of offering reparations, so I do not expect McDowell to disagree on this point.

Cases like this suggest is that (2′) is mistaken. The reasons that count against Φ-ing can do their work and make it wrongful to Φ even if the subject is not cognizant of them. We never act for the reasons against acting, so the motivation for thinking that reasons for action must be reasons we are cognizant of in order for these reasons to justify does not apply to the reasons against acting.[32] It is worth noting that McDowell is committed to the idea that reasons against Φ-ing can do their work even when these reasons are beyond the subject's ken. He thinks that if you are in the bad case, it can look as if *p* even if *-p* and that the (alleged) psychological difference between you and someone in the good case is beyond your ken (even if this difference is not beyond their ken).[33] Thus, for him, the fact that you are hallucinating rather than veridically perceiving is a

---

[32] I owe the point to Gardner 2007.
[33] Remember that if you are in the good case, you know *p* and so know something you would not know in the bad. If you are in the bad case, you do not know *p*, but assuming that the axiom of negative introspection is incorrect, not knowing *p* does not thereby put you in a position to know that you do not know *p*.

fact that contributes negatively to your justificatory standing when you are hallucinating.

McDowell needs to revise (2′) to say that only that which contributes positively to justification is not beyond your ken, in which case the argument for Disjunctivism comes to this:

1′. If a full description of your psychological states entails neither q nor $\sim q$, you cannot know whether q non-inferentially.
2″. If you cannot know whether q non-inferentially, q cannot on its own make a difference to the justificatory status of your beliefs by conferring any sort of epistemic benefit upon you.
3″. (Therefore) If a full description of your psychological states entails neither q nor $\sim q$, q cannot on its own make a difference to the justificatory status of your beliefs by conferring any sort of epistemic benefit upon you.

Once we see why these revisions are needed, we can see why the argument for Disjunctivism fails. Suppose Good Enough is true. We want to know why subjects in the good case have good enough reason to believe when subjects in the bad case do not, and one answer is that in the bad case there are reasons against belief that the subject does not have in the good case. In light of these reasons against believing (which you have because your experiences are non-veridical), your epistemic position in the bad case would be worse than in the good even if we held the reasons you had *for* believing fixed between the two cases. Thus, we do not have to assume that your reasons for believing in the good case are better than the reasons you have in the bad in order to explain Good Enough. While (2′) would have ruled out such an explanation of Good Enough, we know that (2′) is not supported by the examples and that McDowell has good reason to deny (2′).

What about Better Reasons? I have just explained why we do not need Better Reasons to explain Good Enough. Earlier I argued that you need Better Reasons to understand how perceptual knowledge is possible. Does Better Reasons commit you to Disjunctivism? I think not. Better Reasons follows from IKSE and Factivity$_E$ given the further assumption that you have non-inferential knowledge of the external world. If you can see that there is a cat sleeping in the corner, that there is a cat in the corner is among your reasons (because it is a fact you know non-inferentially), but not a reason your counterparts have if they are hallucinating. Since these assumptions tell us nothing about perceptual experience, it is hard to see why we should accept (1′).

McDowell might say that I have helped myself to something I am not entitled to because I assumed that we have non-inferential knowledge of an external world in explaining Better Reasons. Remember that I am engaged in the same project that he is. He assumes that we have perceptual knowledge and then tries to describe the conditions under which it is possible to have this knowledge.[34] This is what I have done. I have described conditions under which we have perceptual knowledge without assuming that we receive any epistemic benefits from anything beyond our ken. Nothing I have said thus far in arguing for Better Reasons and Good Enough commits me to the claim that there is a mental difference between the good case and bad. Yet everything I have said is consistent with McDowell's internalist point. Thus, McDowell's internalist point does not show that Disjunctivism is true.

If we reject (1′) and we can consistently maintain that Better Reasons and Good Enough are true, we avoid the skeptical worries generated by Different Basis. Since nothing we have said thus far commits us to Different Basis, nothing we have said thus far commits us to the kind of infallibilist view that seems to generate inductive skepticism. So, we have seen our way through a tricky dilemma. On the one horn was the disjunctivist view that seemed committed to Infallibilism and inductive skepticism. On the other was the evidential internalist view. It was not committed to Different Basis, but it led to skeptical problems of its own. Insofar as it denies Better Reasons, it can avoid skepticism only by denying Factivity$_E$ or IKSE. Since we have seen that both theses are correct, we know that the fallibilist view evidential internalists defend is not free from its own skeptical problems. Factivity$_J$ does not commit you to the view that the right to believe p depends, inter alia, upon possessing some antecedent reason to believe p that is inconsistent with $-p$. Rejecting Infallibilism does not commit you to the view that you can have the right to believe p simply by having the right sort of basis for your belief regardless of how things are in the external world.

4.5 ACTING FOR REASONS

In this section, I want to look at one final objection to the view that justifying reasons are typically the facts about external matters that you have in mind when you deliberate about whether to do something or whether something is true. What happens when you act or believe for a

---

[34] McDowell 2008, p. 384.

reason? The obvious answer is that there is a reason, you take the reason to bear on whether to Φ or whether *p*, and you believe or act for *it*. Since the things we take to bear on whether to act or believe are typically facts about matters external to you, if we act or believe for these reasons, the reasons for which we act and believe are typically facts about matters external to you. Arguments from error are supposed to show that it is impossible to act or believe for these sorts of reasons, so I need to show that these arguments err.

For the purposes of this discussion, I shall assume that it is possible to act for good reasons and that any view that says likewise has to accommodate these constraints:

Explanatory Constraint: Any normative reason is capable of contributing to the explanation of an action done for that reason.

Normative Constraint: Any motivating reason must be capable of being among the reasons that count in favor of acting.[35]

There are views that violate these constraints. For example, some have defended a view on which motivating reasons consist of psychological states and normative reasons consist of facts.[36] Whether these facts were about the agent's psychology or the agent's situation, these views say that when you acted for a good reason, the reason for which you acted would not *really* be a reason that was good or a good reason to act (i.e., a normative reason). We shall set these views aside for now so that we can see if any view can accommodate these constraints while dealing with cases of error.

There are two versions of Psychologism about motivating reasons that we should consider:

Motivational Psychologism$_S$: Motivating reasons are constituted by your mental states.

Motivational Psychologism$_P$: Motivating reasons are constituted by the propositions you have in mind (regardless of whether these propositions are true).

I shall argue that arguments from error give us no reason to identify normative reasons with an agent's mental states or the false propositions she has in mind when she deliberates about what to do or whether something is true.

---

[35] For a defense of these constraints, see Dancy 2000, p. 101.
[36] See Parfit 1997 and Smith 1987.

Cooper and Leo are running down two very similar hallways in two very similar houses. There is a killer chasing Cooper and he knows it. Leo is Cooper's non-factive mental duplicate, so he believes there is a killer chasing him as well. Cooper is in the epistemically good case. Leo is in the bad case. His belief that there is a killer after him is mistaken. It seems natural to say that Cooper's reason for running down the hall was that there was a killer chasing him. What should we say about Leo? According to Dancy, "The distinction between true and false beliefs on the agent's part cannot affect the form of the explanation which will be appropriate to his actions."[37] I think this point is right. If the form that a rationalizing explanation took depended upon whether an agent's beliefs were correct or not, we would identify different kinds of considerations as being the agent's reasons in the good case and the bad. In the good case, his reasons would be facts about his situation. In the bad case, his reasons for running would be facts about his attitudes and would not include any facts about his situation (e.g., that someone is chasing him). The rationalizing explanation is supposed to explain the agent's behavior in ways that would help us understand the agent's action from the agent's point of view. Since things from the agent's point of view are the same in the good case and bad, we do not capture things from the agent's point of view if we offer different descriptions of the agent's reasons for acting in the good and bad cases. So, it seems that we say this about Leo: Leo's reason for running down the hall was that there was a killer chasing him. Since there was nobody chasing him, this is supposed to be false. If Leo's reason was not that a killer was chasing him, we will have to say that Coop's reason was not that a killer was chasing him. Then, if we want to accommodate our Motivating and Explanatory Constraints, we have to embrace a thoroughgoing Psychologism on which normative and motivating reasons consist of either mental states or propositions (including falsehoods).

As I understand it, the argument from error comes to this:

1. If two agents act for reasons where these agents are psychological duplicates, these agents act for the same reason.
2. Cooper and Leo are in the same mental states and these mental states stand in the same causal relations throughout the story.
3. Cooper runs down the hall for a reason.

---

[37] Dancy 1995, p. 13. He credits the point to Williams 1981, p. 102.

4. (Therefore) Leo runs down the hall for the same reason that Cooper does.
5. There are no external facts that could be Leo's reasons for running.
6. (Therefore) Cooper's reason for running down the hall cannot be an external fact.
7. (Therefore) The reasons that bear on whether Cooper should run cannot be external facts.

We have seen Dancy's defense of (1). We can stipulate that (2) and (3) are true. I see no reason to take issue with (5). There can be no external facts that are Leo's reason for running because such reasons would have to figure in his reasoning and these reasons would have to consist of facts. None of the propositions he considers in deciding to run is true. Given the Explanatory and Normative Constraints, (7) seems to follow from (6). The upshot seems to be a thoroughgoing Psychologism about normative and motivating reasons. The reasons for which we act and for which we believe are never facts about things external to us. Among other things, my argument against Evidential Internalism fails because a crucial premise in that argument is that the reasons for which we believe what we do and the reasons there are to believe as we do are sometimes constituted by external facts.

I want to start by looking at Motivational Psychologism$_S$. On this view, motivating reasons are the psychological states of the agent. Specifically, they are the psychological states that we cite in explaining why Cooper and Leo ran down the hall. I think this view faces some serious problems. If we assume that the Explanatory and Normative Constraints hold, Motivational Psychologism$_S$ has to say that the reasons that bear on whether to run are the sort of psychological states that figure in explanations of our agents' actions. Intuitively, neither these states nor facts about these states count in favor of running. The reasons, however, that constitute reasons to run do so by counting in favor of running. So, this view seems to imply that favorers are not reasons.

Gibbons seems prepared to accept this. If reasons are not reasons because they count in favor, how do they become reasons? He says that reasons are things that make things reasonable.[38] Since the agent's mental states are what determine whether the agent's actions and beliefs are reasonable, they can play the role of reasons. Facts are the wrong sort of thing to make things reasonable, so they are the wrong sorts of thing to be reasons.

---

[38] Gibbons 2010.

This view faces two difficulties. This view identifies motivating reasons with psychological states that explain the agent's behavior. I think this view cannot be made to work because there are ways of explaining the agent's behavior by describing the subject's mental states where we are not explaining the agent's behavior in terms of motivating reasons. Audrey knew that there was a party, but she stayed home anyway. We might say that she stayed home because she was so very shy. We might also say that she stayed home because she thought that there would be lots of strangers at the party.[39] We have two explanations of Audrey's actions, but we do not have two explanations of her actions in terms of her motivating reasons. How does Motivational Psychologism$_S$ distinguish psychological explanations that do not make reference to the agent's motivating reasons from psychological explanations that do make reference to these reasons? You might say that in explaining the actions in terms of the agent's motivating reasons our goal is to show the light in which the agent decided to act as she did, but neither explanation does that.[40] From her perspective, her reason for staying away was that there would be so many strangers there. True, she would not have acted for this reason if she did not believe there would be so many strangers there, but that is true also of her shyness. If she were not so shy, she might have gone. The motivational psychologists cannot help us understand the difference between the two psychological explanations on offer because they identify the agent's motivating reasons with her psychological states. If instead we identify the agent's motivating reasons with what the agent had in mind, it is easy enough to understand the difference between these explanations.

The second difficulty with his view is that it threatens to sever the connection between reasons and rightness. If it is right for you to Φ, you cannot be obligated not to Φ. If you are obligated not to Φ, you have an undefeated reason not to Φ. These points seem relatively uncontroversial. Suppose you think that reasons are things that make things reasonable. On this view, you could never judge that you ought to Φ and be obligated to act against that judgment if that judgment is reasonable. You could never judge reasonably that you ought to Φ if you ought not Φ because (i) it is never reasonable to do other than Φ when you rationally judge that you must Φ and (ii) your judgment could only be mistaken in such a case if there was undefeated reason not to Φ. There could not be such a reason

---

[39] For a helpful discussion of such cases, see Alvarez 2010 and Dancy 2004.
[40] I believe this way of understanding explanations in terms of motivating reasons has been standard since at least McDowell 1978.

because such a reason cannot make it reasonable for you to Φ. (Not in the relevant circumstances, at any rate.)

The trouble that this view faces is that it denies that it is possible for someone to reasonably judge that the case for Φ-ing is weaker than the case against Φ-ing when the opposite is true. Consider an example. Parents have to decide when to send their children out to play on their own. If you keep your children indoors in very safe neighborhoods, you are being overly protective. If you let your children out in very dangerous neighborhoods, you are being insufficiently protective. It is hard to believe that nobody could reasonably judge incorrectly that they ought to keep their children in when they ought to let them out (or vice versa). Once we see that this is possible, it seems that a person can judge and act reasonably without thereby acting rightly. Once we see that acting reasonably and acting rightly are not the same thing, we have to decide whether reasons determine what is reasonable or what is right. What the reasonable agent has in mind when deliberating about what to do are considerations that bear on the rightness of an act or judgment, so things that bear on rightness are better candidates for reasons that move the agent to act.

Motivational Psychologism$_P$ avoids these worries. Those who defend this view say motivating reasons are the considerations the agent has in mind when deliberating about what to do, not the mental states by virtue of which they attend to these considerations.[41] This might allow them to say that the agent's motivating reasons are the things the agent took to favor acting the way she did. In turn, this might also allow them to say that reasons are favorers. In Cooper's case, his reason did favor running. In Leo's case, it did not. However, the reason Cooper had for running *could* have counted in favor of running. If *true*, that very same proposition would have counted in favor of running. An attractive feature of Motivational Psychologism$_P$ is that it can accommodate the view that normative reasons for belief and action consist of facts. Normative and motivating reasons are propositions. Whether the reason could motivate has to do with the attitudes the agent takes towards it. Whether the reason could justify has to do with whether it is true and whether the true proposition counts in favor of the relevant action or belief. Because the view does not imply that false propositions can constitute normative reasons, it seems that many of the standard arguments for Factivity$_E$ and Factivity$_P$ might leave Motivational Psychologism$_P$ untouched. Reasons,

---

[41] See Miller 2008 and Schroeder 2008.

normative and motivating, still belong to the same ontological category, so it accommodates the Explanatory and Normative Constraints.

Contrast this view with Dancy's view.[42] He agrees with the defenders of Motivational Psychologism$_P$ that the following claims are true:

8_C. Cooper's reason for running down the hall was that there was a killer running after him.
8_L. Leo's reason for running down the hall was that there was a killer running after him.

These views differ in their explanations as to why (8_C) and (8_L) are correct. His view seems to differ from Motivational Psychologism$_P$ in that he rejects the idea that false propositions could be the agent's reason for acting. To handle cases of error, he says that there can be correct, non-factive explanations.[43] He would say that it is a mistake to think that the success of the explanation we give when we assert (8_L) depends upon whether there really was a killer running after him. On his view, a better way to explain Leo's action is to say:

8_{DL}. Leo's reason for running down the hall was that, as he supposed, there was a killer running after him. However, there was no one chasing him.

What makes this explanation correct is that it depicts the light in which the agent acted. It is supposed to be a non-factive explanation, however, because the truth of (8_L) and (8_{DL}) does not turn on the truth or falsity of the agent's relevant beliefs.

To my ear, (8_{DL}) is contradictory. Hornsby agrees:

[I]t is a very strange idea that explanations are ever non-factive. To many ears, "He Φ'd because, as he supposed, p" is true only if it is true that p. One plausible account of "as Φ supposes" used parenthetically within a sentence s will treat it [as a sentence adverb such as "luckily" should arguably be treated] as conveying something about what is said in s without affecting its truth-conditions. If so, then given that "p because q" requires the truth of p and of q, introducing a parenthetic "as Φ supposes" within it will not produce anything non-factive.[44]

The linguistic data appear to disconfirm Dancy's view as well as Motivational Psychologism$_P$. Consider two claims:

9_C. Cooper ran down the hall because there was a killer running after him.
9_L. Leo ran down the hall because there was a killer running after him.

---

[42] Dancy 2000.   [43] Dancy 2000, p. 131.   [44] Hornsby 2007, p. 292.

These are both factive. If they are correct, there were killers chasing after both Cooper and Leo. We know, however, that they were not both being chased. Cooper ran from a killer and Leo ran from nobody. This means that Dancy and defenders of Motivational Psychologism$_P$ are forced to say that (8_C) and (8_L) are not logically equivalent to (9_C) and (9_L) when it seems clear that they are equivalent. If (8_L) does not entail that there was a killer after Leo, (8_L) cannot entail (9_L). Yet, the conjunction of (8_L) and $(\sim 9_L)$ clearly seems contradictory. On one perfectly sensible test for entailment, the entailment holds. You cannot reinforce (8_L) with (9_L), so there is further evidence that suggests that the connection between them cannot be weaker than entailment. Moreover, if you were to deny that (8_L) entailed (9_L), you would have to explain what it means to say that (8_L) provides a correct explanation of Leo's action if it fails to identify the reasons that explain his action. (If you deny (9_L), it certainly seems that you have to deny that (8_L) identifies the reason that explains Leo's action.)

To be fair, Dancy and defenders of Motivational Psychologism$_P$ might say that their arguments are powerful enough to override the linguistic evidence. After identifying a variety of perfectly sound reasons for rejecting Motivational Psychologism$_S$, Miller says this on behalf of Motivational Psychologism$_P$:

> [U]nless we are infallible about what facts there are, there will be plenty of instances in which we invoke motivating reasons in our practical deliberation and yet at the same time are quite mistaken about the existence of the facts to which they make putative reference.[45]

The argument does not support his conclusion. Think about Leo. He is mistaken about the facts. Is he mistaken about the reason for which he runs? He is mistaken about the reason for which he runs if he believes falsely that he runs for a reason. On Miller's view, if you were to ask Cooper or Leo what their reasons for running were, they would offer the same correct response – that there is a killer running after them. The problem here is that while Cooper (arguably) asserts something that is true, Leo would assert something false. Just as he is fallible about the facts, he is fallible about the reasons for which he runs. We know that the 'reason' he identifies as his reason could not be the reason that explains his action because what he asserts when he offers a rationalizing explanation of his action is that (9_L) is true. Whatever special authority an agent has in describing his motivating reasons, it does not include authority over

---

[45] Miller 2008, p. 229.

whether any particular behavior can be explained in terms of what he takes his motivating reasons to be. If the Davidsonian view is correct, for example, and rationalizing explanations are causal, certainly the agent has no special authority over whether he is acting for a reason since this is partially a matter of causal relations between his mind and his body he knows nothing about. For all that the agent can tell, the actions he thinks he performed could have resulted from causal manipulation by another agent.

It is telling that if we stop Leo and ask him why he was running, he might assert (8_L) or (9_L). Once we tell him that there was nobody after him, he would not continue to assert that (8_L) or (9_L) are true. He would say that he was running because he believed there was a killer after him. I do not see how Motivational Psychologism$_P$ can explain this. On their view, a speaker who asserts that (8_L) or (9_L) is true is not committed to the proposition that there was a killer after Leo. Someone could say that they do not assert (8_L) or (9_L) because it is misleading, but it seems to me that there is a world of difference between (8_{DL}), "Leo thought that there was a killer after him, but it turned out he was mistaken." Any implication that Leo's belief was correct is cancelled in this case, but not with (8_{DL}).

Of course, those who defend the view that the agent's reasons for actions are either mental states or facts about those states might insist that (8_C) and (8_L) should be taken as elliptical for longer descriptions of these agents' reasons in terms of their mental states. We need to treat this point with some care. Having learned that there was nobody chasing him, Leo might respond to the question, "What reason did you have for running?" by saying "I thought someone was chasing me." If his interrogator does not know that Leo's belief was mistaken and wanted to know why he was running, she might ask Leo, "Who was after you?" and Leo might reply that he thought that there was someone there. Leo was not saying that he was being chased by a non-existent killer, but was instead clarifying that the question about who was after him rested on a mistaken assumption or presupposition. Similarly, when Leo says, "I thought someone was chasing me," Leo might be taken to say that the question about his reasons also rested on a mistaken assumption. With nobody chasing after him, there was no reason at all. Still, his actions made sense because he thought that there was a reason to run.

Perhaps one reason people reject this line is that they think that since Leo was running intentionally, Leo must have been running for a reason.[46] Since none of the facts fit his attitudes, his reasons must have been

---

[46] See Audi 1986 and Davidson 1980.

combinations of attitudes. The problem with this objection is that it rests on the assumption that you act for a reason whenever you act intentionally. Examples suggest that you can do something intentionally without doing what you do for a reason. Alvarez claims that turning a cartwheel just because you want to is something you can do intentionally without doing it for a reason.[47] Hursthouse claims that you might shout at someone as an expression of anger or rage where the shouting is something you do intentionally without doing it for a reason.[48] I would add one more example to this list. You know that you are home alone, but you cannot shake the feeling that someone is standing just behind you watching you, so you run out the door out of fear, knowing that there was no real reason to run. What these cases have in common, Alvarez notes, is the awareness and control typical of intentional action. What they lack is awareness of some consideration that counts in favor or shows the action in a favorable light. The alleged link between acting intentionally and acting for a reason does not strike me as a serious problem for my suggestion that Leo ran but did not run for any reason.

Some say that the problem with saying that there was nothing that was Leo's reason for running is that it collapses the distinction between good and bad reasons. It does not. If Leo ran down the hall screaming because a small puppy was chasing after him, his reason for running might well be that he was being chased. The fact that he was chased by a puppy wanting to play is in the right ontological category to be a reason, but it is a bad reason for fleeing.

An alternative view to consider is a disjunctivist account of acting for reasons. On this account, neither (8_L) nor (9_L) is correct. Instead, we should describe the bad case as follows:

$8_L'$. Leo's reason for running down the hall was that he believed there was a killer running after him.

$9_L'$. Leo ran down the hall because he believed there was a killer running after him.

The disjunctivist account does a nice job of handling the linguistic data, but it is a mark against the view that it denies Dancy's point and insists that the form the explanation takes will depend upon whether the agent's relevant beliefs are correct. If they are, the agent's reason for acting is a fact about the situation, a fact the agent has in mind. If they are mistaken, the agent's reason for acting is a fact about her and her mental states. The

---

[47] Alvarez 2009.   [48] Hursthouse 1991.

cost of this is that it seems to deny that agents who act for reasons are in a privileged position to say what their reasons were for acting if they acted for reasons at all. It is one thing to say that the agent has no special authority over whether she acted for a reason or not and another to say that she has no special authority when it comes to describing her own actions in cases that do not involve self-deception. Barring self-deception, if you acted for a reason and you take yourself to have acted for a reason, the reason you acted for is the reason you take yourself to act for. The reason you take yourself to act for depends upon your psychological states, not further facts about the situation. The disjunctivist denies this. In doing so, they would say that Coop and Leo acted for different reasons even though they are both disposed to describe their actions as acting for the same reasons. By questioning these judgments, they seem to challenge Leo's authority over what his reasons were. I do not see how you can challenge Leo's authority in these cases and say that he did not properly describe his reasons for acting. Not if you claim that your reasons' explanation captures the light in which the agent acted. By Leo's lights, he and Coop act for the same reason. By my lights, Leo was wrong.

There is an alternative view to consider.[49] One problem with the argument from error as written is that it is invalid. We can only establish that (4) is true once we establish that Leo's running was something he did for a reason. If Leo's running was *not* something he did for a reason, we can reject the argument's conclusion without denying (1) and we can accommodate the relevant linguistic data. The main obstacle to this view seems to be that people take it as obvious that we *can* explain Leo's actions. In turn, this is supposed to show that Leo ran for a reason. I do not deny that we can explain Leo's actions. What I deny is that Leo acted for a reason and that this reason explains Leo's actions.

When the agent is motivated to act by a false belief she fails to act for a reason:

10. The reasons for which you Φ when you Φ for a reason are picked out by that-clauses that capture the content of some deliberative belief.
11. When you Φ for a reason, the form that the explanation takes does not vary depending upon whether your deliberative beliefs are correct.
12. The ascriptions that report the reasons for which you Φ are factive.
13. (Therefore) If p is false, "You Φ'd for the reason that p" is false.

---

[49] Alvarez 2010 defends a similar view, although not necessarily for the reasons offered here. Her discussion of the distinction between explanatory and motivating reasons helped me to see how best to deal with the psychologist's objections.

14. If you are the non-factive mental duplicate of a subject that did Φ for the reason that p, "You Φ'd for the reason that p" is the only candidate for explaining your action in terms of motivating reasons.

15. (Therefore) If your deliberative beliefs are mistaken, you might have Φ'd, but you did not Φ for a reason.

Acting for a reason is an achievement in much the way that knowledge is. If you are not properly related to your surroundings, we cannot explain how you know p because you do not know p. If you do not find yourself properly related to your surroundings, we cannot explain how you acted for the reasons you had in mind because there were no reasons you had in mind. Because this view is the only view that accommodates the desiderata we have set out, I think this view is preferable to the alternatives considered.

The main obstacles to my view are these. First, as Dancy says, it sounds 'too harsh' to say that Leo acted for no reason when he ran down the hallway.[50] Perhaps this comes across as too harsh because he was perfectly reasonable to have run down the hall screaming. Second, it seems perfectly obvious that we can explain Leo's running down the hall. He ran down the hall because he believed that the killer was chasing him.

I agree that we can explain Leo's action by saying that he runs because he believes falsely that he is being chased. I agree that there are reasons why he acted as he did. I agree that when we see what these reasons are, we can see why Leo was perfectly reasonable in acting the way he did. What I deny is that Leo acted for a reason. There was nothing in light of which he did what he did. We all know why Leo ran – he ran down the hall because he believed that the killer was after him. This does not explain his action in terms of motivating reasons because it does not tell us what his reasons were – it turned out that he had none. The reasons why Leo acted as he did are facts about Leo's mental states and these provide us with a perfectly good explanation of Leo's behavior. We regard Leo's actions as reasonable because we accept a causal explanation of his behavior according to which Leo's behavior was controlled by the mechanisms responsible for responding to reasons and because we think he was not unreasonable in taking himself to have the reasons that would speak in favor of running.

[50] Personal communication.

4.6 CONCLUSION

We have covered a considerable amount of ground in this chapter. Let me briefly summarize what I have argued for here. Your reasons for action and for belief consist of all and only that which you justifiably believe. Whether you justifiably believe something depends upon whether what you believe is true, because what you justifiably believe depends upon whether what you believe can properly function as a reason in deliberation. Only facts properly figure in deliberation. While some have argued that this view leads to skepticism or avoids skepticism only when combined with Disjunctivism, we have seen that we can resist the argument for Disjunctivism while still maintaining that our reasons for belief are better when our experiences are veridical. We have also seen that arguments from error give us no reason to embrace any psychologized conception of reasons. Reasons are what we take them to be. They are what we act on and what we base our beliefs on, which is to say that they are facts about the situation. Since the justification of belief depends upon whether that belief provides us with reasons, we have to reject the idea that there can be false, justified beliefs along with the orthodox internalist and externalist views that allow for this possibility.

CHAPTER 5

Assertion

5.1 INTRODUCTION

Assertions can be evaluated along a number of dimensions. What matters for our purposes is not that they can be rude or funny, but whether they can be epistemically defective. If so, what standard distinguishes defective assertions from those that are not?

Some of the locals will tell you that the water is not safe to drink and that it would be in your interest to buy bottled water. Suppose you do so. After buying your bottles, you learn that they think the water is unsafe only because it has been fluoridated. We might suppose the water is unsafe for reasons that the locals know nothing about (e.g., toxic materials have found their way into the town's water). In telling you what they did, the locals spoke truthfully. Still, you can reasonably resent that they told you what they did. Given their grounds, they should not have thought the water was unsafe and should not have thought they were telling the truth. The grounds for your resentment have to do with the epistemic standing of the speaker's beliefs. As such, we can put the epistemologists to work in trying to uncover which norms govern assertion.

In this chapter, I want to look at competing accounts of warranted assertion in the hopes that we will gain further insight into the nature of justification. There is some reason to expect that this will bear fruit. The concepts of warrant and justification are both constitutively connected to the concept of obligation. A belief is justified only if it is permissibly held and an assertion is warranted iff it is epistemically permissible. Some of the arguments that shape the Internalism–Externalism debate are designed to show that justification is an internalist notion precisely because justification is a deontological notion. If warrant is a deontological notion and we can show that an assertion can be unwarranted because the speaker spoke falsely, we can see that there are deontological notions that are externalist notions. Second, an increasing number of contributors to the literature on warranted assertion are convinced that assertion and belief are governed by common epistemic standards.[1] If this is right and we see that external conditions determine whether it is proper to assert that something is so, they should help determine whether it is proper to believe that something is so.

Assertions are correct only if they are true. In this respect, assertions are like beliefs. If we say that an assertion is correct iff it is true, we might consider identifying warrant with truth:

TA: Your assertion that p is true is warranted iff p is true.[2]

Many object to TA on the grounds that it is too weak to account for the intuitive data. Our locals' assertion, for example, was unwarranted even though it was true.

While he rejects TA, Williamson defends the idea that there is a truth norm that governs assertion. He thinks TNW is correct because he thinks that the fundamental norm of assertion is the knowledge norm:

TNW: You should not assert p unless p is true.
KA: Your assertion that p is true is warranted iff you know that p is true.[3]

The arguments typically offered in support of KA seem to support the considerably weaker view that the internal components necessary for knowledge are required for warranted assertion:

RA: Your assertion that p is true is warranted iff you reasonably believe p.[4]

The arguments for thinking that the external conditions necessary for knowledge are also required for warranted assertion have been less persuasive. I want to try to help fill a gap in the literature by arguing that truth is required for warranted assertion. Williamson was right and his critics were wrong, but his critics were right to reject KA, nevertheless. This is because assertion and belief are governed by common standards,

---

[1] Adler 2002a; Kvanvig 2009; Sutton 2007; and Williamson 2000a maintain that the same norms govern assertion and belief.
[2] Weiner 2005.
[3] Slote 1979; Sutton 2007; Unger 1975; and Williamson 2000a defend the view that knowledge is the norm of assertion.
[4] Lackey 2007 defends the view that you have warrant to assert p iff p is reasonable to believe, so she defends something only in the neighborhood of RA. Kvanvig 2009 argues that you have warrant to assert p iff you justifiably believe p, so he might defend RA if he thinks that you justifiably believe p iff you reasonably believe p.

and justification determines whether you have sufficient warrant for your assertions:

JA: Your assertion that p is true is warranted iff you justifiably believe that p.

The external conditions that distinguish justification from knowledge are not normatively significant. Since truth is normatively significant, it is among the necessary conditions for warrant and justification.

Most epistemologists would say that JA and TNW are incompatible since they take JA to imply that there can be false, warranted assertions and TNW clearly implies that there cannot be. I think they are compatible. In this chapter, I want to strengthen the case for Factivity$_J$ by arguing for both JA and TNW. The guiding idea is this. Justification is a deontological notion. If you justifiably believe p, you cannot be epistemically obligated to refrain from so believing. Among the norms governing assertion is a norm that enjoins you to refrain from asserting false propositions. Among the norms governing belief is a norm that enjoins you to refrain from believing what you do not have sufficient warrant to assert is true. Since warrant requires truth, so does justification.

5.2 WARRANT AND NORMATIVITY

It is prima facie plausible that knowledge is sufficient for warranted assertion. If knowledge was not enough, you could fail to live up to your epistemic obligations for asserting something without having a sufficiently strong epistemic position to do so even if you knew you spoke the truth. It is hard to see how this could happen. There might be cases where you should not assert that p is true unless you are absolutely certain that p is true. Perhaps the heavens would fall if you spoke falsely. In such a case, knowledge of p's truth might not permit telling someone that p, but it seems the reason this is so has to do with the high practical stakes. There are two theoretical options here, which is either to argue that knowledge depends upon the practical stakes or to argue that the obligation to refrain from asserting in high-stakes cases is a practical obligation rather than an epistemic one.[5] To show that knowledge does not provide sufficient *epistemic* warrant for assertion, we need some reason to say that the higher

---

[5] For arguments that it is harder to know in high-stakes cases, see Fantl and McGrath 2009; Hawthorne 2004; Stanley 2005; and Weatherson 2005. For contextualist treatments of high-stakes cases, see Cohen 1999; DeRose 1995; and Schaffer 2006.

stakes raise the epistemic standards required for warrant without having any effect on whether you meet the conditions necessary for knowledge. Because it seems odd for someone to acknowledge that the speaker knew she spoke correctly and insist that she failed in her epistemic obligations by asserting *p*, I shall assume that knowledge is sufficient for warrant and focus on the more difficult question as to whether it is necessary.

The standard complaint about KA is that it is too demanding. Why does Williamson think that nothing short of knowledge could warrant assertion? One suggestion is that knowledge is the constitutive rule of assertion. The knowledge rule is what distinguishes the speech act of assertion from other speech acts. He formulates the knowledge rule as follows:

KR: You must: assert *p* only if you know that *p*.[6]

Just as the rules of chess tell us what it is to castle, this rule tells us what it is to assert something. Constitutive rules can be broken (e.g., you still count as boxing if you break the rules of boxing and somehow Roller Derby has rules even if everyone is encouraged to break them), so you can assert *p* without knowing *p*. (Indeed, you can assert *p* without intending to assert what you know.) There is, however, a limit on how far you can go in violating a constitutive rule. You cannot castle without a chessboard using a banana or play Roller Derby by yourself in your socks. KR helps us see what assertions are and, perhaps, what they ought to be.

Critics say that KR is implausibly strong. Kvanvig raises the worry that Williamson might be committed to the implausible position that the knowledge rule is indefeasible.[7] Thomson similarly objects that KR is far too strong to be true.[8] If we read KR as she does, she is certainly right. She reads KR as if it marks the second coming of Kant. To say that you 'must' not assert something is supposed to be stronger than saying that you 'ought' not assert it. In effect, she takes KR to say that no case could ever be made for asserting something you do not know. Kant was wrong to deny that you may lie to hide someone from the killer at the door. If this is what KR says, so much the worse for it.

Of course, Williamson never meant to side with Kant.[9] Obscured by a subtle point about the distinction between 'ought' and 'must' is an important issue having to do with the normativity of warrant. Williamson's critics say that it is permissible to assert what you do not

---

[6] Williamson 2000a, p. 243.   [7] Kvanvig 2009, p. 141.
[8] Thomson 2008, p. 88.   [9] Williamson 2000a, p. 240.

know and Williamson rightly responds by saying that he never meant to say otherwise. Whatever reasons you have to refrain from asserting what you do not know can be overridden because whatever reasons you have to refrain from asserting without warrant can be overridden. Even this seems not to go far enough, however, as Kant's example shows. There is no reason to refrain from lying to the killer at the door. Not only is there no absolute prohibition against asserting what you do not know, there is no *pro tanto* reason to refrain from asserting falsehoods.

One problem with arguing for KA on the grounds that KR is the constitutive rule of assertion is that, as formulated, KR is too strong. Sometimes there is no reason whatever to refrain from asserting what you do not know. Another is that constitutive rules do not provide categorical reasons; at least, not the right kind of categorical reasons to explain some of the intuitive data. As Foot observed, some categorical reasons are categorical because they apply to us whatever our ends or desires happen to be.[10] The reasons associated with the rules of etiquette are like this. If someone says that you ought not hold your salad fork with your toes, the speaker does not speak falsely just because you want to eat with your toes. If the reasons associated with the norms of assertion are like the reasons associated with the rules of etiquette, they might have inescapability without having rational authority. Of course, some categorical reasons have rational authority. These are reasons that rational agents are supposed to assign some weight to. There are two questions about the norms of assertion. Do they have rational authority? If so, from where does this authority derive?

I think there are rationally authoritative reasons that can give us reason to conform to the norms of assertion, but they are not provided by these norms on their own. We know that there can be rationally authoritative reasons to conform to the norms of assertion. If there were no rationally authoritative reasons ever to conform to them, we could not reasonably resent it when someone asserts something without warrant. As we saw earlier, however, you can reasonably resent that the locals told you to buy water when clearly they did not have sufficient warrant to assert what they did. Even if KR is the constitutive rule of assertion, there is a gap in the argument from this claim to the further claim that there are rationally authoritative reasons to refrain from asserting without warrant. What fills this gap?

---

[10] Foot 1972. I have borrowed Brink's 1997 terminology.

There is an important difference between the case of Kant's killer and cases in which weighty reasons pressure you to tell your students things that you know are not true. In light of the weighty reasons (e.g., credible threats from fanatics bent on getting you to teach your students that, say, people used to keep dinosaurs as pets), it might be right to lie to your students. In this case, the lie is regrettable. In the case of Kant's killer, it is not. The difference between these cases is not purely epistemic. You know you speak falsely in both cases. The difference is moral. In one case, you have a responsibility to your audience. In the other, you do not.

We wanted to know how to fill in the gap and show that if there are constitutive rules that govern assertion there are also rationally authoritative reasons that sometimes tell you that it is wrong to assert without warrant. Moral norms fill the gap. Constitutive rules tell you what assertions are for, what they are supposed to do. They have no rational authority in themselves, just as the rules for castling do not have any rational authority. Moral norms tell you when you have a responsibility to see to it that your assertions conform to the constitutive rules of assertion. They also tell you whether your responsibility includes a duty to exercise due care or extends beyond this. They have rational authority. You know that when you assert something, your audience can treat what you asserted as a piece of intelligence, a premise that can be used for the purposes of practical or theoretical deliberation. If your assertion is no good for this purpose, it is unwarranted. If morality tells you that you have a responsibility to your audience, this lack of warrant has normative significance and there are rationally authoritative reasons for you not to assert what you did. If, however, morality tells you that you have no responsibility to your audience, the lack of warrant has no normative significance. It is not, for example, a cause for regret.

Because assertions are pieces of intelligence or potential premises others might rely on for the purposes of practical or theoretical deliberation, they are supposed to be true. This is why falsehoods arrived at through careful reasoning and truths typed out by monkeys banging away at keyboards are defective in some sense. The normative question is which defects matter when it comes to the ethics of assertion. One side will say that although false assertions are defective in some way, permissible assertion requires only that you take due care and refrain from asserting without sufficient evidence. The other side says that due care is not enough for warrant or permissibility. You can try to live up to your responsibilities and act in just the way that a responsible person would without meeting your responsibilities.

There are two strategies to show that knowledge is the norm of assertion. You might say that if your responsibility is, say, to provide someone with an effective treatment for their pain, you should know the drugs will be effective before you hand them over. The concept of knowledge does not play a role in determining whether the drug is defective, only in determining whether it is permissible to provide someone with safe and effective drugs. Alternatively, you could say that an assertion is defective if it does not express knowledge. Asserting what you do not know is akin to selling toasters that do not toast. Whichever way you go, to show that knowledge is the norm of assertion, you have to show that your responsibility is not simply to assert what you reasonably take to be true. You have to show that you cannot meet your responsibilities to your audience without knowing that what you say is true.

5.3 THE KNOWLEDGE ACCOUNT

Should we refrain from asserting what we do not know? I think not. The arguments offered in support of KA support weaker accounts of assertion, such as RA or JA. KA also delivers the wrong verdicts in some of the cases where RA delivers the right verdicts.

5.3.1 Truth as the aim

The first argument for the knowledge account works from the assumption that belief and assertion have a common aim and that the fact that they have this aim is normatively significant. In saying that belief or assertion have an aim and that you ought not assert or believe when this aim would not be achieved, it is not at all clear which of these claims is explanatorily prior to the other. It might be that in saying that belief aims at truth or knowledge, I am expressing the thought that beliefs that are not true or do not constitute knowledge are not as they ought to be, but that might be because this talk of aims is a useful metaphor best cashed out in normative terms.

Suppose that belief does aim at the truth.[11] Let us also suppose that belief has no further independent aim of equal significance that it might achieve without being true. Given this, it seems natural to say that even if some good comes of believing a false proposition, such a good has

---

[11] For defense, see Velleman 2000; Wedgwood 2002b; Whiting 2010; and Williams 1973.

little significance when it comes to justifying the belief in question. Our concern is with assertion, not belief. Still, we can make some progress in understanding the norms governing assertion by thinking about the norms that govern belief since, as Williamson notes, "assertion is the exterior analogue of judgment, which stands to belief as act to state."[12] Given this, a reasonable default assumption is that assertion and belief share common aims and are governed by common standards. If belief aims at the truth, so does assertion. If truth is normative for assertion, it is normative for belief. If the assumption that truth is the fundamental norm for belief is too weak to account for all of the normative demands that we are under as believers, we should expect the same to be true for assertion and the demands that we are under if we decide to tell our audience that something is so.

Williamson suggests that if the norms of assertion can be derived from a proper description of the norms and aims of belief, you can derive the knowledge account of assertion from the assumption that truth is among the aims of belief and assertion.[13] If there is such a derivation, it is not straightforward. Utilitarians do not think that the justification of an action depends upon whether the agent *knew* that it was optimific prior to action, only that it was optimific. No one has ever faulted them for this. You are courting disaster if you advance the claim that there are positive duties and claim that all duties must be knowingly discharged. Such a combination of views would seem to lead rather quickly to the untenable view that says that there are unknowable obligations that are only obligations insofar as they are knowable.

We avoid these worries if we assume that our epistemic duties are all negative and that we could meet our obligations simply by refraining from believing or asserting. If there is a truth norm that governs assertion, it enjoins us to say only what is true, not to say that things are true:

TNW: You should not assert p unless p is true.

Williamson suggests that if TNW governs assertion, an evidential norm must govern assertion as well:

ENW: You should not assert p unless you have sufficient evidence for believing that p is true.

In light of this, he thinks knowledge is necessary for warranted assertion:

---

[12] Williamson 2000a, p. 238.   [13] Williamson 2000a, p. 241.

KNW: You should not assert *p* unless you know that *p* is true.

The idea seems to be that the evidential norm is derivative from the truth norm and that somehow we ought to think knowledge is necessary for warranted assertion given that ENW and TNW govern assertion.

If TNW is among the norms that govern assertion, we have to reject the following thesis about epistemic wrongs and fault:

> Fault₁: All epistemic wrongs are fault-implying wrongs (i.e., any condition that makes believing or asserting *p* wrongful is a condition that the believer can be faulted for failing to take account of if she asserts or believes *p* when that condition obtains).

While TNW is incompatible with Fault₁, it is consistent with this thesis about fault and epistemic wrongs:

> Fault₂: Any condition that grounds the charge of epistemic fault is a condition that makes assertion and belief wrongful.

It seems that Williamson's reason for taking ENA to be a consequence of TNA is something along the lines of Fault₂. He says:

> [I]f one must not bury people when they are not dead, then one should not bury them when one lacks evidence that they are dead. It is at best negligent to bury someone without evidence that he is dead, even if he is in fact dead.[14]

While I think this is right, it does not support anything as demanding as KA.

Williamson says we do not satisfy the evidential norm governing assertion unless we have evidence that puts us in a position to know that what we assert is true.[15] If we think about lottery propositions, it seems we do not have adequate evidence to believe or assert such propositions. It seems the best explanation as to why this is just is that the evidence we have for believing lottery propositions does not put us in a position to know that these propositions are true.

There are two ways of reading Williamson's lottery argument. On the first, his remarks concerning lottery propositions gives us a clue as to what he thinks it takes to satisfy Fault₂. If you believe or assert without first gathering evidence that puts you in a position to know that *p*, you seem to be at fault even if your belief turns out to be true. On the second,

---

[14] Williamson 2000a, p. 245. [15] Williamson 2000a, p. 246.

we appeal to ENW directly and let intuition serve as our guide in determining what it takes to satisfy ENW rather than appeal to assumptions linking fault and justification.

On the first reading, the argument amounts to this.

1. You should not assert p unless p is true.
2. If you do not know whether you would violate a strict prohibition by Φ-ing but Φ anyway, you are at fault for Φ-ing.
3. (Therefore) You should not assert p if you do not know p.

So formulated, the argument rests on an implicit assumption about fault and knowledge:

> Fault$_3$: It would be irresponsible to Φ if you do not first know whether Φ-ing is permissible.

Without the assumption, you cannot derive anything stronger than the conjunctive claim that you ought not Φ unless you have conformed to TNW and have sufficient evidence to reasonably take yourself to have conformed to TNW.

There are two reasons to reject Fault$_3$. First, suppose we say that knowledge is a condition necessary for permissible assertion and suppose Fault$_3$ is true. If so, we would have to say either that mere knowledge of p's truth is insufficient for permissibly believing p or we would have to endorse a KK thesis according to which you cannot know p unless you are in a position to know that you know that p is true.

Second, there is a further reason to deny Fault$_3$. If combined with the KA, it commits us to the JTB analysis of knowledge and an infallibilist conception of justification. Epistemic irresponsibility can make an otherwise justifiable belief unjustified. According to Fault$_3$, if you fail to know for any reason, you can be charged with epistemic irresponsibility. Thus, if you cannot be charged with epistemic irresponsibility because you are justified in believing p, the fact that you are justified in holding your belief is logically incompatible with (a) your belief being mistaken or (b) your belief being Gettiered. As a result, you cannot satisfy the justification condition if it is possible that someone should have just your reasons but be mistaken about whether p. Thus, your reasons must entail p if your belief that p is justified. But, no one should believe that you must have entailing grounds to permissibly believe p. Thus, it seems that Fault$_3$ has the consequence that if someone does not know that p, they are not justified in believing p, in which case Gettier cases are impossible.

In light of these problems, we should look at the second reading of Williamson's argument.[16] On this reading, the argumentative burden is shouldered not solely by assumptions about fault and epistemic responsibility, but also by intuitions concerning cases involving lottery propositions. The assumptions about fault are supposed to support the idea that some sort of evidential norm governs belief. Our intuitions about lottery propositions are supposed to help us see what it takes to satisfy this evidential norm. We start from the assumption that you should not assert or believe lottery propositions. The natural explanation for this is that you do not have evidence for believing these propositions that would put you in a position to know that they are true. From here, the argument might go in one of two directions. If someone said that this is why you ought not assert what you do not know, this would repeat the mistakes of the argument we just discussed. All that follows is that you ought not believe *p* if you are in a position to appreciate that your evidence does not put you in a position to know *p*. In Gettier cases and in cases where you do not know that *p* is a lottery proposition, you do not know *p*, you do not know that you are not in a position to know *p*, but it is not obvious that you have violated ENW. If you think you do violate ENW in such cases, you will once again be forced to accept the JTB analysis of knowledge and an infallibilist account of justification.

To avoid these difficulties, someone should instead argue as follows. Intuition, they could say, tells us that evidence is needed for permissible belief. Intuitions about lottery cases tell us that beliefs in lottery propositions are defective because there is not adequate evidence for believing them outright. The best explanation of the observation that you do not satisfy ENW unless your evidence puts you in a position to know is that KA is the fundamental norm of assertion.

This argument rests on a pair of assumptions. First, the argument assumes that beliefs in lottery propositions do not constitute knowledge. Second, it assumes that you ought not believe lottery propositions. If we deny the first assumption, we cannot appeal to intuitive verdicts about lottery cases to motivate KA. If we were to reject the second assumption while accepting the first, lottery cases would provide counterexamples to the claim that you should not believe what you know you do not know.

I want to say two things in responding to this argument. KA cannot give the best explanation of the data if independent considerations show

---

[16] Jonathan Sutton said in conversation that this is the more charitable reading of Williamson's argument.

that KA does not govern assertion. The verdicts the knowledge account delivers for covert lottery beliefs and Gettiered beliefs are counterintuitive. Thus, while the knowledge account delivers the right verdict in some familiar lottery cases, it seems to give the wrong reason for the verdict. Intuitions concerning cases of covert lottery beliefs suggest that the reason we ought not believe lottery propositions is not that they cannot constitute knowledge per se, but that subjects that believe lottery propositions are wrong to do so in light of considerations accessible to them (i.e., considerations about the kinds of grounds they have for believing lottery propositions). While such grounds might not put the subject in a position to know, the normative significance of this is not what the knowledge account takes it to be.

We are all familiar with the distinction between overt and covert lottery beliefs even if we are not familiar with the terminology. Let us say that a covert lottery belief is a belief whose truth or falsity depends on the outcome of a lottery held where the believer is not in a position to appreciate that this is so. Let us say that an overt lottery belief is a belief in a lottery proposition held by someone who has no insider information and knows that the truth of what they believe depends upon the outcome of a lottery. If you look at your bank statement and see that you are down to your last few dollars, you might reasonably believe that you will not be able to go on safari. If your mother has just purchased you a ticket for a lottery drawing being held later this afternoon without telling you, your belief that you cannot afford to go on safari is a covert lottery belief. Were you to believe that the ticket that your mother bought you will lose, that would be an overt lottery belief. (We are assuming that you know that you would be able to afford to go on safari if only you were to win the lottery drawing being held this afternoon.) It seems that overt and covert lottery beliefs will either both constitute knowledge or neither will. If you think that some suitably formulated closure principle holds true, someone will be in a position to know that a covert lottery belief is true only if this subject is in a position to know that an overt lottery belief is true. Assuming, as we are, that overt lottery beliefs fail to constitute knowledge, it seems we have good reason for thinking that covert lottery beliefs similarly fail to constitute knowledge.

If this is correct, the knowledge account implies that you should not hold or form covert lottery beliefs. I think this is a mistake. In defenses of the knowledge account, the focus has been on the judgments that overt lottery beliefs should not be held and cannot constitute knowledge. No intuitive support has been offered to back the claim that neither type of lottery belief ought to be held. In fact, you might think that one of the reasons that the lottery paradox is so interesting is that we are not naturally disposed to think of covert lottery beliefs held by others as beliefs they should not continue to hold for reasons of which only we are aware (i.e., that unbeknown to them the truth of their beliefs is contingent on the outcome of a lottery). The knowledge account's verdict in covert lottery cases is counterintuitive.

To see this, consider a modified version of one of Hawthorne's examples. A friend writes you an email on Monday before a lottery is held and you read their email on Tuesday after the results of that lottery are known to you. It contains the following line of reasoning:

The ticket for tomorrow's lottery is a loser. So if I keep the ticket I will get nothing. But if I sell the ticket I will get a penny. So, I'd better sell the ticket.[17]

You know now that the first premise was not known to be true because of the grounds the subject had for that belief and know that the belief turned out to be true. Retrospectively, it seems you would agree with Hawthorne that this reasoning is unacceptable and would likely further agree that its unacceptability is due to the speaker's belief in the argument's first premise. Assuming that you should not hold beliefs that should not be trusted for the purposes of practical deliberation, we would arrive at the view that the speaker should not have held the first belief. Even without that assumption, you might agree that the subject should not have held the first belief regardless of whether it was fit to figure in practical deliberation.

Now, suppose a different friend writes you an email on Monday before a lottery is held, but you only read it on Tuesday after the results of that lottery are known to you. You had purchased this friend a ticket for this lottery without telling them, but now know that the ticket was a loser. They had written:

I want nothing more than to go on safari. If I were to go on safari, I would want nothing more than to buy a new elephant gun. The gun will be useless, however, since I cannot afford to go on safari. So I guess I will use that money instead to do some repairs around the house.

You know that the subject's belief in the first premise is a covert lottery belief and did not constitute knowledge. The lottery was held and the ticket lost, so the outcome of the lottery would not affect what would be best for your friend to do. I think you would take this reasoning to be

---

[17] The example is taken from Hawthorne 2004, p. 29.

acceptable. However, the knowledge account regards both instances of reasoning as unacceptable for the very same reason. In both cases someone reasons from a premise not known to be true.

That the knowledge account delivers the wrong verdict in the case of covert lottery beliefs suggests that knowledge is not the norm of assertion or belief. Additionally, it suggests that the knowledge account gives the wrong explanation for the unacceptability of the first bit of reasoning. The knowledge account seeks to explain the unacceptability of this reasoning in terms of a fact that is not accessible to the individual engaged in this bit of reasoning (i.e., that one of the beliefs involved in the reasoning is not known to be true). However, if overt and covert lottery beliefs have different normative statuses (i.e., one ought never hold overt lottery beliefs but may permissibly hold some covert lottery beliefs), it seems that the proper explanation as to why you should not reason from overt lottery beliefs should be given in terms of features distinctive of overt lottery beliefs (e.g., the kinds of ground available for overt lottery belief) rather than ignorance, per se. We have not found a route from the truth norm, or the thesis that belief aims at the truth, to the knowledge norm. It is not for a lack of trying. Williamson is right that anyone who thinks there is a truth norm should think there is an additional evidential norm governing belief, but we know from Gettier that there is more to conforming to the knowledge norm than conforming to these two.

5.3.2 *Knowledge as the aim*

Rather than try to derive the knowledge account from the truth norm, we could try a more direct approach. Belief, you might say, does not aim at just the truth. Belief aims at knowledge. Any belief that fails to constitute knowledge is wrongful precisely because there is no distinct aim a belief serves that could potentially provide a justification for believing without knowing.

Since the argument assumes nothing about justification and fault, it should not face the problems the previous argument did. The argument assumes that knowledge is the aim of belief. The norms that govern belief also govern assertion. So, since you should not believe what you do not know, you should not assert what you do not know.

The problem with this argument for KA is quite simply that knowledge is not the aim of belief. To test proposals about aims, we can consult our intuitions to determine what an external observer would or should say if she knew that another's belief fails to constitute knowledge. We know that belief aims at the truth, for example, because we know that if someone knows that someone else's belief about p is not true, this outside observer has sufficient warrant for asserting that this belief is incorrect or mistaken. On the hypothesis that belief also aims at knowledge, we should expect that those who know we don't know that p for any reason will be disposed to say we have made a mistake, we were wrong to believe what we did, or that we should suspend judgment. This is not what we find. If this is how we evaluate claims about the epistemic aim and the epistemic ought, we not only fail to find support for the knowledge account, we find evidence for denying that belief is governed by the knowledge norm. If beliefs that fail to conform to no norms are justified, we find evidence for denying that knowledge of p's truth is necessary for the justification of the belief that p. Suppose you think you saw a barn. You did, but you did not realize that you were in the land of fake barns. Because the hills were filled with convincing fakes, we do not think your belief constitutes knowledge. Knowing this, however, I do not think that your belief failed to fulfill its aim. Knowing that you do not know and why your belief is not knowledge, I would not be inclined to tell you that you are wrong to believe what you do or that you have made a mistake by believing that you see a barn. If a belief such as this does not miss its mark, nothing is left of the view that belief aims at knowledge. The fakes prevent your belief from fulfilling its aim only when they fool you into believing a fake barn is genuine.

If we set aside the question about aims and focus on the normative question, it seems that if someone said that you should not believe it is a barn knowing that your belief fails to constitute knowledge simply because the belief is Gettiered, it seems that they have made the mistake, not you. If that is right, there is nothing left of the view that knowledge is what is necessary for permissible belief. In saying that it is not epistemically wrong to believe p if that belief has been Gettiered, it might seem I am denying something Reynolds says in his discussion of Gettier cases and warranted assertion. He says the locals who know that you have been driving through fake-barn country would not say that you should believe you saw a barn.[18] They know that you were reasonable in holding this belief, but they know that given the grounds on which your belief is based, you did not have the power to distinguish fake from genuine barns. This may be true, but the knowledge account is not necessary for explaining why the locals would not (and ought not) say it is permissible

---

[18] Reynolds 2002, p. 150.

for you to believe you saw a barn. Reynolds says the locals do not know whether the particular belief you have formed is true. They only know that your grounds are not effective for determining whether your belief is true. Because of this, it would be wrong for them to assert that you should believe what you do because they do not have a true and reasonable belief that your belief satisfies the truth norm. Once we give the locals the additional piece of information that your belief is correct and they know that the sole reason you fail to know has to do with factors beyond those that determine whether you are justified or you are right, speakers are not disposed to think you should revise your beliefs and suspend judgment. Without this information, however, we cannot use their responses to evaluate the respective merits of the knowledge account or the weaker truth account.

The claim that knowledge is the aim of belief is not pulled from thin air. There are arguments for this view that we should address. What is wrong with the thesis that belief aims at the truth without aiming at knowledge? Sutton remarks:

> Another assumption is almost as common as the assumption that truth maximization/falsity minimization is a primary epistemic goal – the assumption that a central fact about belief is that it aims at truth. Known unknown beliefs again suggest that this is not so. If belief aims at truth, then the belief that one will lose the lottery … will, in almost all cases, succeed in fulfilling that central aim, and so should be impeccably formed, that is, justified. If, as I will argue, the known unknown beliefs are not justified, and are not justified because they do not constitute knowledge, we should rather say that belief aims at knowledge.[19]

The argument assumes that if something is an aim or, perhaps, a legitimate aim, of Φ-ing, Φ-ing is justified if it fulfills that aim. The thought here is that if there are beliefs that are true, they should be justified whether or not they constitute knowledge if belief's aim is truth but not knowledge. The problem with this argument is that it ignores the possibility of side-constraints that distinguish between legitimate and illegitimate ways of pursuing legitimate aims.

5.4 MOORE'S PARADOX

Some argue that reflection on Moore's Paradox supports the knowledge account of assertion. Consider the statement "Custer died at Little Big Horn, but I believe he did not." It seems contradictory, but it easily could

---

[19] Sutton 2007, p. 22. Vahid 2006 raises the same worry.

have been true. (I know almost nothing about the history of the United States.) What accounts for the appearance of contradiction in the absence of contradiction? One suggestion is that anyone who holds the beliefs associated with Moorean absurd statements holds beliefs that conflict with the rational commitments that come with those very beliefs.[20] For example, it is thought that belief has as its aim the truth, and someone who holds the beliefs associated with "Custer died at Little Big Horn, but I believe he did not" would be committed to denying the accuracy of the belief expressed by the first conjunct. That is akin to a contradiction. The appearance of contradiction is explained in terms of the conscious conflict between the beliefs the subject is cognizant of and the rational commitments that come with the beliefs associated with the Moorean absurd statements (e.g., such as the fact that, by her lights, she has misrepresented how things are by believing Custer died at Little Big Horn).

The arguments discussed in this section purport to show that knowledge is the norm of belief, which is supposed to show that knowledge is a norm of assertion as well. Those who deny either of these theses are supposed to have trouble explaining why Moorean absurd thoughts and assertions are defective. These arguments all rest on a methodological assumption that I shall grant for the purposes of this discussion:

MA: Anyone who holds the beliefs associated with a Moorean absurd statement holds beliefs that conflict with the rational commitments that come with those very beliefs.[21]

Huemer argues that knowledge is the norm of belief by appeal to these two assumptions:

MCP: Consciously believing p rationally commits you, upon reflection, to comprehensively, epistemically endorsing your belief that p.

ETK: Knowledge attribution is the most comprehensive epistemic endorsement.[22]

If you believed p, he says, it would be wrong to hold that belief without endorsing it as knowledge. But, you should not endorse that belief

---

[20] See Adler 2002a; de Almeida 2001; and Huemer 2007b.
[21] Those who think that Moorean absurdity has everything to do with speech and nothing to do with thought will reject the argument for the knowledge account at a stage earlier than I will by rejecting the methodological assumption central to this line of argument. For arguments that the paradox is not about speech alone, see Adler 2002a; Shoemaker 1996; and Sorensen 1988.
[22] Huemer 2007b.

as knowledge unless it is knowledge. Therefore, you ought not believe *p* unless you know *p*.

In defense of MCP, remember that MA tells us that whenever someone utters a Moorean absurdity, they have uttered something absurd because the beliefs associated with that statement conflict with the rational commitments that come with those beliefs. As such, these beliefs cannot be comprehensively endorsed. As for ETK, I agree with Huemer that there is no more comprehensive epistemic endorsement of a belief than to endorse it as constituting knowledge.[23]

Here is an initial worry about Huemer's strategy. His argument implicitly assumes that each of the conditions that figure in a comprehensive epistemic evaluation pertains to the permissibility of belief. Consider moral evaluation. A moral evaluation that focused exclusively on the permissibility of some action would not be a comprehensive evaluation. A comprehensive evaluation of an action should not only tell us whether the act was permitted, but also whether it had moral worth. That my act lacks moral worth does not show that I acted without justification. Similarly, it does not follow from the fact that my action was supererogatory that it calls for a justification. Huemer gives us no reason to think that a comprehensive evaluation of belief would concern only that belief's deontic status. So, even if we assume ETK, it would not be surprising if some of the conditions needed for knowledge were not necessary for permissible belief.

This is not an idle worry. We have already seen some reason to think that the permissibility of belief does not turn on whether that belief can be properly endorsed along all lines of epistemic evaluation. Knowledge, for example, seems to be more valuable than justified belief. Surely a comprehensive epistemic evaluation would consider whether some belief had this value. Thus, we either have to say that a comprehensive epistemic endorsement concerns more than just the deontically relevant properties of belief or deny the evaluative claim that knowledge is distinctively valuable. If a comprehensive epistemic endorsement concerns more than just deontically relevant properties, a permissibly held belief might not be one that deserves a comprehensive endorsement.

There is a second problem with Huemer's argument for the thesis that knowledge is the norm of belief. While the knowledge account seems to follow from MCP and ETK, it also seems to follow from these assumptions that you should not believe *p* unless you know that you know that

---

[23] Huemer 2007b, p. 149.

you know (etc.) that *p*. Since knowledge does not require knowing that you know that you know (etc.), the argument needs to be revised. The needed fix is not hard to find. We can rewrite MCP and say that consciously believing *p* requires that you should not believe yourself to fail to satisfy the standards of a comprehensive epistemic endorsement while also consciously believing *p*. This revision is independently motivated. It is simply not true that if you permissibly believe *p*, you ought to believe that your belief satisfies a comprehensive epistemic endorsement. Failing to have any belief about whether you know *p* when you happen to believe *p* (and happen not to be wrong to do so) is no sin at all. What rationality requires is that you revise your beliefs if you believe that you cannot comprehensively endorse them (i.e., by judging that they are false, that they don't amount to knowledge, etc.). We should replace MCP with:

MCP$_2$: Consciously believing *p* rationally commits you, upon reflection, to refrain from believing both *p* and that *p* cannot satisfy the standards of a comprehensive epistemic endorsement.

MCP$_2$ is too weak to support the argument for the knowledge account. According to ETK and MCP$_2$, all that permissibly believing *p* requires is that you do not believe what you believe yourself not to know. You can satisfy this requirement without knowing *p*. You satisfy this requirement if you do not have any second-order beliefs.

Let's consider a second argument for the knowledge account, one provided by Adler.[24] He thinks we can rely on our intuitive sense of which combinations of attitudes would constitute Moorean absurdities to determine which norms govern those attitudes. His argument seems to be this. According to MA, if any judgment that expresses the belief that *p* is coupled with the acknowledgment that some condition C does not obtain and the resulting conjunction is absurd in the way that Moorean absurdities are, you are cognizant that, by holding these beliefs, you violate rational requirements on holding those beliefs. The judgment expressed by '*p* but I do not know it' is incoherent in the way Moorean absurdities are. Therefore, in judging that you do not know *p*, you know there is something wrongful in believing *p* – namely, that you do not know *p*.

This is an improvement over the previous argument because Adler's argument does not assume the Metacoherence Principle. Instead, it relies on the incoherence test:

[24] Adler 2002a.

IT: If it is incoherent in the way Moorean absurd statements are to Φ while acknowledging that C does not obtain, in acknowledging that C does not obtain, you are cognizant of something that makes it wrong to Φ – namely, that C does not obtain.[25]

Given our methodological assumption, it seems we can test proposals concerning the norms of belief as follows. If it is incoherent in the way a Moorean absurd thought is (i.e., apparently contradictory without being a belief in a contradiction) to simultaneously believe p while believing C does not obtain, there is a norm that enjoins us to refrain from believing p when C does not obtain. For example, it seems incoherent to believe the following:

1. I believe Custer died at Little Big Horn, but he did not.

In representing the belief about Custer as being false, it seems we have an incoherent combination of attitudes without a contradiction. Perhaps this is due to the fact that belief is governed by the truth norm. It seems similarly incoherent to believe:

2. I believe Custer died at Little Big Horn, but there is no reason for me to think that.

On the assumption that the only thing that could be a reason for me to believe is a piece of evidence, we can infer from the fact that (2) is a Moorean absurdity that belief is governed by an evidential norm. It is also incoherent to believe both p and believe that this belief fails to satisfy one of the conditions necessary for knowledge. So, by similar reasoning, it seems that we ought to accept that knowledge is the norm of belief.

Unfortunately, this test is insufficiently discriminating. It might only be useful for uncovering normative requirements governing combinations of belief without uncovering the norms that govern those beliefs individually. Consider:

3. God hates my atheism and it is raining outside.[26]

This is a Moorean absurdity, but there is no norm that enjoins us to refrain from believing that it is raining outside unless God would forgive my atheism. It is no mystery as to why (3) is incoherent. It is incoherent because the belief that God hates my atheism is a Moorean absurdity in its own right. At the very least, IT needs to be reformulated to avoid

[25] Adler 2002a, p. 29.   [26] This example is based on an example in Sorensen 1988.

these sorts of example. Even if we grant that for every incoherent pair of attitudes there is something you are cognizant of that makes one of the attitudes you are conscious of wrongful, we could say what makes it wrongful is precisely that it is held in combination with the belief that C does not obtain. It might be that this belief alone is absurd, irrational, or contravenes an epistemic norm. We might say, as it were, that whenever believing p while believing C does not obtain constitutes a Moorean absurdity, all that follows is that:

4. You should not believe: p and that C does not obtain.

That is different from:

5. If C does not obtain you should not believe p.

The former is a normative requirement and the 'ought' takes wide scope. The latter is a norm where 'ought' takes narrow scope. The former tells us what combinations of attitudes we ought to avoid. The latter tells us what sorts of conditions bear on whether to hold the belief in question. As we are trying to derive norms such as the knowledge norm (i.e., if you do not know p you must not believe p) from judgments about rational combinations of attitudes (i.e., it is irrational to believe both that p is true and not known to be true), we need some reason to think that we can proceed from intuitive judgments about irrational combinations of attitude to judgments about attitudes we have reason to refrain from holding when certain non-mental conditions obtain (i.e., that we have reason to refrain from believing falsehoods).

Maybe these problems are not insuperable. We can revise IT to deal with examples like (3) as follows:

> IT_2: If it is incoherent in the way Moorean absurd statements are to Φ while acknowledging that C does not obtain and the belief that C does not obtain is not itself incoherent, in acknowledging that C does not obtain, you are cognizant of something that makes it wrong to Φ – namely, that C does not obtain.

To deal with the second problem, we might say that the reason it is irrational to believe both that p is true and that C does not obtain is that in representing your present situation as one in which C does not obtain, you thereby appreciate that if that belief is correct, you should expect there to be reason not to believe p. Moreover, if that belief is incorrect it is still by your lights a situation where there is reason not to believe p. To believe against what you take to be good reasons is itself an epistemic wrong.

This might address the problems with IT. Unfortunately, the revised version of the test does not support the knowledge account. To see why, notice that the test applies only when the belief that C does not obtain is a belief that is not incoherent taken on its own. While we might grant that if C is a condition necessary for knowledge it is incoherent to believe both that p is true and that C does not obtain, we only find confirmation of the knowledge account if we assume also that for any condition C such that C is a condition necessary for knowledge it is coherent to believe on its own that C does not obtain. This is not what we find.

It is not incoherent to believe that you do not know p because p is false. So, according to IT$_2$ there is a norm that enjoins us to refrain from believing the false. It is not incoherent to believe that you do not know p because your evidence does not put you in a position to know whether p. So, according to IT$_2$, there is a norm that enjoins us to refrain from believing without evidence.[27] What of the other conditions necessary for knowledge? So far, we have confirmed only that you should not believe the false and not believe without evidence. The belief that my belief about p is Gettiered, like the belief that God will not forgive my atheism, is incoherent taken on its own. There are many ways to Gettier a belief, but I shall focus on two. In the first sort of case, your evidence for believing p is undermined thanks to true propositions of which you are unaware. In the second sort of case, your evidence for believing p only accidentally leads you to the correct judgment concerning p.

It is reasonably clear why you cannot coherently and correctly believe yourself to be in the first sort of case. To believe yourself to be in such a case, you have to believe of some piece of evidence (i) that you are unaware of it and (ii) that it would, if combined with your present evidence, undermine the justification you have for believing p. However, you would have this evidence in mind if you were to believe this. The case is not possible. If you were aware of the evidence you would no longer be justified in believing what you did. This means this would not be a Gettier case.

What about the second sort of Gettier case? In this case, you fail to know p is true due to the accidental connection between your grounds and the truth. You cannot coherently believe that you fail to know that p simply because you are only accidentally related to the truth about p. To believe that your connection to the truth is accidental is (roughly) to

---

[27] Adler 2002a; de Almeida 2001; and Williams 1994 offer explanations along these lines. They do not rely on the knowledge norm to explain the absurdity of the judgments associated with 'p but I do not believe p,' 'I believe p, but ~p,' and 'p but there is no reason to believe p.'

believe that if p turns out to be true, this is not to be expected. The judgment that you are in this sort of Gettier case amounts to the complex judgment that p is true but that you are not in an epistemic position to expect that it is true. This is a Moorean absurdity in its own right. We can account for its absurdity by noting that someone with such attitudes would take their belief that p is true to fail to fulfill the evidential norm since what is to be expected is a function of the evidence available. The subject's taking it to be the case that the truth of the relevant belief is not to be expected is acknowledging that by her lights she cannot expect to be right given her evidence. IT_2 fails to confirm that this condition is necessary for permissible belief.

There is a third and final argument for the knowledge account to consider. It starts with the observation that this is a Moorean absurdity:

6. p, but I do not know p.[28]

The challenge is to explain how (6) could have this status if knowledge is not the norm of belief. I think the challenge can be met. If you take yourself not to know that p because you take yourself not to believe p, say, then we have a situation where your second-order belief is transparently falsified by a fact about your own mind. If you take yourself not to know that p because you take it to be that p is false, we can explain the incoherence by appeal to the truth norm. If you take yourself not to know that p because you have insufficient evidence by your own lights, we can explain this in terms of the evidential norm. That norm in turn can be derived from the truth norm in the way Williamson suggested earlier. And, if you take yourself not to know because you take yourself to be in a Gettier case, we have already seen how the evidential norm can explain the incoherence of that attitude. It seems that we have our bases covered. If we were to assume that the solution of Moore's Paradox should be given in normative terms and assume that MA is true, while the knowledge account might have the resources to explain the absurdity of the thoughts we have thus considered, it seems the knowledge account is unnecessary for explaining why Moorean absurd thoughts strike us as contradictory. It seems we can explain the same data using either the truth norm

---

[28] DeRose 2002 seems to think that assertions of the form of (6) are just the sort of case we need the knowledge norm of assertion to address. His solution is that the assertion of 'p' represents the speaker as knowing p although what the assertion expresses is correct iff p. While it seems this account might have the resources for explaining why asserting (6) is improper, it does not seem to give us any explanation as to why the judgment that (6) is true is also incoherent or absurd.

combined with the evidential norm or the evidential norm taken on its own. So, while some might think that MA is a dubious assumption and dispense with the very idea of using Moore's Paradox as a way of uncovering the norms of belief, MA does not support the hypothesis that knowledge is the norm of belief.

5.5 TRUTH AND REASONABLE BELIEF

In dealing with lottery cases and cases of Moorean absurdity, the real work is done by two assumptions. The first is that you cannot reasonably believe outright what you know you are not in a position to know. The second is that you should not assert what you cannot reasonably believe. Since you can reasonably believe false propositions, it is not clear what work TNW does in an account of warranted assertion. Perhaps Williamson is right that TNW commits you to ENW, but I can think of no reason why ENW would commit you to TNW. Should we say that ENW is the norm that governs assertion and an assertion is warranted iff the speaker is reasonable in believing that the proposition she asserts is true?

The view that has emerged as the main rival to KA takes seriously the idea that belief and assertion are governed by common epistemic standards, notes that belief is governed by a norm that says, in effect, that it is proper to believe *p* iff you justifiably believe *p*, and then says warrant is justification. Those who defend the view say that the external components that distinguish knowledge from justified belief are conditions that have nothing to do with warranted assertion. The view denies TNW on the grounds that either JA or RA is correct. I shall argue that this view is mistaken.

How should we approach this issue? There is a debate between some writers as to whether the point of assertion is to say something true or say something you know. For reasons we have already discussed, I do not think that assertions aim to express knowledge and do not think that there is any norm that tells us that you should refrain from asserting what you do not know. The debate between those who accept a truth norm and those who deny that there is any such norm is not really about the point, aim, purpose, or goal of assertion. Both parties agree that in telling someone *p*, you tell them that *p* is true and so you fail in your aim, in some sense, if you speak falsely. One side thinks this is normatively significant. The other does not. The side that denies that TNW governs assertion does not deny that the norms governing assertion have something to do with truth. If I understand their view, they think that we cannot fail to live up to our responsibilities or fail to meet our duties simply because we speak falsely even if what we are trying to do is speak the truth. The thought is that the right to do something cannot depend upon something external such as truth, but not because there are overriding reasons to speak falsely. There can be, but those are non-epistemic reasons and they are not needed. You can have warrant to assert something that happens to be false provided that you were reasonable in taking yourself to speak the truth because external conditions have no deontic significance.

The debate between those who defend TNW and those who defend RA as an alternative that allows for false, warranted assertions is similar to debates about product liability. One side says that your obligation is to exercise due care and that your obligation ends there. The other side thinks that a strict liability standard determines whether you have lived up to your obligations. On what grounds could they say that your obligation is only to exercise sufficient care? They could deny that a strict liability standard governs assertion by insisting that genuine normative standards are never strict. Those who defend RA seem to think that what is impermissible always involves fault.[29] Lackey writes:

> [T]here is an intimate connection between our assessment of asserters and our assessment of their assertions. In particular, asserters are in violation of a norm of assertion and thereby subject to criticism when their assertions are improper. An analogy with competitive basketball may make this point clear: suppose a player steps over the free throw line when making his foul shot. In such a case, there would be an intimate connection between our assessment of the player and our assessment of the free throw – we would, for instance, say that the player is subject to criticism for making an improper shot.[30]

She argues that TNW does not govern assertion precisely because you cannot be criticized simply for asserting something false. While she is right that a speaker is not properly criticized for asserting something false, per se, her criticism of TNW rests on the assumption that the reasonable is the mark of the permissible. We have seen that you cannot be fully excused for having Φ'd unless it was reasonable for you to think it is permissible to Φ and the excusable is not the mark of the permissible.

Like Lackey, Kvanvig also thinks there is a close connection between the assessment of the speaker and the assertion:

---

[29] In addition to Kvanvig and Lackey, see Douven 2006, p. 477.
[30] Lackey 2007, p. 595.

This point should be self-evident ... norms of assertion are norms governing a certain type of human activity, and thus relate to the speech act itself rather than the content of such an act. Notice that when we look at the four conditions for knowledge above [i.e., truth, belief, absence of defeaters, and justification], the only ones regarding which apology or regret for the speech act itself is appropriate are the belief and justification conditions. There is, therefore, a prima facie case that knowledge is not the norm of assertion, but rather justified belief is.[31]

The upshot is supposed to be that if some condition makes it wrongful to act or assert, the very same condition makes it appropriate to regret having acted or asserted and to apologize. From this it is supposed to follow that the internal conditions necessary for knowledge determine whether an assertion is warranted. The external conditions that distinguish reasonable belief from knowledge are normatively insignificant because you need not apologize for having asserted something false and need not regret having asserted something false.

   I can see why someone would say that what you should apologize for is what you can be faulted for and what you can be faulted for is what you should apologize for. I agree with Kvanvig that you cannot be faulted simply for asserting something false. Having said that, I do not see how to convert his remarks into an argument for the reasonable belief account of warranted assertion. You should not engage in any wrongdoing, excusable or otherwise. If you do engage in excusable wrongdoing, it is not entirely clear that an apology is in order. An explanation might be in order and you might have an obligation to make reparations, but it seems that you offer an apology in recognition of the fact that someone else can properly fault you. If, however, you ought to be excused for your action, it would be inappropriate for someone to fault you. So, it seems that if there is a close conceptual connection between what you should apologize for and what you can be faulted for, there is not a close conceptual connection between the conditions under which it is appropriate to apologize and the conditions under which you act wrongfully. Perhaps whenever you ought to apologize, you committed some wrong, but it is not at all obvious that whenever you commit some wrong, you owe an apology. If I am wrong on that point, it is likely because I am mistaken in thinking that you only ought to apologize when someone can fault you for what you did. If we sever that connection and say that you can owe an apology even for excusable wrongs, it seems that you should sometimes apologize

[31] Kvanvig 2009, p. 147.

for having done something you could not be faulted for. If this is so, there is no argument for Internalism here.

What about regret? Regret is complicated. We have already seen that an agent can act with justification but regret having so acted when duty requires her to act against some defeated reason. The agent might rightly regret having Φ'd even though she knows she must Φ. The regret is not the recognition that she ought to have done things differently. She regrets that she could not have done things differently given what her obligations were and regrets that meeting her obligations necessitated acting against the defeated reason. That you regret having Φ'd does not mean that you ought to have done something else. Perhaps what Kvanvig is saying is this. Regret is not the mark of the impermissible; rather, if something is not the sort of thing that you can properly regret, it is not the sort of thing that has any bearing on whether to Φ. To convert this point into an argument for an internalist approach to warrant, we have to assume that you cannot properly regret asserting something that you reasonably took to be true. The problem with the argument seems to be this very assumption. I think Oedipus can rationally regret that he married his mother. I think I would have regretted telling Oedipus that he and Jocasta would make a great pair. Intuitively, it seems that we can regret bringing about outcomes we did not know we were bringing about. My own intuitions might be idiosyncratic, but if I am wrong on this point, it is not because it is true in general that you should regret only that you Φ'd if you could have known at the time how to avoid Φ-ing. In situations of moral conflict, you know that you cannot avoid wrongdoing whatever you end up doing. Still, you can regret acting against a reason however you decide to act. If the unforeseeable is not regrettable, it is not because you ought not regret what you do not know how to avoid. The unavoidable can be regrettable.

None of the objections to TNW considered thus far seems terribly convincing, but that hardly counts in favor of TNW. What reason is there to think truth is necessary for warrant? Williamson offers a defense of TNW:

Suppose that I rationally believe myself to know that there is snow outside; in fact, there is no snow outside. On the BK and RBK accounts [that say that you have warrant to assert what you believe you know or you reasonably believe yourself to know], my assertion "There is snow outside" satisfies the rule of assertion. Yet something is wrong with my assertion; neither the BK nor RBK account implies that it is. They can allow that something is wrong with my belief that I know that there is snow outside, for it is false, but that is another matter. The BK and RBK accounts lack the resources to explain why we regard the false assertion itself, not just the asserter, as faulty.[32]

While he is right that there is something defective with the assertion, those who deny TNW might say that these defectiveness intuitions are weak evidence. Someone who acts rightly might bring about regrettable side effects and these might be defects of a kind, but by hypothesis, the agent acted rightly. Not only that, Williamson might have given his opponents just what they need. He gave them an explanation as to why the assertion seems faulty. The false assertion would dispose someone who trusted the speaker to believe something false and, as Williamson notes, there is something wrong with the false belief. Since he thinks such beliefs are nevertheless permissibly held, it is not at all clear why the defect he has focused on makes the assertion wrongful.

I want to try to shore up the support for TNW by taking aim at the idea that the test that determines whether someone has lived up to her responsibilities is that the agent acted responsibly in trying to meet them. This seems to be the position of those who defend RA, and I think the view does not get the cases right. Let's start with an example:

Cook: Audrey just moved into the apartment next to Cooper's. To welcome her to the building, Cooper cooked her dinner. He did not realize that the mushrooms he used in making her dinner were poisonous. (So far as this is possible, imagine that he is not culpable or blameworthy for his ignorance. Cooper used a field guide for distinguishing safe from unsafe mushrooms, but it contained a few errors.) Cooper has on hand the stuff to give people who eat poisoned mushrooms, but only enough for one person. It just so happens that her other neighbor, Harry, is suffering from food poisoning because he ate a can of bad peaches. (So far as this is possible, imagine that he is non-culpably ignorant.) Cooper's stuff could help Harry just as well as it could help Audrey. It's good stuff. Now, Harry and Audrey are equally sick and Cooper can help only one. It seems intuitively clear that Cooper has a more stringent duty to assist Audrey than to assist Harry. He did poison Audrey, after all.

The example suggests that when it comes to an agent's action, it is possible for two agents to be internal duplicates up to the point of action but then differ with respect to whether they acted permissibly. We could easily imagine a story similar to Cook in which there were no poisonous mushrooms where it is clear that some internal duplicate of Cooper's does nothing wrong in cooking a dish for his new neighbor.

[32] Williamson 2000a, p. 262.

If Cooper's duty to Audrey was merely a *pro tanto* duty of beneficence, it would be difficult to see how the duty to Audrey could be more stringent since Harry's needs are just as great as hers. Thus, it's tempting to think that Cooper's duty is no mere duty of beneficence. My hypothesis is that the reason that Cooper's duty to Audrey is more stringent is that Cooper is righting a past wrong of his by assisting Audrey. Whereas reasons having to do with beneficence count in favor of helping both Harry and Audrey, the reparative duty gives a reason that breaks the tie. We cannot make sense of how there could be this wrong on any internalist view for the simple reason that it seems there is no ground for wrongdoing that is constituted by or strongly supervenes upon the internal conditions that determine how things seem to Cooper and Cooper's counterpart. The reason he ought to assist Audrey first is that he poisoned Audrey by serving her poisonous mushrooms, and this fact is something that is not accessible to Cooper.

Someone might say that while Cooper has a more stringent duty to assist Audrey, it does not follow that this is a duty to address some prior wrong he has committed. Perhaps it is no mere duty of beneficence, but it is not a reparative duty if such duties are understood as responses to past wrongs. To give this kind of duty a name, we can speak of reparative* duties. A reparative* duty is similar to a reparative duty insofar as they are duties one can be under only if the agent brought about some bad state of affairs, but they are like the duty of beneficence insofar as they can arise without any prior wrongdoing on the agent's part. Why not say that the difference in stringency is due to the fact that there is a prima facie duty to assist both Audrey and Harry, but a stronger duty to Audrey because there is the additional reparative* duty that gives him a *pro tanto* reason to assist Audrey? That way, we can accommodate intuition without giving up Internalism about the justification of action. The problem with this response is with this idea of reparative* duties. If this is merely a reparative* duty, then we would have to say that this is a case in which Cooper did not act against any *pro tanto* reason to refrain from giving Audrey the poisoned dish. (Otherwise, we would have to say that this was a reparative duty.) But, then it seems quite odd to think that Cooper could have such a duty because it would have to combine two features. First, it would have to give Cooper a reason to act that a similarly situated but causally idle agent would not have. (Otherwise, we would say that the reparative* duty was really a mere duty of beneficence. It would be the very duty that, say, a bystander such as Bobby would have if he had just the same amount of stuff to give to someone who has been poisoned as Cooper has.) Second, it would have to be a reason for Cooper to act over and above a reason associated with a mere duty of beneficence to address some bad state of affairs when he could know full well that he never had any reason not to bring that bad state of affairs about in the first place.

On this account, there would be a resultant moral difference between Cooper's and Bobby's duties (i.e., both would have reasons of beneficence to assist either subject but Cooper would have the additional reason to discharge a reparative* duty) that alters the range of permissible options available to them due to a causal difference that was not coupled with any normative difference.[33] That sounds quite odd. Better, I think, to say that the reason that this causal difference between Cooper and Bobby makes a normative difference is because it was in virtue of a causal relation between Cooper and the bad state of affairs that he acted against a *pro tanto* reason unknowingly. Now, he has the knowledge necessary to see that his actions were wrongful and there is a wrong that needs to be addressed. This is why Audrey has a stronger claim on Cooper's assistance than Harry does. But, this is why there is a reparative duty that Cooper ought to discharge, not a reparative* duty.

Let's add a further detail to the story. Suppose Cooper did not know what to make Audrey to welcome her to the building. He asked Leo. Leo said that he should use the mushrooms in the garden to make his dish. Cooper followed his advice. Should Leo have said this? Here is a principle that seems pretty plausible:

> Advice: If an advisee ought not Φ and there is no reason to give insincere advice, the advisor ought not assert that the advisee ought to Φ.

If Advice is false, the reasons that speak against Φ-ing do not constitute reasons to refrain from encouraging someone to act against those reasons by advising them to do so. That seems to go against everything we know about giving sincere advice. Yes, sometimes we should give insincere advice but the principle takes account of that. If the argument above is correct, a kind of non-culpable ignorance works as an excusing condition. When such excusing conditions obtain, the agent can act rightly only if there is some justifying reason for giving the neighbor the poisoned dish. There is none in the story I have just told. That is true of the action and the assertion that the action should be performed.

---

[33] Robert Howell and Sarah Wright independently suggested a response along these lines.

We can now state the case against RA:

1. Circumstances can arise in which a decisive case can be made against Φ-ing where the reasons not to Φ are grounded in considerations the agent is non-culpably ignorant of (e.g., Cook).
2. In such cases, an advisor might also be reasonably ignorant of the reasons that constitute a decisive case against Φ-ing.
3. In such cases, there is nevertheless a decisive case against the advisor's asserting that the advisee ought to Φ.
4. (Therefore) Circumstances can arise in which there is a decisive case against the advisor's assertion that the advisee ought to Φ where the considerations that constitute this case are considerations the advisor is non-culpably ignorant of.

Since you cannot have warrant to assert p when there is a decisive case to refrain from asserting that p, Cook is a counterexample to RA. Now, someone could resist this and say that the assertion was merely morally defective, not epistemically defective. The effect of this would be to undercut the motivation for RA. So far as I can tell, the motivation for RA is the general thought that if an agent is fully responsible in how she conducted herself, she could not have failed to live up to her responsibilities. As we have seen, it is hard to square this view with the intuitive data.

5.6 JUSTIFICATION AND WARRANT

In the previous section, I argued that somebody could reasonably believe p without having sufficient warrant to assert p. The argument is supposed to show that there are cases in which the speaker has a decisive reason not to assert false propositions where the subject is non-culpably ignorant of the fact that she speaks falsely. In this section, I shall argue that justification is sufficient for warrant.

If truth is necessary for warranted assertion, it is necessary for justified belief. Of course, not everyone agrees that there cannot be false, warranted assertions, but a fair number of writers do agree. The aim of this section is to argue that there cannot be false, justified beliefs if there cannot be false, warranted assertions. The basic idea is that you cannot lack warrant for asserting what you have the right to believe. The right to believe requires truth because the right to believe comes with a warrant to assert that what you believe is true.

Consider two further norms:

TNB: You should not believe p unless p is true.
WNB: You should not believe p if you lack sufficient warrant to assert p.

Anyone who violates TNB violates WNB. If you believe a false proposition, you cannot have sufficient warrant to assert that what you believe is true. If you do not have warrant to assert that p is true, you should not believe p. You might believe p even if you should not, but not with justification. If among the norms of assertion is a norm that enjoins us to refrain from asserting falsehoods, there is a norm that similarly enjoins us to refrain from believing falsehoods.

The argument for Factivity$_J$ depends on the idea that the conditions that determine whether our beliefs are justified can do so only if they thereby give us the right to assert that our beliefs are true. WNB seems rather plausible. If you do not have sufficient warrant to assert p, you are epistemically obligated not to assert that p is the case. If you should not assert that p is the case in this sense, there is an undefeated reason for you to refrain from asserting that p is the case. If it is nevertheless the case that your belief is justified, that is either because the reason to refrain from asserting is not a reason to refrain from believing or because there is an overriding reason to believe that does not provide a justification for asserting. The suggestion that the (alleged) reason to refrain from asserting on epistemic grounds would not constitute a reason to refrain from believing is obscure, as is the suggestion that the (alleged) overriding reason to believe could not provide an overriding reason to assert what there is (allegedly) a reason not to assert. So, it seems plausible to maintain that belief and assertion are held to common rather than divergent epistemic standards.

This strikes me as a reasonable theoretical rationale for WNB, but there is another route to Factivity$_J$ to consider. If assertion is governed by TNW, it seems the following principle is true:

Non-Maleficence: If S were to assert that p is true and cause S$'$ an epistemic harm by convincing S$'$ to believe p, S should not assert that p is true.

If someone's assertion convinces you that p is true when in fact p is false, you have suffered an epistemic harm. So, if Non-Maleficence is true, you should not assert false propositions. Suppose I know you are interested in whether p is true and I assert:

1. There is sufficient justification/reason for believing *p*.

As there cannot be sufficient justification for believing *p* unless it is permissible for you to believe *p*, it follows from (1) that:

2. It is permissible for you to believe *p*.

When *p* is false, it seems that my assertion that (1) is true or that (2) is true could cause the very same epistemic harm as my assertion that *p* is true. Thus, if you accept Non-Maleficence, it follows that you cannot have sufficient warrant to assert (1) or (2) if *p* is false.

Suppose that this much is right. Let me add an additional assumption. It is relatively uncontroversial that knowledge is sufficient for warranted assertion. Remember that the notion of propriety that figures in an account of warranted assertion is epistemic, and it is hard to see what more than knowledge that *p* is true could be needed for properly saying that *p* is true. If knowledge, justified belief, or truth suffices for warranted assertion, knowledge suffices for warranted assertion. If knowledge is not enough for warranted assertion, situations should arise where we can properly say something like, "He knew that *p*, but he was in no position to claim that *p* was true." I doubt such situations would arise with any frequency. Combine Non-Maleficence with the thesis that knowledge suffices for warranted assertion and you get the result that you cannot know that (1) or (2) is true if *p* is not true. If *p* is not true, Non-Maleficence says that you cannot have sufficient warrant to assert that (1) or (2) is true. It follows from this and the thesis that knowledge suffices to warrant assertion that you do not know that (1) or (2) is true.

Why is it that you cannot know (1) or (2) if *p* is false? Consider the potential explanations. The first is that your belief in (1) and (2) cannot be justified unless *p* is true. This explanation assumes Factivity$_J$. We often have sufficient warrant to ascribe justification as we do not infrequently ascribe knowledge to one another. If the fact that *p* is false does not prevent someone from justifiably believing *p* on its own, why would it prevent the speaker from having sufficient justification to believe that there is sufficient justification for the first-order belief that *p* is true? The second is that your belief in (1) and (2) cannot be true unless *p* is true. This explanation also assumes Factivity$_J$. The third potential explanation is that you cannot believe (1) and (2) unless *p* is true. This does not assume Factivity$_J$, but surely you are psychologically capable of believing (1) and (2) whether or not *p* is true. The fourth potential explanation is that if *p* is false, anyone who believes (1) or (2) does not know (1) or (2) for purely Gettierish reasons. This has no plausibility whatever. The only two plausible explanations as to why it follows from the fact that p is false that someone cannot have sufficient warrant to assert (1) or (2) assume that you cannot justifiably believe p when $\sim p$.

5.7 CONCLUSION

If truth is required for warranted assertion and common standards govern assertion and belief, truth is required for justification. This is not because you have the right to believe only what you have the right to assert, mind you. This gets the explanatory order backwards. Even if we cannot explain Factivity$_J$ in terms of the norms governing assertion, the fact that truth is required for warrant is further evidence for Factivity$_J$.

CHAPTER 6

Action

6.1 INTRODUCTION

In previous chapters I argued that justification ought to be understood in externalist terms because reasons for action consist of facts, and beliefs have to fit the facts in order to provide us with reasons. Justification ascriptions are supposed to flag those beliefs that can provide premises for practical deliberation. The trouble with orthodox accounts of justification that deny Factivity$_J$ is that they cannot do justice to the idea that justification ascriptions flag these beliefs and that the normative standing of a belief depends upon whether it is fit for deliberation.

In this chapter, we will look at another link between belief and action. I shall argue that orthodox internalist and externalist views fail because they cannot make sense of the normatively significant relation between belief and action. As such, they cannot do justice to our moral intuitions. In order for beliefs to rationalize action, the reasons that bear on whether to act and whether to believe cannot divide the agent against herself and require her to act against her own epistemically right judgment. If the normative standing of action and the normative judgments that rationalize action 'sway together,' epistemic justification is an externalist notion because external conditions determine whether we meet our practical obligations. Rather than argue for Externalism on the grounds that internal conditions alone do not bring us closer to knowledge, we find support for Externalism when we turn our attention inwards and think about the normative significance of the role belief plays in deliberation.

6.2 KNOWLEDGE AND ACTION

When is it epistemically permissible to treat something as a reason for action? According to Hawthorne and Stanley, knowledge is the norm for practical reasoning. Knowledge and action are, they say, related by means of the reasons–knowledge principle:

> RKP: Where your choice is a p-dependent choice, it is appropriate to treat the proposition that p as a reason for action iff you know that p.[1]

To some, the claim that nothing beyond knowledge of p's truth could be necessary for properly acting on p might seem perfectly harmless.[2] The notion of propriety we are concerned with is epistemic, not practical. What more could we possibly need to properly treat p as a reason for action? Superknowledge?

Perhaps the main reason that RKP is controversial is that it asserts that nothing short of knowledge of p's truth could warrant acting on p. In this section, I shall argue that you can have sufficient warrant to act on p even if you do not know that p is true, and address Hawthorne and Stanley's arguments to the contrary.

In support of RKP, Hawthorne and Stanley say:

> Consider … how blame, judgments of negligence and so on interact with knowledge. If a parent allows a child to play near a dog and does not know whether the dog would bite the child, and if a doctor uses a needle that he did not know to be safe, then they are prima facie negligent.[3]

Because of their qualification, it is hard to know what to make of their suggestion that there is a connection between negligence and ignorance. Let us ignore this qualification for now and consider the proposal that:

> Fault$_4$: In cases where you ought not Φ unless p is true, you can be blamed for Φ-ing if you do not first know that p is true.

Given the plausible assumption that it is not proper to treat p as a reason to Φ when you can be blamed for treating p as a reason to Φ, it seems Fault$_4$ does lend support to RKP.

Note that judgments of blame, negligence, and the like also seem to interact with ascriptions of justification:

> Fault$_5$: If you can be properly blamed for believing p, you are not justified in believing p.

[1] Hawthorne and Stanley 2008, p. 578. A choice between options is p-dependent iff the most preferable option conditional on p is not the most preferable option conditional on -p.

[2] Brown 2008 criticizes the claim that knowledge that p is true is sufficient for properly treating p as a reason for action. See Neta 2009 for a response to Brown's criticism.

[3] Hawthorne and Stanley 2008, p. 572.

To deny $Fault_5$, you would have to say that the facts in light of which someone can be properly blamed for believing p do not threaten the justificatory status of that belief. This is a difficult position for anyone to defend. Since knowledge requires justification, it is an impossible position for anyone to defend if $Fault_4$ is correct.

Problems arise for any view that incorporates both $Fault_4$ and $Fault_5$. Combined, these assumptions entail that if your belief that p is true is practically relevant, your belief cannot be justified unless it constitutes knowledge.[4] To use Hawthorne and Stanley's example, suppose that you should not use a needle unless it is clean. From $Fault_4$, it follows that you can be blamed for using the needle if you use it without knowing that it is clean. It seems, intuitively, that you can be properly blamed for using the needle only if you are not blameless in the belief that it is clean. (Think about the contrapositive conditional. If you are blameless in believing the needle is clean, how could you be blamed for acting as if it is?) It follows from $Fault_5$ that you cannot be justified in believing that the needle is clean if you do not know that it is.

Two objections should suffice to show that we should not accept both $Fault_4$ and $Fault_5$. Given that $Fault_5$ is relatively uncontroversial it seems that the objections below, if sound, give us good reason to deny $Fault_4$. First, according to the JTB analysis of knowledge, if Audrey is justified in believing p and her belief is true, she knows p. We know this analysis fails. Audrey and Cooper are on a cross-country trip and stopped this afternoon to have lunch in the land of fake dollar bills. Neither knows that they are in the land of fakes. That is why we can say that they are justified in believing that they have cash and not counterfeit bills in their pockets. Audrey recalls that she owes Coop ten dollars. She reaches into her pocket, pulls out ten dollars, hands it to Coop, and says that they are now even. While her belief that her debt is repaid is true and she is justified in that belief, she does not know that her debt has been repaid. If, however, she does not know that her debt has been repaid, it follows from $Fault_4$ that she can be blamed for acting on her belief that p. In turn, she can be blamed for believing p. In turn, it follows from $Fault_5$ that her belief that p cannot be justified. In turn, it follows that Gettier cases are not possible.

Consider a second objection. In arguing against Supervenience Internalism, I have argued that epistemic justification does not supervene

---

[4] Let's say that your belief that p is the case is practically relevant iff you are faced with some p-dependent choice.

upon your non-factive mental states. Those who think that epistemic justification does supervene on your non-factive mental states will typically also assert that the conditions that determine culpability and blameworthiness supervene on these internal conditions. They will say that if two subjects are in the same non-factive mental states and act for the same reasons, the first subject is blameworthy iff the second subject is. Externalists about epistemic justification often accuse internalists of conflating this perfectly harmless claim about blame with the perfectly false claim that justification supervenes on the same internal conditions. As part of the error theory that purports to explain why the internalists are mistaken about epistemic justification, they will say that the conditions that determine culpability and blameworthiness that do supervene on the internal states are distinct from the conditions that determine the justificatory status of a belief. The internalist's mistake about justification is due to their mistaken view that conditions you cannot be culpable for failing to take account of cannot affect the justificatory status of your beliefs. Justification and permissibility, they will say, can come apart from culpability.

Suppose, as seems plausible, that the conditions that determine blameworthiness and culpability supervene upon a subject's non-factive mental states. If you combine this supervenience thesis with Fault$_4$, you get the result that you can only blamelessly believe p if every possible internal duplicate of you knows p. This in turn commits you to an infallibilist conception of personal and doxastic justification according to which it is permissible to believe p only if a complete description of your non-factive mental states entails p. Such a view about justification is quite clearly at odds with ordinary intuition and leads to external-world skepticism given the plausible additional assumption that descriptions of our mental states entail that few of our external-world beliefs are correct.

Hawthorne and Stanley might remind us of an important qualification. They said that someone who acts on p without knowing p is "prima facie negligent." If what they meant to say was that someone who violates RKP *appears* negligent, I think this is still a mistake. You do not appear negligent if your beliefs have been Gettiered and you act on them. Moreover, if they qualify their position in this way, this undercuts their contention that blame judgments interact with knowledge. Perhaps what they should say (and seem to say in some passages) is that anyone who violates RKP reasons in ways she should not reason. She might not be blameworthy for reasoning from things she does not know. Perhaps the subject should be excused. Nevertheless, she violates an epistemic norm governing practical reason. Let us assume that this is the picture that they are working with.

If they reject Fault$_4$, they can avoid the difficulties we have considered thus far, but RKP still faces serious objections. Consider this passage:

> Consider also how knowledge interacts with conditional orders. Suppose a prison guard is ordered to shoot a prisoner if and only if they are trying to escape. If the guard knows someone is trying to escape and yet does not shoot he will be held accountable. Suppose meanwhile he does not know that someone is trying to escape but shoots them anyway, acting on a belief grounded in a baseless hunch that they were trying to escape. Here again the person will be faulted, even if the person is in fact trying to escape. Our common practice is to require knowledge of the antecedent of a conditional order in order to discharge it. If a guard shoots a prisoner on a baseless hunch they can be faulted for doing this, but there is a world of difference between knowingly shooting a prisoner trying to escape and doing so on a baseless hunch.[5]

You do not need RKP to explain what is wrong with shooting an escaping prisoner on a baseless hunch. If RKP is correct and the guard has good reason to believe mistakenly that a prisoner is trying to escape, the guard ought not shoot the prisoner if the guard's belief is mistaken. The fact that the guard was reasonable in assuming that they were doing what they ought is an excuse for the shooting, not a justification for it. This seems right. Suppose that as the guard raises the rifle to take a shot at Bobby he looks just like a prisoner escaping. A second guard standing nearby the first knows that Bobby is in fact an aspiring actor spending the weekend in the prison preparing for his upcoming role in a film. The second guard might mace the first guard to stop him from shooting Bobby. The reason it is not wrong for him to mace the guard knowing how painful it will be for the guard to be sprayed with mace is that the first guard is about to do something he ought not. He has lost the right to non-interference as a result.

While RKP gets this case right, it gets it right for the wrong reason. Forget about cases of reasonable, mistaken beliefs. Forget about the cases of aspiring actors that look like prisoners trying to escape and think about aspiring escapees who surround themselves with aspiring actors. According to the order, Leo, who is a prisoner and not an actor, ought to be shot if he tries to escape. According to the order, Bobby, who is an actor but not a prisoner, ought not be shot even if it looks like he is trying to escape. Leo tries to escape. According to the order, the guard ought to

---

[5] Hawthorne and Stanley 2008, p. 572.

shoot him before he makes his escape. The guards do not know that there are aspiring actors such as Bobby dressed like prisoners, so they do not know that it is a prisoner trying to escape. So, the guard does not know Leo ought to be shot. He merely reasonably and correctly believes Leo ought to be shot. According to RKP, it is wrong to act on the one premise that could justify shooting Leo (i.e., that he is a prisoner trying to escape). Leo ought not to be shot. It seems to follow that the guard ought to shoot Leo and ought not shoot Leo. In general, you are going to run into trouble if you combine RKP with the view that it is possible for there to be positive duties to Φ if p is true if someone can non-culpably fail to know that p is true when indeed it is true. If it is possible for circumstances to arise in which p is true where p cannot be known to be true, it follows that you both ought to Φ and ought not Φ.

Similar difficulties will arise if you combine RKP with the knowledge account of assertion. According to the knowledge account, you ought not assert p unless you know p. It follows that you have a conclusive reason to refrain from asserting p if you do not know p. It follows from this and RKP that you ought not assert p unless your belief that you know p constitutes knowledge. Since not everything you know is something you are in a position to know that you know, a problem arises, which is that knowledge of p's truth is not invariably going to ensure that you have sufficient warrant for asserting p. However, the view that knowledge is sufficient for having epistemic warrant for asserting p is certainly more plausible than the view that knowledge of p's truth is necessary for having that warrant. So, it seems you ought not accept both RKP and the knowledge account of assertion. It seems the easiest way to sort out this mess is to deny RKP.

Earlier I suggested that if you combined RKP with Fault$_4$, you had to deny that Gettier cases were possible. That seems pretty costly. You can avoid paying that cost if you deny Fault$_4$, but by denying Fault$_4$ you do not avoid all the difficulties caused by Gettier cases. It seems that if RKP is true, there is a prima facie reason for anyone who fails to know p to refrain from reasoning from p. If your belief about p is mistaken, I can see that the consequences of acting on the mistaken belief might be terrible. Because of this, we might be inclined to say that it was wrong for you to have acted on your mistaken belief. If your belief about p is unreasonably held, I can see how your acting on p might manifest the kinds of bad motives or intentions that show that you can be faulted for having acted on p. It is not hard to see why someone might think that RKP rightly says that you ought not act from unreasonably held beliefs or mistaken beliefs.

It is hard to accept the suggestion that all of the conditions necessary for knowledge are deontically significant.

If Audrey hands Coop the ten dollars she owes him, her bills are genuine, and she has no reason to think anything is amiss, precisely what is it that was wrong with her acting from the belief that by handing that bill over she would repay her debt? I cannot see what could possibly be wrong with her action. From Coop's point of view, it is not as if he would think Audrey knowingly or unwittingly wronged him in any way. If I imagine myself as an outside observer who knows that Audrey does not know she will repay the debt merely because she is trying to repay that debt in the land of fake bills, I am not at all inclined to think that the advisory judgment "You should not act from the assumption that you will repay that debt" is correct. It seems that the very same examples that show that we cannot identify knowledge with true beliefs we are justified in holding show that knowledge of p's truth is not needed to properly rely on p in practical reasoning. Surely we have all we need to rightly reason from p if our belief about p is true and not unreasonably held.

We have seen there is some reason to think RKP is mistaken, so we have some reason to be suspicious of the arguments for RKP. Hawthorne and Stanley argue for RKP by appeal to observations about ordinary usage:

> Suppose … Hannah and Sarah are trying to find a restaurant, at which they have time-limited reservations. Instead of asking someone for directions, Hannah goes on her hunch that the restaurant is down a street on the left. After walking for some amount of time, it becomes quite clear that they went down the wrong street. A natural way for Sarah to point out that Hannah made the wrong decision is to say, "You shouldn't have gone down this street, since you didn't know that the restaurant was here."[6]

It is natural enough for Sarah to say this and for us to construe this as criticism of Hannah. The case provides little support for RKP, however, because Hannah's belief fails to constitute knowledge for a variety of reasons (e.g., her belief is really no better than a hunch and her hunch is mistaken). To test RKP properly, it seems we should consider three variants on the example:

> Restaurant₁: Hannah and Sarah are trying to find a restaurant, at which they have time-limited reservations. Instead of asking someone for directions, Hannah relies on her usually impeccable memory and decides to go left. She has been eating at this restaurant regularly for years. After walking for some time,

---

[6] Hawthorne and Stanley 2008, p. 571.

it becomes quite clear that they went down the wrong street. Unbeknown to Hannah, the restaurant had caught fire three days ago and reopened at an alternative location two blocks away.

Restaurant$_2$: Hannah and Sarah are trying to find a restaurant, at which they have time-limited reservations. Instead of asking someone for directions, Hannah goes on her hunch that the restaurant is down a street on the left. They find the restaurant just in time. Hannah declares, "That was lucky, I was just guessing that it would be this way."

Restaurant$_3$: Hannah and Sarah are trying to find a restaurant, at which they have time-limited reservations. Hannah checked the restaurant's website to verify its address. Minutes later, that website was hacked and the hackers posted the wrong address to try to lure customers to a rival restaurant. If Hannah had checked the website only slightly later, she would have believed that the restaurant was at the wrong location.

In Restaurant$_{1-3}$, Hannah does not know that the restaurant is to the left. However, it is only in Restaurant$_1$ and Restaurant$_2$ that it seems natural for Sarah to say, "You should not have gone down this street, since you did not know that the restaurant was here." The defender of RKP cannot say that the reason it seems unnatural to say this in Restaurant$_3$ is that Hannah is blameless in that example, because she is blameless in Restaurant$_1$ and yet Sarah's remark seems natural. The defender of RKP cannot say that the reason it seems unnatural to say this in Restaurant$_3$ is that there is no reason for Sarah to say this so long as they arrived at the restaurant because it is natural for Sarah to say this in Restaurant$_2$. The restaurant cases provide no more support to RKP than they do to the thesis that knowledge is merely a matter of, say, true beliefs that are not unreasonably held.

There is a perfectly reasonable explanation for this pattern that does not assume RKP. We often use 'knows' loosely as if it served to pick out true beliefs or not horribly unreasonable true beliefs.[7] Unfaithful lovers will speak this way when they think someone 'knows' of their secret rendezvous. Thieves speak this way of cops who 'know' about the heist. In conversational contexts such as these, the propriety of using 'knows' does not depend upon what is known. That Sarah's remarks seem proper only in Restaurant$_1$ and Restaurant$_2$ suggests that we are dealing with conversational contexts such as these. Observing how 'knows' functions in such contexts provides no real support for RKP. At least, no more support than it does for the hopeless view that knowledge is merely a matter of firmly held true belief.

---

[7] Goldman 2002, p. 183.

6.3 JUSTIFICATION AND ACTION

Any condition that distinguishes knowledge from justified belief is normatively insignificant. If this is right, justification is the norm of practical reason, not knowledge:

RJP: Where your choice is a p-dependent choice, it is appropriate to treat the proposition that p as a reason for action if you justifiably believe that p.[8]

This view or views similar to it have been defended by a number of people as an alternative to the knowledge account defended by Hawthorne and Stanley. Those who have defended the view have worked with an orthodox account of justification and hoped to use that notion to shed some light on what it is to properly treat something as a reason for action. I think we should run things the other direction and try to understand what is involved in justification by trying to understand what is involved in properly relying on a belief for the purposes of practical deliberation. We shall see that RJP is true only if we reject the orthodox view that insists that there can be false, justified beliefs. If the arguments below are successful, the project of trying to use the concept of justification to make sense of when it is proper to treat something as a reason for action is a failure. We should work from the other direction. What it is for a belief to be justified is for a belief to be fit for the purposes of deliberation. Once we have an account of when it is improper to treat something as a reason for action, we should have a better idea of what justification is.

6.4 THE INCOHERENCE AND THE SUBTRACTION ARGUMENTS

Suppose there is a difference between knowing p and justifiably believing p. According to RKP, it is proper for you to treat p as a reason for action if you know p and your choice is p-dependent, but improper to treat p as a reason if you merely justifiably believe p even if you know your choice is p-dependent. Suppose you know you ought to Φ if p but ought to ψ instead if $\neg p$. You justifiably believe p, know that you ought to Φ if p, but it seems RKP says that you should not treat p as a reason for deciding to

---

[8] Fantl and McGrath 2009; Gibbons 2010; Littlejohn 2009; Dustin Locke, "It's Still Not What You Know That Counts" (unpublished manuscript); and Neta 2009 defend principles similar to this one.

Φ since you do not know p. Suppose p is true. Suppose you reason from your belief that p is true and your belief that you ought to Φ if p to the conclusion that you should Φ. The conclusion is a belief, not an action or intention. It is a belief with a practical subject matter, but a belief nevertheless. Is it wrong to treat p as a reason to believe that?

No, of course not. Modest closure principles tell us this much. So, it seems that taken in combination, RKP and modest closure principles for justification (e.g., that justification is closed under obvious entailment) tell us that you should not treat p as a reason for Φ-ing even if you permissibly treat p as a reason for believing you should Φ. This strikes me as incoherent. If you justifiably believe p, you can justifiably include your belief about p in deliberation when you know p bears on the proper outcome of that deliberation. According to RKP, if you can properly treat p as a reason for action in the course of deliberating about whether to Φ and either intending to Φ or Φ-ing, you know p. According to our modest closure principle, you can properly treat p as a reason for beliefs about whether to Φ if you justifiably believe p and know that you should Φ if p. If justified belief sufficed for knowledge, there would be no problem here, but justified belief is not knowledge. So, if you think that having the right to treat p as a reason for judging that you should Φ comes with the right to treat p as a reason for intending to Φ or for Φ-ing, it seems you either need to say that justified belief suffices for knowledge, deny that justification is closed under obvious entailment, or deny RKP. Of the options, denying RKP seems best.

Three claims form an inconsistent triad. The first is that justified belief is not sufficient for knowledge. The second is that justified belief is all you need for it to be epistemically proper to treat something as a reason for action. The third is that you know p if it is epistemically proper for you to treat p as a reason. It seems odd for someone to acknowledge that justified belief both falls short of knowledge and falls short of giving you the right to rely on p in your deliberations, especially once we are clear that the kind of propriety or permissibility at issue is epistemic. So, I would reject the third claim to remove the inconsistency.

The incoherence argument urges those who think justified belief falls short of knowledge to reject the idea that knowledge rather than justified belief is the epistemic norm for practical reasoning. It is strikingly similar to the incoherence argument from the previous chapter that purported to show that it is a mistake to say that knowledge rather than justified belief is the norm of assertion. If knowledge is justified belief, it makes sense to say that knowledge determines a normative standard for belief, assertion, action, etc., but Gettier cases seem to show that the antecedent of that conditional is false.

Hawthorne and Stanley tentatively suggest that there is a principled link between knowledge and reasons for belief that is akin to their principle linking knowledge and reasons for action.[9] This would be fine if they were willing to go further and say that since you have to know p to properly treat p as a reason for belief, you have to know p to justifiably believe p, as Sutton does. I see no indication that they are willing to say that knowledge is necessary for justification and Gettier cases suggest that they would be wrong to do so. So, their view seems susceptible to the incoherence objection. Sutton's view avoids it because he denies that there is any difference between justified belief and knowledge, but we have already seen that this view is not kind to our intuitions.

The incoherence argument is similar to an argument of Fantl and McGrath's.[10] In support of something in the neighborhood of RJP, they run the subtraction argument:

1. If you know p, it is permissible for you to treat p as a reason for action or for belief.
2. Holding fixed knowledge-level justification while subtracting from knowledge any combination of truth, belief, and being unGettiered makes no difference as to whether it is permissible to treat p as a reason for action.
3. If p is knowledge-level justified, it is permissible to treat p as a reason for action or for belief.[11]

The key difference between their argument and mine is that they work with an orthodox conception of justification on which you can justifiably believe p even if you do not happen to believe p, your belief is Gettiered, or p is not true. In my argument, the notion of justification operative is a purely deontic notion. A justified belief is a belief you can hold while fulfilling your epistemic duties (whatever those duties happen to be). I made no substantive assumptions about what justification is, such assumptions are defended on the grounds that we need them to understand how justified beliefs do what justified beliefs are supposed to do. We have too tenuous a grip on the notion of justification to use that concept to cash out the permissible use of a belief in deliberation and so would be wary

---

[9] Hawthorne and Stanley 2008, p. 577.
[10] For a defense, see Fantl and McGrath 2009, p. 72.
[11] Fantl and McGrath 2009, p. 99.

of using some independent notion of justification to argue that, say, the truth of p does not matter when it comes to properly treating p as a reason for action.

I shall argue that their subtraction argument is unsound. While it does not matter whether your belief is Gettiered when it comes to treating things as reasons for action, the truth matters. Since the truth matters to what you can properly include in your deliberations, beliefs must be true to be justifiably held.

6.4.1 Segregationism

Fantl and McGrath defend RJP on the grounds of the subtraction argument as well as an argument similar to my incoherence argument. As they see it, the right to believe p comes with the right to treat p as a reason for action or belief. They do not say, however, that p must itself be a reason if it is to be justifiably treated as one. So, while we agree that RJP is true, we still find plenty to disagree about. One of the primary points of disagreement between us has to do with our understanding of the relation between the normative standing of normative judgments and the normative standing of the intentions and actions they rationalize. For reasons that will emerge, they defend Segregationism and I defend Unificationism:

> Segregationism: The demands of practical and theoretical reason can diverge in such a way that it can be practically improper to treat p as a reason for action even if it is epistemically proper to treat p as a reason for action.[12]
> Unificationism: The demands of practical and theoretical reason cannot diverge and so if it is epistemically proper to treat p as a reason for action, it is practically proper to do so as well.

It might appear at first that they defend Unificationism because they say:

[A]ny proposition that is warranted enough to be a reason you have for belief is also warranted enough to be a reason you have for action or anything else. We can see the plausibility of the Unity thesis by reflecting on our habits of deliberation. When trying to determine what is true ... we draw conclusions from the reasons we have. The same goes for trying to decide what to do ... We bring reasons into our reasoning knowing that we might draw all sorts of conclusions from them along the way, some practical and some theoretical.[13]

---

[12] We saw earlier that Feldman 1988a also defends Segregationism.
[13] Fantl and McGrath 2009, p. 125.

Appearances can be misleading. While they think you have sufficient epistemic warrant to treat what you justifiably believe as a reason for action, belief, or anything else, they think there are counterexamples to the stronger claim that you also have sufficient practical warrant to treat what you justifiably believe as a reason for action. Because of this, they cannot link the normative standing of normative judgment to action in the way the unificationists do.

In the course of explaining why they think that you can justifiably believe *p* even if *p* is not a genuine reason, they ask us to consider this example:

Gin and Tonic: Coop tries to make two gin and tonics. He uses the last of the gin on the first. He grabs a new bottle to make the second, but accidentally mixes Audrey a Bernard (i.e., a petrol with tonic and fresh lime). Fill in the details however you like so that Coop is perfectly reasonable in thinking that he has just made two gin and tonics. He gives Audrey her Bernard believing it to be a gin and tonic. She drinks and she becomes violently ill. This date is not going well, Coop nearly killed Audrey.[14]

For reasons already discussed, I would not say that Coop's belief that the stuff he gave to Audrey was a gin and tonic was justified and so I need not agree with them in saying that it was proper for Coop to treat that this is a gin and tonic as a reason to give Audrey the poisonous concoction. Myself, I think he should not have given her the drink and so should not have thought that he should, should not have thought that the stuff was gin, etc. They disagree. They say that Coop's action was perfectly justified:

Notice if we asked the unlucky fellow why he did such a thing, he might reply with indignation: "Well, it was the perfectly rational thing to do; I had every reason to think the glass contained gin; why in the world should I think that someone would be going around putting petrol in the gin bottles!?" Here the unlucky subject, in our view, is not providing an excuse for his action … he is defending it as the action that made the most sense for him to do and the proposition that made most sense to treat as a reason. He is providing a justification, not an excuse.[15]

I think this is wrong. The action could not be excused unless Coop could have reasonably thought that he was acting rightly.

This is something to return to later, but notice that if Fantl and McGrath reject Unificationism it is not because of the way that Unificationism treats cases of mistaken non-normative belief. If they reject Unificationism

---

[14] Inspired by Williams 1981.   [15] Fantl and McGrath 2009, p. 125.

and say that the epistemic warrant someone has to treat p as a reason for action does not always come with a further practical warrant to treat p as a reason for action, there must be cases where the epistemic and practical warrant come apart. In conversation, they said that they did not think cases of mistaken non-normative belief were the right sort of case to provide a counterexample. They look to cases of mistaken normative belief to motivate their segregationist view:

Austin and Boston: Coop has a prima facie duty to be in Austin and a prima facie duty to be in Boston. He cannot be in both places. He knows of both duties and their grounds. He thinks there is a weightier reason to be in Austin and, let us assume, that this is something he is reasonable to believe. There are, however, weightier reasons to be in Boston. So, that is where he ought to be.

Suppose Coop acts on his reasonable but mistaken belief about where he ought to be. Fantl and McGrath are waiting for him in Boston and they accuse him of wrongdoing. I can imagine Coop saying in response, "Well, it was the perfectly rational thing to do; I had every reason to think I ought to be here in Boston rather than Austin for as you both agree, this was the rational thing to believe. Here I am, the unlucky subject, and I am not providing an excuse for an action. I'm defending it as the thing it made most sense for me to do given not just what I believe, but what I ought to believe." If Coop's defense works in Gin and Tonic, it works just as well in Austin and Boston. I think it works as a way of defending Coop from criticism (i.e., as an excuse), but think it succeeds in neither case as a defense of what Coop did (i.e., a justification). I might be wrong about this, but I doubt their defense succeeds in one case rather than the other. Perhaps they ought to be convinced by the defenses they offered on Coop's behalf initially in defending his behavior in Gin and Tonic. Perhaps they should say that cases of mistaken belief are not counterexamples to the unificationists' view. If they reject the Segregationist view, they can opt either for a view that classifies Coop's actions in both cases as justified or says that he didn't act with justification in either case. My preference is for the latter view, but this preference should be defended.

6.4.2 Unificationism

There has to be some connection between the normative status of the beliefs that rationalize action and the actions and intentions such beliefs rationalize. If you judge that you ought to Φ and you then ψ instead, knowing that you were ψ-ing rather than Φ-ing, it seems that you would be deeply irrational in acting in the way that you have. It seems plausible that you should not be irrational in this way. So, if there is some normative relation between beliefs that rationalize actions and the actions rationalized, what is it? Could it be this?

NSO: If you believe you ought to Φ, you ought to Φ.

I think not. NSO allows for factual detachment. For counterexamples to NSO, see any movie about Nazis.

If 'ought' takes wide scope, we can block factual detachment:

WSO: You ought to see to it that: if you believe you ought to Φ, you Φ.

If someone believes he should Φ but it is not the case that he should believe this, WSO does not allow us to detach the conclusion that he should Φ. The trouble with WSO is not that it allows factual detachment; it is that it is not clear that it represents any normatively significant relation between normative beliefs and the actions these beliefs rationalize. Suppose that, in some sense, someone ought to believe she ought to Φ. If she ought to believe and does believe, can we detach the conclusion that she ought to Φ in accordance with her judgment? If she ought not Φ and so ought not Φ in accordance with her judgment, can we say that she ought not believe she ought to Φ? It is unclear.

Those who accept WSO might say that once you determine what you ought to do and then you do it accordingly, this is not some fallacy of practical reason. This is precisely how reasoning should go. As such, there has to be some principle that allows for a kind of detachment. You cannot rightly detach the conclusion that you ought to Φ simply given that you believe you ought to Φ, but surely you can if you believe it and you ought to.

The trouble here is making sense of what happens when an agent reasons to a belief about what to do and then acts accordingly. Is judging that you ought to Φ and conforming to WSO anything like judging that you ought to Φ knowing that you ought to ψ if you Φ and ψ-ing accordingly? They seem different. The instrumental principle says that you have a practical obligation to take the known necessary means to fulfilling your obligations. In the case of conforming to WSO, if you put an epistemic obligation in and get an epistemic obligation out, you have to say that there are epistemic obligations to act. There are no such things. If you want to get a practical obligation out, you can try to put a practical obligation in, but there are no practical obligations to believe. WSO cannot help us understand the normatively significant relation between beliefs about what to do and the actions they rationalize.

The principles that capture the spirit of the unificationist view have to allow for mixed deontic detachment. That is to say, they have to allow us to detach a practical obligation from statements about epistemic obligation and some linking premise that tells us how the epistemic and practical obligations mesh. They also have to allow us to detach an epistemic obligation from statements about practical obligation and the same linking premise that tells us how the practical and epistemic obligations mesh. Unificationism should accept the following conditionals as they allow for mixed deontic detachment:

> MDD_1: If you believe you $ought_{practical}$ to Φ and $ought_{epistemic}$ to believe you $ought_{practical}$ to Φ, you $ought_{practical}$ to Φ.[16]
>
> MDD_2: If you $ought_{practical}$ not Φ, you $ought_{epistemic}$ not believe you $ought_{practical}$ to Φ.

Segregationists deny that these conditionals are true. Fantl and McGrath thought Austin and Boston constituted counterexamples to MDD_1 and MDD_2. To take one of these cases to be a counterexample requires cutting the link between the reasonable and the permitted. One rationale for MDD_1 and MDD_2 might be the thought that if the reasonable is the mark of the permissible in either the practical or theoretical domain, it is the mark of the permissible in both. Those who take it to be the mark of the permissible in both might be attracted to these principles since it seems that denying them requires allowing that it is possible that the thing you ought to do is to act against your own impeccable normative judgment. Such a thing could never be reasonable. If the reasonable were the mark of the permissible, you would be permitted to act on your judgment. The putative counterexamples would be defused.

Of course, some of us deny that the reasonable is the mark of the permissible. Those of us who deny that the reasonable is the mark of the permissible have to defend MDD_1 and MDD_2 on different grounds. Some of this involves deflecting objections. A common objection that I have encountered is that MDD_1 and MDD_2 clash with the idea that the reasons

---

[16] Since I think there are no positive epistemic duties, I take MDD_1 to be trivially true. Unificationists who think that the rational is the mark of the permissible are committed to positive epistemic duties, so they think MDD_1 is non-trivially true.

that bear on whether to believe or act depend upon our perspective or have to pass through some sort of "epistemic filter."[17] This is a mistake. If you are committed to MDD_1 or MDD_2 you can still say that the reasons that apply to you depend upon your perspective. It might seem that there is a tension here between views that take reasons to be accessible and MDD_2 because MDD_2 lets you say that you ought not believe something simply because there is a practical obligation you are under not to act on that belief. Notice, however, that all MDD_2 says is that the reasons that oblige you not to act must have passed through an epistemic filter if that is what reasons must do to oblige you. To deny MDD_2 it seems you would have to say that the reasons that determine what to do will not thereby determine what to believe, and that would seem to require reasons that determine your obligations that are not available to you. So, if you think reasons depend upon perspectives, you should probably like MDD_1 and MDD_2.

Of course, some of us deny that reasons have to pass through an epistemic filter to determine what you ought to do or believe. Some of us deny that the reasons that apply to you depend upon your perspective. I think we have some sense of how we can respond to putative counterexamples and know better than to think that MDD_1 and MDD_2 force you to deny that reasons have to be available to you. I know of no other objections to MDD_1 and MDD_2, but the reader might have doubts. Let me offer two points in support of Unificationism.

First, think about the incoherence argument for RJP and against RKP. Assuming that we do not need to know p to treat p as a reason for action, I said that there was something strange to the view that says that you can properly treat p as a reason in deliberation if that deliberation is concerned with determining what to believe but not if it is concerned with determining what to do. I think similar worries arise for Segregationism.

With apologies to Judith Thomson, consider an example:

COOPER: Harry, I have a problem. We're at war with a villainous country called Bad, and my superiors have ordered me to drop some bombs at Placetown in Bad. Now there is a munitions factory at Placetown, but there is a hospital for children there, too. Some people tell me that I should drop the bombs to help with the war effort but some tell me that we should avoid killing innocents. I just do not know what to think. Should I think of this as a necessary evil?

---

[17] Dancy 2000, p. 57.

HARRY: Look, Cooper, given what you have said, it is clear that you should think of dropping the bombs as a necessary evil.

Weeks later:

GORDON: Coop, you really should not have dropped those bombs. You killed scores of children in that attack on the munitions factory.
COOPER: Harry, can I get a little help here?
HARRY: What's the problem?
GORDON: I told Cooper that he should not have dropped the bombs.
HARRY: He's right, you shouldn't have.
COOPER: But you told me that I should think of dropping the bombs as a necessary evil.
HARRY: That's right, and I stick by that. That is what you should have believed. Isn't that right, Gordon?
GORDON: Certainly, that's just what you should have believed. But, as I'm sure Harry would agree, what you should have done is not dropped the bombs. I'm concerned with action. Harry is concerned with belief. We agreed to not disagree. I think Harry has the epistemology right and we both think I have the ethics right.
HARRY: Precisely.[18]

My sympathies lie with Coop, not Gordon and Harry. The thought that the epistemologist and the ethicist can agree not to disagree by denying that the oughts that concern the one have any bearing on the oughts that concern the other is deeply troubling. If you think that if someone ought to think of something as a necessary evil, she should gnash her teeth and do what she thinks she must, you probably have some sympathy for Unificationism.

Let me offer a second rationale for MDD_1 and MDD_2. If either MDD_1 or MDD_2 is false, it has to be possible for situations to arise where there is a decisive case against acting that does not constitute a decisive case against believing you should act in that way. In other words, there is sufficient epistemic reason to believe you ought to Φ but sufficient practical reason not to Φ. Suppose, then, we imagine two cases. In the first, the subject knows she ought to Φ and knows that the reasons by virtue of which she ought to Φ are the reasons by virtue of which she should believe she should Φ. In the bad case, the subject believes mistakenly that she should Φ. Really, she should not Φ. Perhaps what the subject should believe in the good case and bad is determined by the evidence, or her perspective,

---

[18] Inspired by an example from Thomson 1991. She used her example to tell us something about intention and permissibility, not something about the relation between the normative standing of belief and action.

or how things seem. What the subject should do, we might say, depends upon the facts. Since the facts do not fit the beliefs in the bad case, we need a bad case to cause trouble for MDD$_1$ and MDD$_2$.

At this point the segregationists have to explain why one sort of reason depends upon things available to us when the other does not. I take it that such differences cannot be brute.[19] The explanation, however, either has to appeal to something about the reasonness of reasons, the epistemicness of epistemic reasons, or the practicality of practical reasons. The explanation cannot be grounded in something having to do with the concept of a reason: both epistemic and practical reasons are reasons. We cannot say that the epistemicness of epistemic reasons or the practicality of practical reasons will provide us with the explanation we seek. The difference between the epistemic and the practical is that the former is concerned with truth and knowledge whereas the latter is concerned with the good. That difference does not help us see why one sort of reason applies to us only if it is available to us when the other does not. So, since it cannot be a brute fact that the reasons differ this way, and it seems there is nothing that could explain why the reasons bearing on belief and action would differ in this way, perhaps the alleged fact about reasons is no fact at all. Either both sorts of reason depend upon your perspective rather than the facts, they depend upon the facts rather than your perspective, or they depend upon both.

6.4.3 From Unificationism to Externalism

In this section, I shall argue that unificationists should be externalists. Specifically, they should endorse Factivity$_J$. The cases of mistaken belief and ignorance we shall consider below are better conceptualized as cases of excusable wrongdoing rather than regrettable right action. Given MDD$_1$ and MDD$_2$, we shall see that if an agent who reasonably judges she should Φ nevertheless fails to meet her practical obligations, she has failed to meet her epistemic obligations as well. Among her obligations is the obligation to refrain from including those beliefs in reasoning that pass off counterfeit reasons as if they were real. Mistaken normative judgments ought to be excluded from deliberation, and facts about what you

---

[19] This expands on an argument from Gibbons 2010. He thinks "Don't be an idiot" is a categorical imperative and that anyone who acts against their own justified judgment about what to do violates this imperative.

should do depend (in part) upon contingent facts external to you, not just facts about you and your own mental states.

Let's begin with a story:

Loan Shark: Harry is behind in his payments to Bobby, the loan shark. Bobby gave Harry a severe beating last week and a warning that if he missed another payment, Bobby would kill him. The payment is due today and Harry does not have the money. He borrows a revolver and hangs out at Audrey's restaurant hoping that Bobby will leave him alone in public. He is shocked when he sees a man with a menacing look he takes to be Bobby come in and walk straight towards him. Harry says "I won't let you get me, Bobby!" and he pulls out his revolver and takes aim.[20]

Suppose the story continues as follows:

Loan Shark$_1$: Audrey has a pipe. She knows that the man Harry takes to be Bobby is really Bobby's twin brother. She knows that while he might look dangerous, he is a threat to no one. She knows that to stop Harry from firing at Bobby's twin, she will need to club him with her pipe. She does so, intervening on behalf of Bobby's brother.

Concerning Loan Shark$_1$, it seems natural to say this:

1. Audrey would act rightly if she intervened on behalf of the man Harry intends to shoot (i.e., on behalf of Bobby's twin).

The story could have unfolded differently.

Loan Shark$_2$: We could have changed our cast of characters a bit: Audrey knows that the man Harry takes to be Bobby is really Bobby, not Bobby's twin. As Bobby approaches, Harry produces the revolver, pulls the trigger, but nothing happens. He is out of bullets. Audrey intervenes and knocks Bobby unconscious with her pipe.

Concerning Loan Shark$_2$, it seems intuitive to say:

2. Audrey would only act rightly if she decided to intervene on behalf of Harry.

What explains these intuitions? The reason that the range of permissible options open to Audrey differs in these stories is that Harry loses the right

---

[20] The example is taken from Robinson 1996. He uses the example to show that the permissibility of acting depends upon features of the agent's situation that the agent might be non-culpably ignorant of. I think the examples can also be used to show that the permissibility of belief depends upon these features. I think he assumes that it is not permissible to use force to prevent someone from acting permissibly. We will see below that this assumption is inessential to the argument.

to non-interference in Loan Shark$_1$ but not in Loan Shark$_2$. I think that this tells us something about the deontic status of the acts Harry intends to perform in Loan Shark$_1$ and Loan Shark$_2$. This can be contested, of course, but suppose for a moment that this is right.

Suppose Harry is permitted to use force in one case but not the other. If so, this looks to be a promising argument that unificationists ought to accept Factivity$_J$:

3. It is consistent with views that deny Factivity$_J$ that Harry's beliefs are justified in both cases.
4. (Therefore) Views that deny Factivity$_J$ should say that Harry justifiably judges that he should use force to defend himself from the man approaching in both Loan Shark$_1$ and Loan Shark$_2$.
5. Given Unificationism, however, this means Harry is permitted to use force in Loan Shark$_1$ and Loan Shark$_2$.
6. This is a mistake. In one case he is permitted to use force and in the other he is not.
7. (Therefore) Given Unificationism, views that deny Factivity$_J$ have to say that reasonably held mistaken beliefs do not merely excuse, they obviate the need to justify acting against undefeated reasons.
8. Thus, given Unificationism, views that deny Factivity$_J$ cannot do justice to our moral intuitions.

We might agree that there is something bad about shooting someone who just happens to look exactly like a loan shark, but how do we decide whether the shooting would have been bad and impermissible or merely regrettable? From my own experience, the intuitions that favor internalist views are strongest when we ask what someone should do or believe and do not let the story continue from there. Externalist intuitions start to get their grip on us when they let the story continue and ask what should be done in the wake of some untoward chain of events. Think about the injuries that Bobby suffers in Loan Shark$_2$. He gets a nasty bump on the head and a massive headache waiting for him if he ever wakes up. Suppose we add in some detail to Loan Shark$_1$. In Loan Shark$_1$, Leo sees Audrey swinging her pipe at Harry. Leo believes that Bobby's twin is Bobby and believes that Audrey must be helping the loan shark kill Harry. Leo grabs a pipe and swings it at Audrey on the reasonable but mistaken belief that he is helping to defend Harry from a loan shark and an accomplice. Leo connects and knocks Audrey unconscious, but only after Audrey connects and knocks Harry unconscious. The story is complicated, but at the end of the story we have two unconscious subjects. Harry was knocked unconscious by Audrey because she knew that Harry was going to shoot an innocent person if she did not intervene. Leo knocked Audrey unconscious just as she was striking Harry.

After the police come, Leo sees Bobby and Audrey begin to stir. He has enough pain reliever to help one of these subjects but not enough to help both. It seems intuitive to say:

9. Given just enough pain reliever to help one, Leo ought to assist Audrey rather than Harry.

Why is his duty to Audrey stronger than his duty to Harry? If his duties to Audrey and Harry were mere duties of beneficence, it seems that since he can help both equally and both are equally badly off, we would be at a loss to explain why (9) is true. If, however, his duty to Audrey is a duty of reparation, it is easy to see why (9) is true. Since duties of reparation are duties to respond to previous wrongs, I do not see how any view that denies that the justification of action can depend upon facts external to the agent she is non-culpably ignorant of can explain how Leo's actions were wrongful. Leo, we might assume, was perfectly reasonable in his beliefs and had his beliefs been correct we might all agree that he did just the thing that he should have done. Unfortunately for Audrey, however, his beliefs were not correct. If we say that Leo acted impermissibly we can say that the intuitions that support (1), (2), and (9) cause trouble for views that deny that the truth of a belief matters to whether it can properly figure in deliberation.

In conversation, some have suggested that the intuition that Leo owes something to Audrey rather than Harry has everything to do with the fact that there is a causal chain that connects Leo to Audrey. Perhaps the thought is that our intuition is sensitive to this fact and this fact about the source of our intuition helps explain it away and undercut the intuitive support for (9). Myself, I think this does little to blunt the force of the intuition. We might easily imagine that Leo is ambidextrous and wields two clubs. Striking both someone engaged in wrongdoing and someone trying to help stop wrongdoing, we can imagine there are causal chains leading from one agent to two bumps. We can ask again which of these bumps Leo should do something about first, which bump he has stronger reason to respond to, etc. If your intuitions are anything like mine, intuition suggests that Leo has a stronger duty to the party trying to help rather than the party up to no good.

We have two sorts of intuition that suggest that unificationists ought to accept Factivity$_J$. There are intuitions about the justified use of force in intervention and intuitions about reparative duties owed in the wake of acting on mistaken beliefs. With the argument now before us, we can consider some of the ways in which someone might try to resist the conclusion. Some contest the intuitions, some contest their significance, and I suspect some will contest both.

6.4.4 Conflicts of justification

One way to resist the argument is to push back against the idea that intuitions about the permissible use of force in intervention help us determine the justificatory status of an agent's actions. In appealing to intuitions about Loan Shark to support Factivity$_J$, I seemed to assume something like this principle:

> Non-Interference: It is permissible for an agent to use force to prevent another agent from acting only if that agent's intended course of action was impermissible.[21]

Non-Interference is false. Even if the only way for two agents to resolve some conflict is by the use of force, it is not obvious that one of these agents intended to do something impermissible. If this is so, it is hard to see how someone could argue from the observation that an agent lost the right to non-interference by intending to Φ to the conclusion that it would have been wrong for her to Φ.

Various examples cause trouble for the view that justifications cannot conflict.[22] Suppose Cooper's niece has been kidnapped and hypnotized. She has been sent to steal medication from Harry. Without this medication, Harry will surely die. Harry is quite frail and he can only defend himself from Cooper's niece by shooting her. Cooper's niece, we might imagine, would not survive the shooting and Cooper feels obliged to protect his niece. Must we really say that morality obliges Cooper to do nothing to protect his innocent niece? Must we really say that morality obliges Harry to do nothing to protect himself from this little innocent aggressor? Or, suppose there is only one life preserver left and both Bobby and Leo need it to survive. Does morality really require them to find a coin to flip and condemn them if they wrestle for it? Morality might condemn one of them for kicking, biting, or gouging during the struggle and

---

[21] Robinson 1996 appeals to a principle similar to Non-Interference to argue mistaken beliefs excuse wrongdoing.

[22] For a discussion of conflicts of justification (and whether these cases involve conflicting justifications), see Husak 1999.

would surely condemn Bobby if he threw sand in Leo's eyes, but I do not think it would condemn Leo for being quicker and more agile if he used agility and speed to get the last remaining life preserver.

While I agree that Non-Interference is false, some of the counterexamples to Non-Interference give us a clue as to how to save the argument for Factivity$_J$. Consider:

Anti-Aircraft: Cooper intends to bomb a munitions factory. Destroying the factory is an important step towards winning a just war. If the bombs hit the factory, the explosion will destroy the apartments that abut the factory. Audrey is among the non-combatants who live in those apartments, whose deaths count as acceptable losses. Audrey realizes that she can defend herself and her family by manning an anti-aircraft gun and firing at Cooper's plane. Someone could say that Audrey's decision to try to stop Coop from carrying out his mission was justified and that Coop's decision to bomb the factory was justified.

According to Non-Interference, Audrey's intervention would be justified only if Coop's intended course of action was not justified. But that seems like a mistake. It is not wrong for the non-combatants who might be permissibly killed in a just war to take arms against just actors who would kill them. Surely if Audrey decides to allow herself to be killed by Coop's actions because she hoped that his side would win, she has gone beyond the call of duty. Surely circumstances can arise in which Coop could justifiably act in a way that would predictably cause Audrey's death.

Notice that in this example, Audrey has a range of permissible options available to her. She can intervene on behalf of Coop and die for the cause. She can intervene to protect herself and her loved ones from Coop. It would be wrong, however, for her to intervene on behalf of the forces of the despotic tyrant that is sending planes to intercept Coop. In Loan Shark$_1$ and Loan Shark$_2$, there is a range of permissible options available as well. The agent can rightly do nothing or rightly intervene on behalf of one party, but they do not have free choice as to which party to assist. So, perhaps the way to state the challenge to those who think that it would not be wrong in Loan Shark$_1$ for Harry to shoot Bobby's harmless twin brother is this. The best explanation as to why agents are permitted to assist different parties in Loan Shark$_1$ and Loan Shark$_2$ has to do with the fact that it is wrong to assist someone engaged in wrongdoing and the parties engaged in wrongdoing differ in these cases. The argument for Factivity$_J$ does not rest on the mistaken assumption that you can never justifiably use force to interfere with someone who is also acting (or trying to act) with justification.

6.4.5 Obligations and outcomes

In trying to bolster the intuition that the conditions that determine the permissibility of an action include conditions that the agent was non-culpably ignorant of at the time of action, I appealed to intuitions about reparative duties. It is possible for two agents to be perfectly alike in all respects that matter to the justification of their beliefs apart from the truth of their beliefs, for these agents to judge that they ought to Φ, for them to Φ accordingly, and for only one of them to owe reparations for what they did. The agent who owed reparations acted impermissibly. The other agent did not. Thus, only one of these agents judged permissibly that they ought to Φ. Thus, the truth of that judgment is required for that judgment to be justified. Thus, the permissibility of action and belief can depend (in part) upon whether the subject's normative judgments are correct, not just whether they were reasonable at the time of action.

This kind of argument can be resisted in two ways. First, someone could try to account for the intuition that these reparative duties are owed in an internalist framework. Second, someone could argue that we have no such reparative duties in these cases.

Herman outlines a strategy for Kantians to account for duties of reparation.[23] Kantians think that all wrongs are due to defects in an agent's will. Although Kantians think that the deontic status of an action depends upon the maxims on which an agent acts and not upon the effects of acting on these maxims, Herman suggests that if an agent must Φ, she must form a suitable maxim to see to it that she does, and this involves forming an initial plan for Φ-ing as well as 'maxims of response.' Think of maxims of response as plans to pursue an end if the initial efforts fail. If her initial efforts fail, we know that the agent must either change her end or adopt new means. If her end is one she is required to pursue, she is required to adopt new means and try again. If she fails again, she formulates another maxim and tries again. Eventually, the agent will meet her obligation. (Or so one hopes.)

To see how this works, suppose someone fully intends to return a borrowed clock and has a maxim that seems to be adequate for her to achieve her intended end. On the occasion of executing the return, however, she trips and the clock breaks. If the moral assessment of actions is based on the assessment of the agent's maxim, there is no way for the theory to register or assess the failure of execution because the maxim might not

---

[23] Herman 1993.

have been defective. Nevertheless, the agent cannot wash her hands of the situation and walk away. In the wake of the failure, she must formulate a new maxim and try again. Perhaps if the clock is broken and cannot be replaced, this involves acting on a maxim so as to make reparations.

There are two problems with this approach. First, in her example, we might say that the promise was to return a particular clock. If the agent tries on Monday to return it and discovers on Tuesday that the clock was destroyed, she discovers that she tried to keep a promise, she failed to deliver what she promised, and she discovers that it is now impossible for her to deliver what is promised. The suggestion seems to be that (i) the agent who wills the end must will the means necessary for that end and (ii) if the end is mandatory, the agent cannot revise her end so as to refrain from adopting means taken to be adequate to that end that she has not yet achieved. Thus, the story goes, she must try again. It is not clear, however, that the agent failed to meet her obligation because it is not clear that the Kantian can say that her obligation was to return a clock rather than simply to try. She did try. If returning the clock is not the required end and the required end is simply that of trying to return, when the agent learns that she cannot return the clock, I do not see how the Kantian can explain why she must make reparations. Moreover, making reparations is not a way of achieving her end, so it is not clear that trying to make reparations would be covered by a maxim of response. If there was an obligation to bring about some state of affairs, it was an obligation to bring about the return of the clock, not return something of similar value.

The second problem with this approach is that it has quite limited applicability. The obligation to act on maxims of response requires an obligation to pursue some end. If an agent must Φ, she must adopt the means adequate for Φ-ing and cannot wash her hands of the situation until she Φ's. So, for example, if someone tried to return a clock but hopped onto the wrong bus, they cannot decide to turn around and go home rather than hop on yet another bus and try to get the clock back to its owner. Notice that the reason that the agent is required to formulate and act on maxims of response is that there is this mandatory end hanging over them. In the cases I described, the agents were not under any obligation to act initially. Their obligations only came about in the wake of their actions. In Loan Shark, for example, Audrey is under no obligation to get involved and try to protect anyone from harm. She is permitted to do so, but not required. If she tries to help and fails, she is free to try again or decide against trying again. Suppose she tries to help and not only fails to help, but makes things worse. If there was nothing wrong with her initial maxim and the situation was not one she was obligated to do anything about initially, the Kantian cannot explain how she could be obligated to do something about it now. Given that she was never required to intervene, the Kantian account implies that she can wash her hands of the situation and walk away. But, this seems highly counterintuitive. If someone gets involved and makes things worse, they are now obligated to try to make reparations. So, it seems that you cannot do justice to our intuitions about reparation without recognizing that it is possible for someone to have duties of reparation simply because of the unintended and unforeseen consequences of their actions.

Rather than try to accommodate the intuition that the outcomes matter and that you can have reparative duties when your good intentions make things worse, some simply deny it. According to Zimmerman, none of us has the right not to be harmed by others and we have no right to be compensated by those who harm us. At most, he says, we have the right not to be put at risk of harm. So, he rejects the first thesis but accepts the second:

> Harm Thesis: We have moral rights against others that they not cause us harm.
> Risk Thesis: We have moral rights against others that they not impose risks of harms on us.[24]

Whether someone is put at risk of harm is determined not by the epistemic position of the victim, but of the agent who harms or risks harming. If this is right, the problem with my argument was not that I drew the wrong moral from a perfectly sound intuition. The problem with my argument was that there were no reparative duties owed to a victim in cases such as Cook.

Zimmerman raises three objections to the Harm Thesis. First, he says that the Harm Thesis leaves some needy parties (e.g., Leo) "out in the cold" even if this party is just as deserving of compensation as those that the Harm Thesis suggests we have reparative duties to. So, for example, in Cook, we had two parties who were equally deserving of assistance and it seems strange to him to suggest that one of these parties has a stronger claim on receiving that assistance. Zimmerman thinks that rights are correlative with duties:

<hr />

[24] Zimmerman 2008, p. 80.

> Correlativity Thesis: One party has a moral right against another agent
> that this agent Φ iff this agent has an obligation to this party to Φ.[25]

If there is no duty to the party harmed, they had no right not to be harmed. If they had no right not to be harmed, there might be duties in the wake of an action, but not duties to the injured parties that I have claimed there are in my examples. Since reparative duties are duties that relate agents to particular parties, it looks as if an attack on the Harm Thesis is an attack on the idea that you have reparative duties to those you harm. Second, he says that the party that harmed may have been just as innocent as the party harmed. The significance of this, I take it, is that it makes no sense to hold one party accountable for making reparations to another if both are equally innocent. Third, he says that there might be some further party who is just as much at fault as the party that causes the injury that is just as deserving to be made to make amends. Why not haul them in and make them pay reparations?

I am not persuaded by these objections to the Harm Thesis. The problem with the second and third objection is that we cannot determine what an agent's obligations are by determining whether she deserves to be under these obligations. Nobody deserves to be under a duty of beneficence. Duties of beneficence arise without any prior relation between you and the potential beneficiary. Thus, the duty does not require that there is any relation between you and anyone else by virtue of which you deserve to be obligated to look after their well-being. We are, nevertheless, often duty-bound to assist others when we are not responsible for the fact that they need assistance. The problem with the first objection is that it would prove too much. Suppose Harry had tried to poison Cooper and succeeded in so doing. If Leo and Cooper are equally faultless in finding themselves poisoned, surely they are equally deserving of assistance, but nobody would say that Harry's obligations to Cooper are for that reason not stronger than the duties he has to those he has not tried to kill. If we took the first objection to be a decisive objection to the Harm Thesis, it would equally work as an objection to the Risk Thesis. Since it is uncontroversial that one of these theses is true, this objection is not a cogent objection to the Harm Thesis.

We have looked at two ways of trying to block the argument for Factivity$_J$. The first was to accommodate intuitions about reparation in a framework that denies that the permissibility of an action depends upon

---

[25] Zimmerman 2008, p. 78.

the outcomes and the second was to reject the Harm Thesis. Neither of these responses shows that you do not have duties not to harm. If there are duties not to harm, the unificationist says that there are duties not to judge that you should act in ways that will be harmful. If you judge that you ought to Φ and thereby harm someone by Φ-ing, you might be excused for having done so, but your actions and beliefs would be excusable at best. The reasons to refrain from acting were reasons to refrain from intending to act and to refrain from judging that you should act.

6.4.6 Against Internalist Unificationism

Some unificationists harbor internalist sympathies. They think that we ought to say that justified beliefs justify actions, but they think we ought to allow for the possibility of false, justified belief.[26] Indeed, they think that we ought to think of justification as an internalist notion. Either they do not share the intuitions that your actions can be wrongful in virtue of factors that you were non-culpably ignorant of at the time of acting or they think they have overriding reason to discount these intuitions. In this section, I shall argue that unificationists ought to accept Factivity$_J$.

One reason unificationists should not reject Factivity$_J$ is that unificationists who reject Factivity$_J$ have to sanction wrongdoing. Subjects with defective moral views can be reasonable in holding their views, their (seemingly) mistaken moral beliefs can be produced by reliable processes, and if you say that their moral beliefs are justified, the unificationist has to say that they have the right to act on them. The result is that the unificationist condones all manner of morally abhorrent behavior.

There is a further reason for unificationists to embrace Externalism. To see what the problem is, let me sketch an account of 'ought to believe':

SE$_1$: You ought to believe p if you have sufficient evidence, you are concerned to settle the question whether p, and you have given the matter sufficient reflection.

---

[26] Gibbons 2010 is the chief advocate of such a view. He rejects Supervenience Internalism, but he also rejects Factivity$_J$ and thinks that you cannot be obligated to do something if you could not reasonably work out that it is your obligation. He defends mixed deontic detachment. Zimmerman 1996 notes some subjective views of 'ought' (e.g., the view that S ought to Φ if S believes she ought to Φ) violate OIC and I think this point can be extended to views that reject this subjectivist view of 'ought' but retain the thought that all obligations are grounded in subjective states of the subject. In conversation, Feldman suggested that he is no longer convinced that the justification of action depends upon facts that the agent is non-culpably ignorant of, so he might be moving towards some unificationist view.

SE$_2$: You have sufficient evidence if you have precisely the same evidence for believing p as someone who knows p.

I think this is the account many internalists would accept, particularly if they thought that rational beliefs are justified beliefs. As we saw in Chapter 1, anyone who holds this view has to say that you can have positive epistemic obligations to believe if you are cognizant of sufficiently strong evidence.

Consider an example. Coop gets in line to buy a snack from the vending machine. He sees that there is an infant, a puppy, and a kitten trapped inside. He knows the machine is in good working order because he has seen people using it all morning and knows that the machine was serviced yesterday. He knows he has just enough change to save the infant, the kitten, or the puppy but not enough to save two. He thinks that puppies are worth more than kittens but thinks that infants are worth more than puppies. So, let us say:

1. In w$_1$, Coop believes correctly and on exceptionally good evidence that it is better to save the infant.
2. In w$_1$, Coop believes correctly and on exceptionally good evidence that he can save the infant.
3. In w$_1$, Coop believes correctly and on exceptionally good evidence that he ought to save the infant.

This much I can stipulate. It is tempting to say that if he reasons from his belief that it is best to save the infant and his belief that he can save the infant that he ought to save the infant. Indeed, it is tempting to say that he knows that he ought to save the infant. But, imagine that in some possible world where Coop is in the same mental states as he is in w$_1$ the following is true:

4. In w$_2$, Coop has just the same evidence for his beliefs as he does in w$_1$.
5. If Coop knows in w$_1$ that it is best to save the infant, that he can do that, and that is what he ought to do, Coop ought to believe these very same things in w$_2$.
6. If Coop knows in w$_1$ that it is best to save the infant, that he can do that, and that is what he ought to do, Coop ought to save the infant in w$_2$.

It is consistent with everything that has been said that:

7. In w$_2$, Coop cannot save the infant because the vending machine is broken.

It follows that if 'ought' implies 'can':

8. It is false that Coop ought to save the infant in w_2.
9. It is false that Coop ought to believe he ought to save the infant in w_2.
10. It is false that Coop could know both that he ought to save the infant and that the best thing to do is save the infant.

Unificationists who accept SE_1 and SE_2 have to say that if you know that infants matter more than kittens or puppies, you cannot have sufficient evidence to believe you can get things out of vending machines.

Somebody could say that you can never know that you will get something out of a vending machine when you put your money in, but this is an implausibly high standard for knowledge! We could rewrite the argument to deal with such worries. Suppose Coop cannot save the infant because there is a transparent piece of glass that covers the coin slot. He cannot get his coins into the machine. It would follow that there is no possible world in which Coop's counterpart knows he can put coins into a machine. Suppose instead that Coop cannot save the infant because he cannot move his arm. The sight of the infant trapped in a vending machine set off a strange chain of events in his nervous system that left him temporarily paralyzed. It would follow that there is no possible world in which one of Coop's counterparts knows he can lift his arm. Suppose Coop cannot save the infant because in the nanosecond between judging he ought to try and trying Zeus strikes him dead. Should we say that there is no possible world in which Coop's counterpart knows he can try to save the infant?

The cost that internalist unificationists have to pay for denying Factivity$_J$ is skepticism. The reason why Coop cannot know that he can free the infant is that an epistemic counterpart of his could have just his evidence for believing this proposition in a world in which that proposition is false. In this world, Coop's counterpart would be mistaken in thinking he can and should save the infant where these mistaken beliefs would rationalize an action that the agent cannot perform. Thus, it turns out that you know p only if you have no epistemic counterparts in any possible world who falsely believe p on your evidence and whose belief that p would rationalize forming the intention to perform an action that cannot be performed under those circumstances. If that's right, is there anything we can know about the external world? Little. All it took to show that Coop did not know p was to find some possible world in which he mistakenly believes p on the basis of the same evidence. Thus, it looks like the internalist unificationist is committed to the unfortunate view that we have sufficient evidence to believe p only when our evidence for believing p entails p.

6.5 CONCLUSION

In this chapter, I defended two claims. The first is that consequential moral luck is possible. It is possible for you and your epistemic counterparts to act on the same intentions and for you to do better in meeting your practical obligations than they do. The second is that there is a principled link between epistemic and practical obligation. If you have the right to believe something, you have the right not only to treat what you believe as a reason for further beliefs, but also as a basis for action. If, however, your obligation is to refrain from acting, your obligation is to refrain from intending to act and judging that you ought to act. When you combine the externalist account of the justification of action with the further view that your epistemic obligation is to refrain from judging that you should $\sqrt{}$ when obligation requires you to refrain from $\sqrt{}$-ing, the result is that there are no false, justified normative judgments.

CHAPTER 7

Justification

7.1 INTRODUCTION

Most of what we want to say about justification can be said in terms of reasons. Your obligation will never be to refrain from believing what you have no reason not to believe. Obligations come with reasons, so when you have no reasons not to believe, you have the permission to believe. Since justified beliefs are permissibly held beliefs, you justifiably believe something whenever you have no reason not to believe as you do. If, however, there is some undefeated reason not to believe as you do and you are obligated not to believe, your belief is excusable at best. If we can identify the reasons that bear on whether to believe and say what it is these reasons demand, we should be able to say what it takes to believe with justification.

Some reasons are demanding things, but it is not obvious what they demand and which reasons make demands on you. I shall assume that these reasons are associated with norms.[1] Norms identify conditions under which you have some reason (*pro tanto* or conclusive) and tell you something the reason demands from you. For example, the knowledge norm of assertion tells us that it would be wrong (*pro tanto* or all things considered) to assert *p* if you do not know *p*, so it tells you that you have a conclusive reason to refrain from asserting *p* if *p* is false or you lack sufficient evidence to believe *p*. If there is no reason (conclusive or otherwise) to refrain from asserting what you do not know, knowledge cannot be the norm of assertion. I shall also assume that some form of generalism

---

[1] Individual pieces of evidence are reasons that have normative significance, but they are not the only reasons that bear on whether to believe. Evidentialists, for example, say that you should not believe *p* without sufficient evidence to do so. You can say that the bits of evidence that support the hypothesis that *p* is true are reasons, but there is also a reason not to believe without sufficient evidence and this is not just a further bit of evidence. See Owens 2000.

is true and the reasons that determine whether to believe are captured by norms that can apply on more than one occasion.

If a norm says that you should not believe something or act some way, there is at least some reason not to believe or act that way. If you violate a norm, might your actions or attitudes nevertheless be justified? Perhaps. You might justifiably break a promise or a toe if you have strong enough reasons that require broken promises or toes. What if you violate a norm without any overriding reason to do so? I would say that the best you could hope for is an excuse, but this assumes controversially that the reasons require conformity. On one view, this is precisely what reasons do. Reasons demand conformity and their demands end there. If a reason is a reason to Φ, you conform to its demands iff you Φ. Suppose you promised to meet someone for lunch, but you would rather not go because he is an epistemologist. If there is reason to keep a promise, you conform to this reason's demands iff you keep the promise. If you grit your teeth and try unsuccessfully to keep your promise, you have not managed to do all that the reason required of you. If you try to break your promise and fate brings you two to the same restaurant, you can fail to break the promise. The conformity account says that you thereby did everything the reasons of fidelity required of you.

Critics criticize the conformity account on two fronts. Some reject the idea that reasons could demand conformity because it seems that whether you conform to some norm depends upon more than just the quality of your will or your efforts. If you did what could reasonably be expected of you in trying to keep a promise, say, just as nobody could fault you for trying and failing, the reasons could not really have been reasons to try and to succeed. Yoda was wrong. Others reject the idea that reasons demand only conformity. If you try to act against some reason and you fail to act against it because of your ignorance or incompetence, it certainly seems strange to suggest that you did everything the reasons required. Perhaps reasons require that you comply with their demands, doing what they demand because that is what they demand from you.

My own view is that reasons demand more than mere conformity. Normative appraisal is concerned with the quality of the agent's efforts, but not exclusively. It is also concerned with whether agents conform to certain norms. So, while normative appraisal will partially be a matter of looking to see if the agent was moved by the right reasons, it will also be concerned with whether the agent's reasons moved the agent to the right place. After defending this view, we shall look at a recent debate having to do with the norm of belief. I shall argue that the fundamental norm of belief is the truth norm, not the knowledge norm or some evidential norm. Once we see what this norm demands, we should have a better idea of what is involved in the justification of belief.

We shall start by considering three competing accounts of what reasons demand:

The Conformity Account: In Φ-ing, you do all the reasons require iff you conform to the relevant reasons.

The Due Care Account: In Φ-ing, you do all that the reasons require iff you are nothing less than fully reasonable and responsible for having Φ'd.

The Compliance Account: In Φ-ing, you do all that the reasons require iff you comply with the relevant reasons.

The relevant reasons for our purposes are undefeated reasons for the agent to Φ or refrain from Φ-ing. The Due Care Account says, in effect, that if there is some undefeated reason to Φ, whether you Φ or not is strictly speaking immaterial. All that anyone can demand from you is that you tried your best, not that you tried and succeeded. Maybe reasons should be like people in that respect. Presumably whether you tried your best is determined by the ends you pursued and the way you pursued them, not on whether you brought about some external state of affairs as the result of your efforts. Like the Due Care Account, the Compliance Account says that normative appraisal is concerned with the quality of the agent's efforts, but differs from the Due Care Account in that it insists that reasons demand full conformity.

Some would prefer the Due Care Account to its rivals because they think the alternative approaches do not do justice to the deontological character of justification. Deontologists about justification sometimes say that theirs is a view on which a justified belief is "epistemically permissible, a belief for which the subject cannot justly be blamed, or a belief the subject is not obliged to drop."[2] In motivating this view, Steup says:

In ethics, it is particularly clear, and, as Linda Zagzebski has pointed out, nearly unquestioned, that responsibility and duty fulfillment demand direct

---

[2] Steup 1999, p. 375.

recognizability ... No one defends the view that what makes an *action* unjustified is something the agent cannot directly recognize.[3]

This tendency to identify justified beliefs with beliefs held by those who meet their epistemic responsibilities is understandable, but there is a danger of falling prey to a fallacious argument that purports to show that justified beliefs are responsibly held beliefs.

According to the Compliance and Conformity Accounts, a subject can rationally judge that she should Φ and her obligation could be to refrain from Φ-ing. Suppose, if only for *reductio*, that this is possible. That she ought to refrain from Φ-ing means that there is an undefeated reason for her not to Φ. When the agent acts on her rational judgment about what to do and thereby acts against this reason by Φ-ing, she would be in breach of her obligations. But, the objection says, this cannot be. It cannot be her duty or responsibility to refrain from Φ-ing because everyone agrees that nobody could accuse her of being irresponsible for having Φ'd. She acted on a rational belief that she ought to Φ. Thus, we should reject the Compliance and Conformity Accounts and accept the Due Care Account.

This argument equivocates, conflating two senses of 'responsibility.' In its forward-looking sense, a 'responsibility' is a duty or an obligation. In its backward-looking sense, 'responsibility' has to do with blame and accountability. If you say that I am responsible for my dog's ill health, that might be taken to mean that I am culpable for the fact that she is ill or that I have a special duty to look after her health because she is my dog. If taken one way, blame is imparted. Taken another way, it is not. If this is the argument for the Due Care Account, there is no basis in such an account.

Perhaps the real reason people accept the Due Care Account is not because of some simple equivocation, but because they think their account best accounts for intuitions or because it is a consequence of some substantive account of what makes the right the right that you cannot nonculpably fail to see what duty requires.[4] In previous chapters, we have

---

[3] Steup 1999, p. 375. See Zagzebski 1996, p. 42. For a defense of the view that what makes an action unjustified can depend upon something the agent does not directly recognize, see Darley and Robinson 1998; Gardner 2007; G. E. Moore 1993; M. Moore 1997; Ross 1930; Sorensen 1995; Thomson 2001; and Zimmerman 2002.

[4] For instances of the former, consider the view that says that your obligation is to maximize expectable value defended by Zimmerman 2008 on the grounds that it accommodates intuitions that objectivist approaches to 'ought' do not. For instances of the latter, consider the Kantian view Herman 1993 defends according to which all moral evaluation is concerned with the agent's will and whether it is defective.

seen that these points are mistaken and cannot support an argument for the Due Care Account.

First, the Due Care Account has to take the rational to be the mark of the permissible. Suppose you rationally judge that you ought to Φ. In light of this, it seems that it should be rational to Φ. If the rational is the mark of the permissible, you are within your rights to Φ. Individuals with different normative evidence can reach very different conclusions about morality's demands. Assuming that it is possible for a subject to judge rationally that Φ-ing is something she must do and another to judge that Φ-ing is something that must not be done, the Due Care Account implies one subject is now obliged to Φ and the other is forbidden from Φ-ing. The Due Care Account seems to lead rather quickly to the sort of relativist view on which rational judgments about obligation become infallible indicators of where your obligations are.

Second, there was the three-case argument we discussed in the first chapter. Consider three cases:

C1: Bobby sees Maddy aim her revolver at Audrey and strikes her knowing that this is the only way he can prevent Maddy from shooting Audrey. He saves Audrey's life, but injures Maddy in the process.

C2: Donna sees Bobby raising a pipe to strike Maddy but does not realize that Bobby is trying to protect Audrey. Believing that Bobby is trying to murder Maddy, she picks up a wrench and swings it at Bobby, mistakenly believing that this is justified on grounds of protecting an innocent party.

C3: In an unrelated incident, Cooper was drugged and in his drug-induced state tried to attack Harry.

In the end, we have three injuries and nobody can be blamed for causing them. The drugs that were slipped into Coop's drink undermined the capacities that would allow him to assume responsibility for his actions. Bobby cannot be blamed because his actions were justified on the grounds that he was defending someone else. Donna's actions differ from Coop's because she could assume responsibility for her actions. Misguided as they were, they were nevertheless quite brave and spoke well of her. Thus, we want to say that the ways we remove blame in (C2) and (C3) differ. We do not, however, want to say that Donna's actions were justified for reasons discussed in previous chapters. So, we want to say that the ways we remove blame in (C1) and (C2) differ.

The first case is a case of a justified wrong and the second is a case of excusable wrongdoing. Since the Due Care Account takes the mark of permissibility to be something along the lines of responsible behavior, it cannot explain why (C1) differs from (C2). Thus, it cannot do justice to the idea that justifications differ from excuses and exemptions while doing justice to the distinction between exemptions and excuses. In cases of excusable wrongdoing, the agent can be held accountable for her deeds. For her to be excused, then, we cannot say that the agent was powerless or helpless. We have to show how her actions show her in a positive light. We do this not by showing that there was overriding reason for her to do what she did (that would be to offer a crypto-justification), but by showing that her actions spoke well of her as a person. The Due Care Account makes a muddle of the distinction between justifications and excuses because it sees in the excuse everything needed for a justification.

These cases also show that the Due Care Account conflicts with an attractive account of reasons. Regardless of whether you think normative reasons are facts, states of affairs, attitudes, propositions, etc., you need to say something about what makes these reasons. Typically, something constitutes a reason because it counts in favor of some prospective course of action. The Due Care Account says that since Donna exercised due care and did what the virtuous person would have done, she did all that the reasons required of her. There was nothing that counted in favor of what she did. So, whatever reasons she had would not have been favorers. Suppose the facts had fit Donna's beliefs. The Due Care Account does not say that she has better reasons to act in such a situation, so while there would be things that counted in favor of her actions, they would not be reasons. The Due Care Account screens off the external facts and says that they are not among the facts that determine what reasons there were for the agent to act. Since favorers are almost always external facts, the Due Care Account denies that reasons to act are typically considerations that count in favor. Since, however, favorers are almost always the reasons that determine what to do, reason does not favor the Due Care Account.

These objections suggest that reasons do demand full conformity. It is hard to see how things could be otherwise. To say that reasons demand less is to say that reasons to Φ do not demand that you Φ. Is that even coherent? Perhaps what people mean to say when they say that your obligations cannot extend beyond what could have been reasonably expected from you given your circumstances is not that reasons demand something less than conformity, but that the real reasons that apply to us are reasons we could not be rationally mistaken about. So, these reasons do demand conformity, but we cannot mistake their demands if we take due care. This position is not incoherent, but it is still hard to see how this position can accommodate the idea that reasons are favorers (we can certainly be mistaken about what, if anything, counts in favor of acting) and we know that this account cannot deal with the three-case argument. Setting the Due Care Account aside, the question now is whether reasons demand more than just conformity.

One way to motivate the Conformity Account would be by attacking its rivals, the Due Care and Compliance Accounts. The Compliance Account does face some serious difficulties.[5] It says, not implausibly, that in determining the deontic status of an action, we need to know whether the agent conformed to the norms governing her actions and what the agent's reasons for acting were. If you have reason to Φ, that reason demands that you Φ for that very reason.

Two kinds of case cause serious trouble for the view. First, you have reasons not to murder your neighbors and eat their pets. Hopefully, these reasons play no role in explaining your actions and moving you through your day. If they do not, that is all to the good. There is no reason whose demands you do not meet if you are not moved by the reasons you have not to murder your neighbors and eat their pets because your actions are not *pro tanto* wrong simply because these reasons never cross your mind much less move you to act.[6] Thus, no reasons demand that you refrain from murdering your neighbors and eating their pets from that very reason, but there are plenty of reasons that demand that you do not murder your neighbors and eat their pets.

Second, think about cases of overdetermination.[7] If you have multiple reasons to Φ but only Φ for one of these reasons, the other reasons are not 'let down' simply because they were motivationally idle. If you Φ as you have overriding reason to do acting for only one of the reasons to Φ, your actions are not *pro tanto* wrong simply because you did not act for all of the reasons there were to Φ. If jumping into the river to save a child in danger of drowning would be both morally right and financially rewarding, you do not fail to do what the reasons require if you act for pecuniary motives.

---

[5] In Chapter 1 we saw that Pollock thinks we ought to be internalists because he thinks that epistemic norms are procedural norms. The objections to the Compliance Account suggest that this is a mistake. Norms as such give us reason to conform without giving us reason to be guided by them in conforming.

[6] Raz 1990, p. 180. [7] Raz 1999, p. 91.

While the Compliance Account posits too many demands, the Conformity Account posits too few. If we knew that Audrey swung her arm with the intention of socking Bobby in the jaw, we might know that her action was *pro tanto* wrong without knowing if she made contact with his jaw. It seems intuitive that we can show that someone's actions were wrongful without having to demonstrate that they violated a norm if we know independently that they tried to. If the Conformity Account is not concerned with the quality of an agent's deliberative efforts and what reasons moved them to act, the account will have a hard time explaining how malice, negligence, and recklessness can have any deontic significance. It is one thing to say that the reasons do not require that we act for their sake and another to say that the reasons do not care if we try to act against them.

Since deontic status depends upon whether we conform and also upon what moves us to act, we have to reject the Conformity Account and the Due Care Account. Since the Compliance Account generates too many demands, we need a fourth option. We could modify the Compliance Account and say that you should always act or believe for some undefeated reason or other.[8] On this view, your reasons for acting have to correspond to an undefeated reason to act that way. This account does not succumb to the objections we have considered thus far. It also helps us to distinguish between two kinds of case. Bobby might jump into a river to save a drowning child in the hopes of being paid. There are better reasons to jump in, but surely that reason is good enough. The agent's actions were not wrong simply for not being heroic. Contrast this with the following case. A trolley is headed towards five who will be crushed and killed if nothing is done. Ben could divert the trolley away from the five if he pulled the lever, but doing so would mean getting dirty and Ben is wearing something rather nice. He notices that his old rival is trapped on the sidetrack and would be killed if he diverted the trolley away from the five. So, he springs into action. He pulls the lever and diverts the trolley. He acts with the intention to kill his rival, something he would attempt only under the cover of saving the greater number. Intuitively, I think his actions are not justified.[9] The modified Compliance Account delivers the

---

[8] Gardner 2007. Raz 1990 once held this view, but I think he does not hold this view any longer.

[9] I am grateful to Matthew Liao for the example. For a discussion as to how an agent's motivations can partially determine the deontic status of her actions, see Sverdlik 2011. Thomson 1991 argues that the agent's intentions have no deontic significance. She observes that we would not say that Ben should have chosen to act differently (e.g., let the trolley crush the five) just because he was moved to act by malice. I agree, but I still think his action could have different deontic properties from the action that someone else would have performed under those circumstances if they were

right verdict. The reason for which he acted was not an undefeated reason to divert the trolley.

There are two problems with the modified Compliance Account. The first is theoretical. The view denies that reasons individually demand compliance. It must in order to deal with the overdetermination cases. Why must we act for some undefeated reason at all, then, if the individual reasons do not demand it? The obvious response would be an instrumentalist one.[10] We always ought to act for some undefeated reason or other because by so doing we better conform to the reasons that bear on what to do or believe. The problem with this is that the instrumentalist rationale supports a view that cannot account for the intuitions that caused trouble for the Conformity Account. If Ben pulls the switch with the intention to dispatch his rival knowing that there is sufficient reason to pull the switch (i.e., that doing so would save the greater number), we want to say that his actions were not justified because he acted for such horrible reasons. Still, he knows that his actions conform to an undefeated reason. (He would not have tried to dispatch his rival unless there were such reasons because he would only murder under the cover of what seemed to be right action.) If the only reason there is to act for undefeated reasons is an instrumental one, it is not clear how this account could account for the intuition that Ben's action was wrongful. He knew that he would conform to the demands of an undefeated reason.

The second problem has to do with intuitions about cases. Audrey is supposed to meet Coop for coffee when she hears that Bobby has been rushed to the hospital. Out of a sense of religious duty, she heads to the hospital to be by Bobby's side. There might have been overriding reason for Audrey to do what she did, but we can suppose that there are no religious duties of the sort she thinks there are.[11] If there are no such duties, she did what there was overriding reason to do without acting for an undefeated reason. The problem is that while it seems she acts rightly and acts with justification, there is no correspondence between reasons that moved her to act and undefeated reasons to act as she did. Somehow

---

not led to do the right thing for horrible reasons. It could be, for example, that someone who acts like Ben creates duties he should not feel free to create even if such duties do not give him overriding reason to refrain from diverting the trolley (e.g., in turning the trolley towards someone with the intention to kill them, you might incur a duty to make amends, seek forgiveness, make reparations, etc.).

[10] Gardner 2007, p. 101.

[11] While I am pretty certain there are no gods in reality, I am certainly certain there are no gods in my story.

reasons have to demand less than the modified Compliance Account suggests and more than mere conformity.

If the motivation for the idea that normative evaluation is concerned with the agent's motivating reasons is that normative evaluation is concerned with the quality of the agent's deliberative efforts, then the last example seems to show that a mere lack of fit between motivating reasons and undefeated normative reasons does not by itself reveal any defects in the agent's will that make the agent's actions wrongful. It might show that she has the facts wrong rather than has the wrong values. That she is moved by spurious reasons might not show that she is willing to act against genuine reasons. Audrey might have misplaced concerns because she feels a sense of duty to non-existent divine beings but her deliberative efforts are certainly not defective in the way that Ben's were as his actions manifested a willingness to murder another.

Perhaps the account that best fits the intuitive data is an account on which reasons place upon us a pair of conceptually related demands. If there is reason not to Φ, something calls on you to refrain from Φ-ing and to refrain from deliberating in ways that manifest a willingness or indifference to acting against that reason. The right view seems to be that there are always two ways to go wrong, either by acting against a reason or manifesting a willingness to do so.[12] We might imagine that both Leo and Bobby take aim at Coop hoping to assassinate him. If only one bullet strikes him, we still know both acted wrongfully. We do not have to hunt around two sets of features, one that explains why it is wrong to shoot Coop and another set of features that make it wrong to try to shoot him. As a working hypothesis, let us assume that this dual-demand view is the correct one and see if it can shed some light on epistemic norms and justification.

7.3 EPISTEMIC NORMS

Whatever it is that reasons demand, it will be impossible to say what it takes to meet their demands if we do not know what these reasons are. We know that these reasons will be associated with general norms that tell us what (*pro tanto* or all things considered) duty requires. Often people say that true belief or knowledge is the fundamental norm of belief, saying in

---

[12] I owe this way of putting it to Mark van Roojen, who thinks Philippa Foot once said something to this effect. If she did not, it is good that somebody did.

effect that whatever norms govern belief do so because these norms govern belief:

TN: You ought not believe *p* unless *p*.
KN: You ought not believe *p* unless you know *p*.

There is a strange disconnect in the literature on epistemic norms and justification. While a considerable number of epistemologists are willing to defend the view that KN or TN is the fundamental norm of belief, few are willing to say that truth or knowledge is required for justification. For reasons you might now expect, I think this is deeply problematic.

The first view I want to look at is the evidentialist view according to which justification depends entirely upon relations between your evidence and your beliefs, not on any further conditions external to them. According to the evidentialist, the considerations that bear on whether to believe *p* consist of considerations taken to bear on the truth of *p* and can only consist of such considerations. Considerations that point to the practical benefits of believing *p*, however, do not give reason to believe *p*. At best, they give us reason to manipulate ourselves in ways to try to causally induce the belief that *p*. Why is it that practical considerations never give us reason to believe? What explains the hegemony of evidence in doxastic deliberation?

Here is one possible explanation.[13] First, we assume that TN governs belief.[14] Second, it is supposed to be in virtue of our grasp of this normative truth that considerations taken to be irrelevant to the truth of a claim (e.g., practical considerations) are excluded from deliberation so that only considerations taken to bear on the truth of the relevant proposition are included in doxastic deliberation. Third, nothing can be a reason unless it can figure in reasoning.[15] If we add this additional assumption that a consideration can constitute a reason to believe only if it is capable of being a reason for which we believe, we have our argument for Evidentialism. What we ought to believe is a function of the reasons there are, and considerations unrelated to truth have just been disqualified as potential reasons. Thus, Shah concludes, "only evidence for and against the truth of *p* is relevant to answering the doxastic question whether to believe that *p*."[16]

---

[13] Adler 2002a and Shah 2006 offer this sort of explanation. I do not believe their intention is to defend the view that justification supervenes upon the evidence, only that practical considerations cannot constitute reasons to believe.
[14] Boghossian 2003; Velleman 2000; Wedgwood 2002b; Whiting 2010; and Williams 1973 defend the view that TN governs belief.
[15] Shah 2006, p. 484, attributes this assumption to Williams 1981.
[16] Shah 2006, p. 498.

This is a promising argument for the view that only truth-related considerations constitute reasons to believe, but not for the further evidentialist thesis that conditions that do not supervene upon your evidence have no bearing on the justification of your beliefs. If belief is governed by the truth norm, there is a reason to refrain from believing falsehoods. Whether your beliefs about the external world are false does not supervene upon your evidence. So, the evidentialist cannot say *both* that belief is governed by the truth norm and that only evidence for or against a belief bears on whether to believe some proposition. The evidentialist cannot motivate their view by saying that the truth norm governs belief if they deny that we have reasons to refrain from believing falsehoods. If they say that a belief's justification depends on the evidence and not also on whether a belief is correct, they would have to say that reasons demand less than full conformity.

If TN governs belief, there is a reason not to believe falsehoods since reasons do demand conformity. If that reason is not defeated by some further reason, Factivity$_J$ must be true. Does TN give us conclusive reason to refrain from believing falsehoods? The evidentialist could plausibly say that the reasons provided by the evidence for p give you reason to believe p even if $-p$, but the question is whether such evidential reasons override the reasons we have to conform to TN. I do not think these evidential reasons can override the reasons we have to conform to TN. First, norms do not typically give us overriding reason to violate them. Second, if the reasons provided by the evidence really did override the reasons provided by TN, an outside observer who knows of both reasons should think that the right way to respond would be to believe the falsehood supported by the evidence. Yet, anyone who knows both that $-p$ and knows that some subject's evidence suggests otherwise will appreciate that these reasons do not give overriding reason to believe p. Third, if there were overriding reasons to believe falsehoods, these would have to be reasons that required you to believe. (Otherwise, they would not override.) These reasons would have to be associated with norms that identified positive epistemic duties. Since there are no such duties, there are no such norms, and there are no such reasons.

At this point, the evidentialist might deny that TN is among the norms governing belief.[17] Rather than say that the reasons associated with TN demand less than conformity, they can say that *only* evidential norms

---

[17] See Conee and Feldman 2004.

govern belief.[18] This move avoids one set of problems, but introduces new ones. First, this would undercut an attractive explanation as to why only truth-related considerations can figure in doxastic deliberation. Second, we have seen that the reasons that bear on whether to act do not supervene upon facts about the subject's evidence alone, so there is pressure on the evidentialist to endorse the segregationist view. The evidentialist would have to say that situations will arise in which your judgment that you must Φ is the one that rationality requires even though the reasons require that you refrain from Φ-ing. This view is deeply problematic. Rationality requires us to conform to the enkratic requirement (i.e., rationality requires that if you judge you ought to Φ then you intend to act and do act accordingly).[19] The natural explanation as to why there is such a rational requirement is that the reasons that bear on whether to act and intend bear on whether to believe that you should act.[20] Also, it is important to remember that the primary motivation for Evidentialism is the simple thought that following the evidence is the way to believe rationally. If you think that the rational is the mark of the permissible, you have to endorse Unificationism. The combination of Unificationism and Evidentialism is unattractive for a variety of reasons (e.g., it denies outcome luck and so cannot account for intuitions about reparation, it commits you to relativism, and it leads to skepticism). If, however, you reject Unificationism to avoid these problems, you have to reject the idea that the rational is the mark of the permissible. This would seem to undermine the primary motivation for Evidentialism.

The problem with Evidentialism is that it restricts the scope of epistemic evaluation to relations between a belief and the evidence to the exclusion of further relations between your beliefs and the matters that your beliefs concern. A second view seems to avoid this problem. According to the knowledge account of belief, KN is the fundamental norm of belief.[21] Because knowledge is factive, the knowledge account takes epistemic evaluation to be concerned with more than relations between beliefs and the evidence we have on hand. It would also be concerned with relations between these states of mind and the states of the world they represent.

---

[18] Feldman 1988b says that we might have truth as a kind of goal, but insists that the truth or falsity of a belief has no bearing on what we ought to believe because a belief could be false without our knowing it.

[19] See Broome 2007 for discussion.

[20] This is consistent with the idea that only truth-related considerations bear on whether to believe. The reasons that bear on whether to Φ bear on whether it is true that you should Φ.

[21] For defenses, see Bird 2007; Haddock 2010; Smithies in press; Sutton 2007; and Williamson 2000a.

While this view has the resources to deal with some of the difficulties that arise for the evidentialist, it suffers from structural problems nevertheless.

Typically, those who say that KN is the fundamental norm of belief deny that knowledge is necessary for justified belief. Bird puts it this way:

Anything short of knowledge is failure. But some failures are worse than others. And in particular some failures can be laid at the door of the believer, because the source of failure is one or more of the believer's mental states, and some failures can be ascribed to mischance, in that the failure is due to some mentally extraneous factor. The role of the concept of justification is to mark the difference between these different sources of failure.[22]

The problem with this position is that it either implies that something can be fully justified even if it does not do all that the undefeated reasons require or it assumes that these reasons demand something less than conformity. Surely if knowledge is the norm of belief, there is a reason to refrain from believing what you do not know that constitutes a conclusive reason to refrain from believing unless it is overridden by a sufficiently strong reason to violate the knowledge norm. There are such overriding reasons. We know this because there are no positive epistemic duties and because those who endorse the knowledge account say that KN is the fundamental norm of belief. So, the only way to make sense of this view is to say either that we can successfully justify Φ-ing in the face of undefeated reasons not to Φ or that reasons demand less than conformity. The first option conflicts with the thought that justifications indicate a permissible or right response to undefeated reasons. The second option could only be correct if reasons do not demand conformity. Thus, you either have to deny that knowledge is the norm of belief or accept that a belief's failure to constitute knowledge constitutes a conclusive reason for abandoning that belief. If knowledge is the norm of belief, you cannot justifiably believe what you do not know.

Some have embraced the idea that a justified belief just *is* an item of knowledge, taking this, as I do, to be a consequence of the view that KN is the norm of belief.[23] As it is obscure what norms would do if not establish the permissibility of the beliefs they govern and obscure what a justification would do if it did not indicate which belief conformed with those same norms, the only intelligible form the knowledge account could take is one on which you can only justifiably believe what you know. The problem with this view is not that it is incoherent. The problem with this view is that it delivers the wrong verdicts in Gettier cases. Having just finished her lunch, Audrey hands the waitress a ten-dollar bill. She believes that she has paid her bill. She has paid her bill with genuine currency. However, unbeknown to her, she is dining in the land of fake ten-dollar bills. Although her currency is genuine, she believes it is genuine, and she is not unreasonable in believing this, she does not know she has handed the waitress a genuine ten-dollar bill because there are fake bills in the other diners' pockets that would easily pass for the real thing. So, she does not know that she has really paid her bill. Think about her belief that she has paid her bill. Do we really think, knowing what we know, that there is something to be excused here? If she acted on her belief that what she gave the waitress would cover the check and she should not have believed that, it seems she also should not have handed the money to the waitress. If the waitress knew all of the relevant facts, it is hard to see how the waitress could say that Audrey failed to do something she should not have. She cannot demand an apology or explanation from Audrey. Knowing what we know, it seems she believes permissibly and that her belief is not mistaken. This first point suggests that there was no breach to excuse, much less justify. Thus, KN says there are conclusive reasons to refrain from believing what we actually have no reason not to believe. The second point suggests that belief does not aim at knowledge. If it did, we would either think that beliefs that failed to constitute knowledge for *any* reason ought not be held or would be mistaken, as such beliefs would miss their metaphorical targets. Yet, this is not what we find.

We might sum up the problems for the knowledge account and Evidentialism as follows. We can think of a belief's justification in terms of doing all that the norms governing belief demand. We do all that is demanded if our beliefs conform to the undefeated reasons associated with a norm and have taken all due care to see to this. The problem that the evidentialists face is that it seems that if they take truth to be the norm of belief, they have to insist that the justification of belief involves more than just relations between that belief and the evidence. If, however, they insist that a belief's justification involves just relations between the belief and the evidence, they either have to deny that reasons demand conformity or deny that belief is a state governed by the truth norm. The knowledge account faces a structurally similar problem. If they take knowledge to be the norm of belief, they have to say that if you fail to know for any reason, there is a conclusive reason to abandon the belief. To bring that in line with intuition, they have to say that reasons demand less than full conformity. As reasons do demand conformity and there is less to justification than knowledge, knowledge is not the norm of belief.

It seems that the norms of belief are concerned with more than just relations between beliefs and bodies of evidence but less than that which turns a belief into knowledge. So, what is the norm of belief? I think TN is the fundamental norm of belief. Belief aims at the truth, not knowledge. We can unpack this metaphor in normative terms. True beliefs can do what beliefs are supposed to do. False beliefs cannot. What beliefs are supposed to do is represent how things are so that we might rely on them for the purpose of deliberation.

One of the main obstacles you face if you say that TN is the fundamental norm of belief is that TN seems to be too weak to account for many of our intuitions about justification. For example, some have objected that it cannot explain why we should not believe without evidence.[24] If my objections to the Conformity Account were sound, this objection is baseless. The reasons associated with TN place upon us a pair of related demands. We are required to refrain from believing falsehoods and required to believe responsibly. Since this requires having beliefs backed by the evidence that a responsible person would have if they were to believe, there is no reason to think that a belief's truth suffices for its justification.

We can get a better sense of what it takes to satisfy TN if we consider an example. Audrey runs a story in the local paper saying that Coop has turned to drink because he cannot deal with the pressures of life in the public eye. If Coop has not turned to drink, he can reasonably demand that the paper prints a correction and issues an apology. He has been wronged even if the writers had it on good evidence that their story was accurate. Suppose that the writers had no evidence whatever for thinking that Coop has turned to drink, but he has. Again, if Coop knows that nobody has any reason to think he has turned to drink, he can reasonably complain about that story. He can reasonably complain if the story misrepresents his deeds or makes statements about his deeds that are not grounded in evidence.

Is there a third way to go wrong here? If not, the account is complete. Unfortunately, it seems there is a third way to go wrong. The story is

---

[24] See Sutton 2007 and Vahid 2006.

not quite complete. Coop has turned to drink, but he has managed to keep this secret from everyone. The otherwise reliable Ben tells Audrey that Coop has turned to drink. Audrey runs the story. Coop demands an apology after he shows to Audrey's satisfaction that Ben had no reason to think that Coop had turned to drink. Although Audrey's belief was reasonable and correct, it was based on faulty intelligence and so amends should be made. So, there is a third way for an assertion or a story to go wrong. If beliefs are like assertions, there is a third way for beliefs to go wrong.

Can we explain how there could be a third way to go wrong given just the resources of TN and the idea that reasons place upon us a pair of demands? I think so. If the fundamental norm of belief is the truth norm, the justification of any particular belief depends upon whether it is true and whether it is reasonably held. In the typical case, it would not be surprising if your beliefs had these two features. In abnormal cases, however, it might be surprising that something you reasonably take to be true is true. The fields are filled with rocks disguised to look like sheep. Seeing what you take to be a sheep, you believe there are sheep in the field. You know that where there are sheep there will be wolves nearby. It just so happens that the wolves have come looking for lunch. They were also fooled by the fakes. Your belief is true. We can assume that it is reasonably held. Still, there seems to be but an accidental connection between the facts in light of which your belief is reasonable and the facts in light of which your belief is correct.[25] My inclination is to say that your belief is not justified.

Suppose neuroscientists induced in you a series of hallucinatory experiences indistinguishable from the experience you would have had if you saw a lemon sitting on a plate in optimal viewing conditions. Suppose one of them happens to place a lemon right where it seems to you a lemon is. It might be that your non-inferential belief that there is a lemon right there on the plate is correct and reasonably held. Nevertheless, it seems unjustified. Again, there is more to justification than just reasonably forming a true belief.

To cover these cases, suppose TN is the fundamental norm of belief and that the reasons associated with this norm place upon us a pair of demands. In cases such as these, you take yourself to have solid reasons to believe that there are wolves nearby or that there is a lemon on the plate in front of you. If we took these seemingly solid reasons away, you could not reasonably judge that there would be wolves nearby or that there is a

---

[25] An example modified from Chisholm 1989, p. 93.

lemon on the plate. If you cannot reasonably judge that something is so, you cannot justifiably judge that something is so. So, the reasons (real and counterfeit) that you have are essential to doxastic justification because they are essential to personal justification. The reasons (which might be a mix of real and counterfeit) in light of which your judgments are reasonable led you to the truth, but they led you there in the wrong way. Your reasons led you to the truth without showing you the truth.

There is a principled explanation as to why there is more to justification than rationally held true belief. TN says that (i) you should not believe *p* unless it would be reasonable to take *p* to be true and (ii) you should not believe *p* unless *p* is true. If you satisfy (i), it is reasonable for you to take *p* to be true. It would only be reasonable to do that if it was reasonable for you to take it that your reasons for believing *p* show that *p* is true. If they do that, you satisfy (i) and (ii) and you believe for reasons that show that *p*. Suppose, however, that what you take as your reasons for believing *p* do not show that *p* is true. They merely make it reasonable to take it that *p* is true. In taking these things to show that *p* is true and treating them as your reasons for believing *p*, they do not show that *p* is true and so TN would say that you should not take them to show that *p* is true. Since you should not believe *p* unless you take something to show that you are right in believing *p* and there is nothing that you should take to show that *p*, you cannot justifiably believe *p*. Thus, whenever you satisfy (i) and (ii), you believe for reasons that show that your belief is correct.[26]

If TN is the norm of belief, you can only justifiably believe *p* when the reasons you take to show that you are right do show that you are right.[27] There is an internal dimension to justification because being shown that something is true requires a proper receptivity on your part. Nothing shows you the truth unless it makes it reasonable for someone in your position to accept it. This requirement on doxastic justification should be satisfied if you are personally justified in believing a proposition. To be personally justified in believing *p*, you cannot have any available defeaters and it has to seem to you that what you believe is correct. Whether it seems to you that you are right and are free from any available defeaters turns on what your mental life is like. Whether your meet all of the requirements on doxastic justification, however, depends upon whether the mental states by virtue of which you meet the requirements

---

[26] My argument assumes that the following principle is correct: if you should not Φ unless you also ψ, you should not Φ if you should not ψ.

[27] This is similar to Fogelin's view, which is that justification requires grounds that establish the truth of what you believe. See Fogelin 1994, p. 19.

on personal justification direct your attention to the facts that show that your relevant beliefs are correct.

It would be nice to have an account of what it takes for something to show someone that something is correct. We know what the basic elements are. There has to be an appropriately receptive subject. There has to be something to show the subject. Finally, there has to be something that puts the person and the facts in the right relation. Whether you are related in the appropriate way depends upon whether the connection between you and the facts is sufficiently non-accidental. To complete the account of doxastic justification, we need to say something about the non-accidentality requirement.

Considerable work has been done on anti-luck conditions for knowledge, but what we need is a suitable anti-luck condition for justification.[28] The condition has to meet two desiderata. First, since justification is required for knowledge, you have to satisfy this anti-luck condition in order to have knowledge. Second, since doxastic justification is not sufficient for knowledge, it should be possible to satisfy this anti-luck condition and have a justified belief without having knowledge. Will any of the anti-luck conditions suit our purposes?

Consider sensitivity.[29] If you believe p, you believe p sensitively iff had it not been the case that p, you would not have believed p. It gets some of our cases right. Suppose you believe on the basis of hallucination that there is a lemon on the plate (roughly) where a lemon happens to be. Your belief is both rational and correct. Given that you believe what you do because you take yourself to see something that you cannot see, my inclination is to say that your belief is not justifiably held. Given that you would have held this belief even if the lemon had not been on the plate, your belief is not sensitive. So far, so good.

There are two problems with the sensitivity account. First, the sensitivity account is not sufficiently discriminating. Think about fake-barn cases. It might be that the only barn Coop saw was the only real barn in fake-barn country. It might be that in the nearest world where his belief is false, he believes there are barns in the hills because he saw a fake. Still, his belief is justified. Second, the sensitivity account does not meet one of our desiderata. If the arguments from earlier are correct and you justifiably believe whatever you know, the sensitivity account of justified belief could only be correct if sensitivity were required for knowledge. I

---

[28] See Engel 1992b; Pritchard 2005; and Unger 1968.
[29] For early discussions of sensitivity conditions on knowledge, see Dretske 1971 and Nozick 1981.

know that Agnes does not speak German. (She is clever, but she is a dog.) My belief that Agnes does not speak German is sensitive. (If she did, I would not believe that she did not.) My belief that Agnes does not speak German in secret, however, is insensitive. Nevertheless, I know that she does not speak German in secret.[30]

You might think that the reason intuition causes trouble for the sensitivity account is that when you evaluate a belief to determine if it is justifiably held, you are not terribly concerned about whether your reasons would lead you astray in very remote possibilities. You might doubt that remote possibilities of error threaten justification but worry that nearby possibilities of error do. If so, you might think safety would be a better anti-luck condition for justification. If you believe p, you believe p safely iff you would have believed p only if p.[31] The safety conditional is the contrapositive of the sensitivity conditional. Because subjunctive conditionals do not contrapose, the safety and sensitivity conditionals are not equivalent.[32] Still, the many cases of insensitive belief are cases of unsafe belief and so safety should be able to explain much of the same data that sensitivity is supposed to. To determine whether you safely believe p, we ask whether there are nearby worlds in which you believe p for the sorts of reasons you actually do where it turns out that $\sim p$. In our case of veridical hallucination and inference through a falsehood to the conclusion that there are wolves nearby, there are nearby worlds where your reasons lead you astray. The safety account of justification predicts that beliefs in these cases will not be justified. Because there are no nearby possibilities in which Agnes speaks German, there is no reason to think that my belief that she does not speak German secretly is unsafe. Thus, it avoids an objection to sensitivity.

---

[30] I thought this example was Neta's, but his example involved a cat that spoke Portuguese. The hypothesis that Agnes speaks German *secretly* explains why we would mistakenly believe the hypothesis to be false in the nearest worlds in which it is true. Because of this, the case causes trouble for the weakened sensitivity conditions of the sort DeRose 2010 defends. Another potential objection to the sensitivity account of justification is that justification would not be closed under known entailment if justified beliefs were sensitive beliefs. Since it is controversial whether there are unrestricted closure principles for justification and controversial whether sensitivity is incompatible with closure, I thought it would be best to set these issues aside. For discussion of sensitivity and closure, see Black and Murphy 2007.

[31] This is Sosa's 2007 gloss on the notion.

[32] To see this, suppose multiple assassins have their pistols trained on Coop and pull their triggers simultaneously from close range. Now it might be true that if the first assassin's gun jammed, Coop would have been shot anyway. It would not be true, however, that if Coop had not been shot, the first assassin's gun would not have jammed. See Lewis 1973, p. 35.

I do not think safety satisfies our desiderata because there seem to be cases of unsafe knowledge.[33] If such cases are possible, there can be justified, unsafe belief. Coop is headed to Audrey's costume party, a party that Audrey is hoping to keep secret from deputy Andy. Donna is directing everyone to Audrey's house, which we should assume is nearly impossible to find owing to the fog and the poorly marked roads. Audrey has secretly instructed her that if she sees Andy heading their way she should direct traffic away from the house and the party will be cancelled. Andy has nodded off, so there is no danger of him discovering the party. Coop, however, has decided to disguise himself as Andy. The disguise is realistic enough that it would fool Donna. If Donna spots him, the party will be cancelled and he will be sent off down the wrong road. Moments before Donna can spot him, Coop's wig blows off and so Donna easily recognizes Coop. She gives him the directions to the party. Intuitively, it seems that Coop knows that this is the way to the party. Nevertheless, it seems Coop easily could have formed a false belief on the very basis he formed his correct belief (i.e., testimony from Donna). If Coop knows on the basis of Donna's testimony where the party is, he justifiably believes that the party is where he is heading. Justification does not require safety. Another problem with the safety account is that it does not deliver the right verdict in the fake-barn cases. In nearby worlds, Coop will falsely believe on the basis of seeming to see a barn that he is looking at a barn. While I think Coop can justifiably believe he sees a barn in fake-barn country, I do not think that the safety account delivers this result. Finally, safety will not eliminate deviant connections to the truth. A helpful angel who can predict when you would err without assistance can change the world to fit your mind or whisper in your ear to change your mind. Your beliefs would be safe either way, but only justified if based on angelic testimony.

Comesaña notes that when there are nearby possibilities in which the process you used would have been rendered unreliable, your beliefs could have been reliably produced without being safe.[34] Sometimes it will seem that your unsafe beliefs constitute knowledge. Might a reliability condition do a better job as an anti-luck condition than safety or sensitivity? It is hard to think of examples in which you have knowledge without reliability and not terribly hard to think of examples in which a reasonably

---

[33] I owe this example to Comesaña 2005b. Similar examples are presented in Neta and Rohrbaugh 2004.

[34] Comesaña 2005b, p. 402.

held and reliably formed true belief fails to constitute knowledge. So, it seems that a reliability condition meets our two desiderata. It will not do, however, to say that the justified belief is the reliably produced and reasonably held true belief. Owing to intervening factors it might be that a reasonable, reliably produced, true belief nevertheless is true only as a matter of good luck. So, reliability on its own will not deal with some of the cases of justification undermining lucky connections.

The safety and sensitivity conditions will not work as anti-luck conditions for justification because these conditions are insensitive to a difference between two kinds of knowledge undermining veritic luck, environmental and intervening luck.[35] In cases of environmental luck, the subject is lucky to be right because she is in an environment in which she easily could have been misled. In cases of intervening luck, something intervenes between the exercise of your cognitive abilities and the resulting cognitive success so that you do not succeed through or from your abilities.[36] While I think intervening luck undermines both justification and knowledge, environmental luck seems to undermine knowledge without undermining justification.

Archery cases are helpful for getting a feel for the difference between these two types of luck.[37] Think about a skilled archer who fires at her target. In one case, pranksters flip on a wind machine to try to steer the arrow off target. They also clumsily bump the target so that it moves into the path of the arrow that had been blown off course. The shot might have been skillful and might have hit its target, but the arrow's hitting the target is not a manifestation of the archer's skill. In the second, pranksters try to put force fields around all of the targets and manage to block all the targets but one before the archers take aim. The archer hits the target as she intends and displays great skill. Because she easily could have shot at a target protected by a force field, it seems she is lucky for having hit a target.[38]

Shifting to epistemic cases, think about the difference between the kind of luck present in the case where the subject judges correctly that there will be wolves nearby because she judges incorrectly that there are sheep nearby and the luck exemplified by fake-barn cases. In the former, cognitive success is not from ability. In the latter, there is a real danger of

---

[35] For a discussion of these types of veritic luck, see Pritchard 2005, p. 146.
[36] Pritchard 2008, p. 445.
[37] See Greco 2010; Pritchard 2008; Sosa 2007; and Dennis Whitcomb, "Knowledge, Virtue, and Truth" (unpublished manuscript).
[38] Pritchard 2008.

making a mistake, but the conditions by virtue of which there is a danger of making a mistake do not seem to show that the resulting success is less than a manifestation of your cognitive abilities. The problem with the safety account, the sensitivity account, and the reliability account is that none of them captures the idea that justification depends upon whether the subject's success is due to her abilities.

The cognitive abilities that matter for justification are abilities to identify reasons and respond to them appropriately. When you believe p with non-inferential justification, you correctly believe p through the exercise of, say, a perceptual faculty that makes p evident to you. When you believe p with inferential justification, you correctly believe p on the basis of reasons provided ultimately by non-inferentially justified beliefs and arrive at this belief by means of the exercise of your capacity for reasoning.

Some prefer to think of cognitive abilities as abilities to acquire knowledge.[39] On such a view, if you judge that p without coming to know that p, you did not manifest the same abilities you would have done if you had instead come to know p. One worry I have about this account is that it suggests that whether you exercise a given cognitive ability depends upon factors that are potentially quite remote. Think about Harman's newspaper case. If you judge correctly that the dictator has been assassinated on the basis of what you read in a reliable paper you might not know that the dictator has been assassinated if a sufficient stock of misleading evidence is also made available. If by divine or authorial intervention such evidence is removed, knowledge is restored. Intuitively, I would chalk up success to the same abilities so long as the links between facts, reporter, and the reports you read are held fixed.

If justified beliefs are what I say they are, they are beliefs that Sosa thinks constitute knowledge. If he is right, then the suggestion that you can only justifiably believe p if the correctness of your belief is through your ability to identify and respond to reasons does not satisfy one of my desiderata. This account would collapse the distinction between justification and knowledge. According to Sosa, apt* belief constitutes knowledge. Your belief is apt* iff accurate because adroit, where correctness can be attributed to skill or ability.[40] These abilities will be rooted in something in the individual's faculties (e.g., the ability to identify red things by how they look or rotten things by their smell) or, perhaps, something

---

[39] Millar 2009.

[40] First-order knowledge or animal knowledge is understood as apt* belief. Reflective knowledge, knowing that you believe aptly*, involves apt* belief aptly* noted.

developed through training (e.g., the ability to correctly judge that the structure you see is a barn or to judge that these splotches are a rash). One potential difference between his view and my own is that I think you have reasons for whatever you justifiably believe and that these reasons play in important role in explaining what it takes to believe with justification. Sosa does not emphasize the role that reasons play in his account of knowledge, but this might just be a difference in emphasis as opposed to a substantive difference. If Sosa said that apt* beliefs provided you with reasons and inferential apt* beliefs are formed when you respond properly to the reasons you have, I would agree.

The main differences between Sosa and me seem to be that I doubt that all apt* beliefs constitute knowledge and I suspect he would deny that only apt* beliefs are justified. On his account, the correctness of a belief is attributable to the subject's exercise of her cognitive abilities only if she exercises them in the appropriate conditions. I agree that this is required for justification, otherwise your capacity for identifying reasons and responding when they are made available would not show you that you are in the right. For Sosa, these conditions will either be the conditions normal for the exercise of these abilities or abnormal conditions where the abnormalities can be suitably compensated for.[41] (For example, Audrey's ability to hit the target she intends might not be the ability to hit that target during a tropical storm unless she can compensate for the gale-force winds and still hit her marks reliably.) If I follow his lead and I say that the correctness of Coop's belief in fake-barn country is a manifestation of his cognitive abilities, I have to say that Coop correctly judges that the structure he sees is a barn under normal conditions. Is this the right thing to say?

I confess that my own sense of when conditions are appropriate is a bit unstable, but I think this position is not entirely unmotivated. Suppose you head into a furniture store to look for a table. One of Sosa's jokesters has recently been promoted to store manager and this is what happens:

You see a surface that looks red in ostensibly normal conditions. But it is a kaleidoscope surface controlled by a jokester who also controls the ambient light, and might as easily have presented you with a red-light+white-surface combination as with the actual white-light+red-surface combination. Do you then know the surface you see to be red when he presents you with that good combination, despite the fact that, even more easily, he might have presented you with the bad combination?[42]

---

[41] Sosa 2007, p. 29.   [42] Sosa 2007, p. 31.

The jokester could have easily presented you with the bad combination, but we know that the device was never activated and you were presented with the good combination. Because the device was never activated, Sosa observes that the jokester did not interfere with the normal exercise of your perceptual faculties. While it is true that the conditions easily could have been abnormal, the fact that the conditions could have easily been abnormal does not mean that the conditions actually were abnormal. Suppose that in many stores nearby many more jokesters are activating their devices, laughing as they trick their customers into thinking that the white furniture they see is red. That they are doing so still does not make the conditions for the operation of your perceptual faculties abnormal, but the jokesters are starting to make things look like fake-barn country. If nearby jokesters do not create abnormal conditions, it is not obviously wrong to say that the conditions were normal in fake-barn country. If the conditions are normal, we can say that this is a case where someone had cognitive success from their ability, in which case we could think of this as a case of justification.

It is controversial whether the true beliefs Coop forms in fake-barn country are examples of cognitive success through ability. Greco thinks that they are not. He thinks that Coop does not have the ability to identify fake barns in fake-barn country, so we cannot attribute the correctness of his beliefs to his abilities. If not, I should not say that his belief is justified. This runs contrary to my own intuitions about justification. Moreover, if Greco is right and this is not a case of success through ability, it is not a case of justification without knowledge, so (again) there is a very real risk of undermining the distinction between knowledge and justification.

I face a problem. I need cases of environmental luck to show that there is a distinction between doxastic justification and knowledge. Given my account of doxastic justification, I want to say that in cases of environmental luck, there is cognitive success through ability that is not knowledge. Greco agrees that environmental luck undermines knowledge, but insists that these very same cases are not cases of success from ability. Sosa, on the other hand, insists that these are cases of success from ability and classifies them as cases of knowledge. In order to show that my account does not collapse the distinction between justification and knowledge, I need to show that knowledge is not just cognitive success from ability (KSA).

Pritchard and Whitcomb argue that KSA is mistaken and that the ability condition on knowledge does not give Greco and Sosa the anti-luck condition they need.[43] If they are right, then perhaps I can avoid the collapse worry. Sosa's ability condition could provide me with the anti-luck condition I need for justification without thereby providing a suitable anti-luck condition for knowledge. Whitcomb offers an example that I think helps us see why KSA is mistaken:

> Weights: Hoodlums at the shooting range put weights in most of the arrows' tips. Champion archers shoot, and due to the weights they miss. Audrey gets to shoot, and by luck she gets the one quiver of unweighted arrows. Through skills that almost always bring target hits, she makes those hits. Her shots are successful and, moreover, they are successful through virtue.[44]

He says that this case is a case of practical success from ability and that it is analogous to Harman's newspaper case. (Pritchard thinks that the case described earlier in which the targets are protected by force fields is analogous to the fake-barn case.[45]) Assuming that this is a case of practical success that manifests the agent's abilities (which seems quite intuitive), we can state the Pritchard–Whitcomb argument against KSA as follows:

1. Weights and Fake Barns are analogous in all relevant respects.
2. Weights is a case of success from ability.
3. (Therefore) Fake Barns is a case of success from ability.
4. Fake Barns is not a case of knowledge.
5. (Therefore) Fake Barns is a case of success from ability without knowledge.

Because they defend KSA, Greco and Sosa have to reject (5) and reject one of the argument's premises. Greco rejects (1).[46] Sosa rejects (4).[47]

Greco's strategy for responding to the Pritchard–Whitcomb argument is to say that the practical and epistemic cases are not analogous. Abilities, cognitive or otherwise, should be understood as dispositions to reliably bring about some result under suitable circumstances. Cognitive abilities are understood as dispositions to bring about true beliefs in appropriate conditions and environments. Practical abilities can be understood as dispositions to bring about intended ends in appropriate conditions and environments. While Coop might have the ability to identify barns in, say, real-barn country, Greco says that he does not have the ability to identify them in fake-barn country. As such, judging correctly that the

---

[43] Pritchard 2008 and Whitcomb, "Knowledge, Virtue, and Truth."
[44] Whitcomb's example is discussed in Greco 2010, p. 86.
[45] Pritchard 2008.   [46] Greco 2010, p. 88.   [47] Sosa 2007, p. 96.

structure he sees is a barn is not success due to ability, just as, say, Coop hitting a baseball blindfolded cannot be attributed to his ability to hit baseballs.

As for Audrey's shot, he says this:

> The ability to hit a target, like any ability, is defined relative to conditions that are appropriate for that sort of ability. In particular, we do not require that an archer is reliable (relative to an environment) in conditions involving arrow-weighting hoodlums. Accordingly, worlds where meddling hoodlums affect performance are not deemed relevant to determine whether [someone] has the ability in question, even if meddling hoodlums are in [her] actual environment ... This is similar to Jeter's ability to hit baseballs in Yankee Stadium – it does not matter whether there is some trickster in the stadium who could easily shut off the lights.[48]

It is not clear to me whether our intuitions about the fake-barns case are due to the fact that we think Coop does not have the cognitive ability to identify barns in the conditions or environment in which he forms his belief. We can describe the case that way, but it is not obvious to me that we have to in order to elicit the relevant intuition. Perhaps the best way to show that there could be cases of epistemic success from ability that are analogous to practical cases of success from ability and that threaten KSA is to focus on Weights.

Greco agrees that when Audrey hits the target she intends this is a case of success from ability. While he thinks that the Audrey's shot is not analogous to Coop's belief, I think he would think that if Audrey had beliefs about whether her arrows will hit her intended targets that these beliefs will be analogous to Coop's beliefs. So, let's think about Audrey's beliefs in Weights. In drawing back the string, she thinks to herself that if she aims just like this while pulling the string back just like so that she will hit her mark if she releases the string. If Audrey truly is a skilled archer it might be that she would readjust her shot if she did not believe this. I want to ask two questions about her means–end belief. Her means–end belief is correct in the case we described. Is it a case of cognitive success from ability? Is it a case of knowledge?

To keep things clear, consider three propositions:

6. Audrey's hitting the target is successful through her ability.
7. Audrey's means–end belief is successful through her ability.
8. Audrey's means–end belief constitutes knowledge.

---

[48] Greco 2010, p. 87.

My intuition, which I think Pritchard and Whitcomb share, is that while (6) and (7) are true, (8) is not. I expect that Greco would agree that (8) is mistaken. Given his commitment to KSA, he has to reject (7). I think he should accept (6). Not only is it intuitive, his objection to the Pritchard–Whitcomb argument was that the cases are not analogous. Since he rejects (1), he should concede that there can be cases of practical success from ability where the agent's actions are guided by beliefs that are not an example of cognitive success from ability. Perhaps the four of us can agree that her belief does not constitute knowledge because she easily could have drawn a weighted arrow, in which case her belief would have been mistaken and she would have failed to bring about her intended end in the way she intended. The problem with Greco's position is that (6) would only be true if (7) were true.

If Audrey's shot truly is a case of success from ability, there should be no principled objection to saying that she hit her intended target intentionally. Assume she did hit her target intentionally. Let's think about how things have to be for her to hit her intended targets intentionally. If things had gone differently and she had grabbed a weighted arrow, she would have had a false means–end belief. If she had a false means–end belief, one of two things would have happened. She would have missed her mark or she would have hit her mark without hitting it in the way she intended to. Either way, she would not have hit her mark intentionally because she would not have had the necessary control over whether her intended ends would be realized.

While you will not intentionally Φ by ψ-ing when you act with the intention to Φ by ψ-ing and believe falsely that you will Φ by ψ-ing, you do not regain the necessary control simply by forming a true means–end belief and acting on it. Suppose Audrey grabbed a weighted arrow, fired, and the arrow cut just the path towards the target that she intended. Suppose it did this because the arrows were weighted with iron and a powerful magnet was placed just behind the spot that Audrey intended to hit. She hit what she intended to hit, her means–end belief might well have been true, but she knew nothing about the magnet and she did not intentionally hit her mark.

What does it take to put Audrey back in control if not a true means–end belief? Suppose Audrey needs to get into the safe, believes for no reason whatever that the combination to the safe is 12–34–56, and she unlocks the safe acting on her baseless belief. We would not say that she intentionally punched in the correct combination. Too much luck was involved. We might say that if she has a correct means–end belief that is rationally held we can deal with this case, but there are more cases in the offing that cause trouble for this proposal.

Suppose Audrey had excellent evidence that the combination was 12–34–56. Coop told her that this was the combination on Monday. Unfortunately, Coop was mistaken on Monday when he said this. On Monday, the combination was 12–34–55. The note that he fished from Ben's coat pocket with the combination was smudged. Fearing that Coop discovered the combination to the safe Ben changed the combination moments before Audrey entered his office to 12–34–56. She punched in the correct code believing reasonably and correctly that the code was correct, but it still seems she did not intentionally enter the correct code. The connection between what she intended to do and what it would take for her to bring about what she intended seems too accidental for us to say that she had the right kind of control to have brought about her intended end intentionally.[49]

What do we need to add so that the agent who acts on a means–end belief brings about her intended end intentionally? Knowledge would do the trick.[50] If Audrey knew that she would hit the target by firing in just the way she did, she would hit her target intentionally. If she knew that by typing in 12–34–56, the safe would open, we could say she intentionally entered in the right combination. If nothing short of knowledge will do the trick, however, Greco's defense of KSA is bound to fail. If nothing short of knowledge would do, we would have to say that (6) is true in Weights only because (8) is. Remember that Greco rejects (7) and (8). Thus, he needs to explain how Audrey hitting the target could be a case of success from ability if the correctness of the means–end beliefs that guided her actions was not itself a manifestation of her cognitive abilities. I think it cannot be done. When we think that the correctness of the agent's means–end belief is not an instance of cognitive success through ability, we will be disinclined to say that the actions guided by these beliefs will be cases of success from ability. Thus, it seems (6) and (7) stand or fall together.

For his part, Sosa might agree that (7) is correct. He responds to the Pritchard–Whitcomb argument against KSA by denying that environmental luck undermines knowledge. Since he rejects (4), he might accept

---

[49] See Mele and Moser 1994. [50] Gibbons 2001.

(6)–(8).[51] If there is a close enough conceptual connection between knowledge and intentional action, this would be a point in his favor. Is the knowledge so intimately connected to intentional action that (6) and (7) would commit us to (8)?

Few people think that you can only intentionally Φ if you act on your intention to Φ in the knowledge that you will succeed. As Davidson observed, you might intentionally produce ten copies by pressing hard on the carbon paper while you write even if you do not believe that you can produce that many copies.[52] If you can intentionally Φ without believing you will, surely you can intentionally Φ without knowing you will. There is an important difference between Davidson's case and Weights. Audrey believes she will succeed. In most of the cases where an agent acts on a means–end belief that does not constitute knowledge, we do not say that the agent intentionally brought her end about. Moreover, there is the linguistic oddity of saying that Audrey hit the target intentionally in just the spot she believed she would hit but did not know that she would hit the target.

We have seen before that we often use 'knows' to refer to beliefs that fall short of knowledge, so perhaps the linguistic oddity is not all that bothersome. The main difficulty with Sosa's position seems to be that it is hard on intuition. Does Audrey really know that her arrows will hit their mark if most of the arrows at the range have been weighted? I think not. Perhaps cases of environmental luck show us two things. First, they show that there is more to knowledge than cognitive success from ability. Second, they show that something less than knowledge can guide your actions when you bring about your intended ends intentionally. The

[51] Sosa 2007, p. 96. Why do we think Coop does not have knowledge in fake-barn cases? Sosa (2007, p. 32) suggests that in cases of environmental luck, we can have apt* belief without being in a position to aptly* believe that our relevant first-order beliefs are apt*. Thus, environmental luck undermines higher-order knowledge, but not first-order knowledge, and we mistakenly take first-order knowledge to be undermined because we rightly register that something is amiss in these cases. Battaly 2009 argues that Sosa's explanation as to how we could be in a position to believe aptly* without being in a position to aptly* believe we aptly* believe in the kaleidoscope case fails. If she is right, this causes trouble for Sosa's treatment of Fake Barns. Sosa says that if you believe *p* correctly, the correctness of that belief is attributable to a competence only if it derives from an exercise of that competence under suitable conditions, and an exercise under these conditions would not have easily resulted in a false belief (2007, p. 33). If you cannot have second-order knowledge because the jokester in control of the kaleidoscope prevents you from satisfying the second conjunct in believing that your perceptual belief is apt*, it would also prevent your first-order perceptual belief from being apt*. If her criticism is sound, Sosa has not shown that he can accommodate the intuition that something is amiss in his case by arguing that we only lack reflective or second-order knowledge.

[52] Davidson 1980, p. 92.

environmental luck does not prevent you from intentionally achieving your ends because these are not cases in which a deviant causal chain links together your attempt and your success. We can see your achieving your end as something under your control or something that manifests your abilities. Environmental luck undermines knowledge, however, because in cases of environmental luck there is a real danger of forming a false belief. If our intuitions about these cases are not to be trusted and it turns out that knowledge is success from cognitive ability, I have failed to show that justification is an externalist notion distinct from knowledge. It would nevertheless be the externalist notion that I have argued it is.

References

Adler, Jonathan. 2002a. *Belief's Own Ethics*. MIT Press.

2002b. Akratic Believing? *Philosophical Studies* 110: 1–27.

Alston, William. 1989. *Epistemic Justification*. Cornell University Press.

1993. Epistemic Desiderata. *Philosophy and Phenomenological Research* 53: 527–51.

Alvarez, Maria. 2009. Acting Intentionally and Acting for a Reason. *Inquiry* 52: 293–305.

2010. *Kinds of Reasons*. Oxford University Press.

Aristotle. 2009. *Nichomachean Ethics*, trans. W. D. Ross. Oxford University Press.

Armstrong, D. M. 1963. Is Introspective Knowledge Incorrigible? *Philosophical Review* 72: 417–32.

1973. *Belief, Truth, and Knowledge*. Cambridge University Press.

Audi, Robert. 1986. Acting for Reasons. *Philosophical Review* 95: 511–46.

1993. *The Structure of Justification*. Cambridge University Press.

1995. Memorial Justification. *Philosophical Topics* 23: 31–45

2001. An Internalist Theory of Normative Grounds. *Philosophical Topics* 29: 19–46.

Austin, J. L. 1956. A Plea for Excuses. *Proceedings of the Aristotelian Society* 57: 1–30.

Bach, Kent. 1985. A Rationale for Reliabilism. *The Monist* 68: 246–63.

Baron, Marcia. 1995. *Kantian Ethics Almost without Apology*. Cornell University Press.

Battaly, Heather. 2009. Review of Ernest Sosa, *A Virtue Epistemology: Apt Belief and Reflective Knowledge*. *Analysis* 69: 382–5.

Bennett, Jonathan. 1988. *Events and Their Names*. Hackett.

1995. *The Act Itself*. Oxford University Press.

Bergmann, Michael. 2006. *Justification without Awareness*. Oxford University Press.

Bird, Alexander. 2007. Justified Judging. *Philosophy and Phenomenological Research* 74: 81–110.

Black, Tim and Peter Murphy. 2007. In Defense of Sensitivity. *Synthese* 154: 53–71.

Boghossian, Paul. 2003. The Normativity of Content. *Philosophical Issues* 13: 31–45.

BonJour, Laurence. 1980. Externalist Theories of Empirical Knowledge. *Midwest Studies in Philosophy* 5: 53–73.

1985. *The Structure of Empirical Knowledge*. Harvard University Press.

2002. Internalism and Externalism. In P. Moser (ed.), *The Oxford Handbook of Epistemology*. Oxford University Press, pp. 234–64.

Bradley, Ben. 2009. *Well-Being and Death*. Oxford University Press.

Brewer, Bill. 1999. *Perception and Reason*. Oxford University Press.

Brink, David. 1997. Kantian Rationalism: Inescapability, Authority, and Supremacy. In G. Cullity and B. Gaut (eds.), *Ethics and Practical Reason*. Oxford University Press, pp. 255–93.

Broome, John. 1999. Normative Requirements. *Ratio* 12: 398–419.

2007. Does Rationality Consist in Responding Correctly to Reasons? *Journal of Moral Philosophy* 4: 349–74.

Brown, Jessica. 2008. Subject-Sensitive Invariantism and the Knowledge Norm for Practical Reasoning. *Noûs* 42: 167–89.

Brueckner, Anthony. 1996. Deontologism and Internalism in Epistemology. *Noûs* 30: 527–36.

2009. E = K and Perceptual Knowledge. In P. Greenough and D. Pritchard (eds.), *Williamson on Knowledge*. Oxford University Press, pp. 5–12.

Burge, Tyler. 1979. Individualism and the Mental. *Midwest Studies in Philosophy* 4: 73–121.

Byrne, Alex and Heather Logue. 2008. Either/Or. In A. Haddock and F. Macpherson (eds.), *Disjunctivism: Perception, Action, and Knowledge*. Oxford University Press, pp. 57–94.

Carlson, Erik. 1995. *Consequentialism Reconsidered*. Kluwer.

Chisholm, Roderick. 1988. The Indispensability of Internal Justification. *Synthese* 74: 285–96.

1989. *Theory of Knowledge*, 3rd edn. Prentice-Hall.

Chuard, Philippe and Nicholas Southwood. 2009. Epistemic Norms without Voluntary Control. *Noûs* 43: 599–632.

Cohen, Stewart. 1984. Justification and Truth. *Philosophical Studies* 46: 279–95.

1988. How to Be a Fallibilist. *Philosophical Perspectives* 2: 91–123.

1999. Contextualism, Skepticism, and the Structure of Reasons. *Philosophical Perspectives* 13: 57–89.

Cohen, Stewart and Keith Lehrer. 1983. Justification, Truth, and Coherence. *Synthese* 55: 191–207.

Collins, Arthur. 1997. The Psychological Reality of Reasons. *Ratio* 10: 108–23.

Comesaña, Juan. 2002. The Diagonal and the Demon. *Philosophical Studies* 110: 249–66.

2005a. Justified versus Warranted Perceptual Belief: A Case against Disjunctivism. *Philosophy and Phenomenological Research* 71: 367–83.

2005b. Unsafe Knowledge. *Synthese* 146: 395–404.

Comesaña, Juan and Holly Kantin. 2010. Is Evidence Knowledge? *Philosophy and Phenomenological Research* 80: 447–54.

Conee, Earl. 2007. Disjunctivism and Anti-Skepticism. *Philosophical Issues* 17: 16–36.

Conee, Earl and Richard Feldman. 2001. Internalism Defended. *American Philosophical Quarterly* 38: 1–18.

2004. *Evidentialism*. Oxford University Press.

2008. Evidence. In Q. Smith (ed.), *Epistemology: New Essays*. Oxford University Press, pp. 83–104.

2011. Replies. In T. Dougherty (ed.), *Evidentialism and Its Discontents*. Oxford University Press, pp. 283–324.

Cruz, Joe and John Pollock. 2004. The Chimerical Appeal of Epistemic Externalism. In R. Schantz (ed.), *The Externalist Challenge*. De Gruyter, pp. 125–42.

Dancy, Jonathan. 1995. Why There Is Really No Such Thing as the Theory of Motivation. *Proceedings of the Aristotelian Society* 95: 1–18.

2000. *Practical Reality*. Oxford University Press.

2004. *Ethics without Principles*. Oxford University Press.

Darley, John and Paul Robinson. 1998. Testing Competing Theories of Justification. *North Carolina Law Review* 76: 1095–143.

Davidson, Donald. 1980. *Essays on Actions and Events*. Oxford University Press.

2001. *Subjective, Intersubjective, Objective*. Oxford University Press.

de Almeida, Claudio. 2001. What Moore's Paradox Is About. *Philosophy and Phenomenological Research* 62: 33–58.

DePaul, Michael. 2004. Truth Consequentialism, Withholding, and Proportioning Belief to the Evidence. *Philosophical Issues* 14: 91–112.

DeRose, Keith. 1991. Epistemic Possibilities. *Philosophical Review* 100: 581–605.

1995. Solving the Skeptical Problem. *Philosophical Review* 104: 1–52.

2002. Assertion, Knowledge, and Context. *Philosophical Review* 111: 167–203.

2010. Insensitivity Is Back, Baby! *Philosophical Perspectives* 24: 161–87.

Dougherty, Trent. 2011. In Defense of Propositionalism about Evidence. In T. Dougherty (ed.), *Evidentialism and Its Discontents*. Oxford University Press, pp. 226–35.

Dougherty, Trent and Patrick Rysiew. 2009. Fallibilism, Epistemic Possibility, and Concessive Knowledge Attributions. *Philosophy and Phenomenological Research* 78: 123–32.

Douven, Igor. 2006. Assertion, Knowledge, and Rational Credibility. *Philosophical Review* 115: 449–85.

Dreher, John. 1974. Evidence and Justified Belief. *Philosophical Studies* 25: 435–9.

Dretske, Fred. 1971. Conclusive Reasons. *Australasian Journal of Philosophy* 49: 1–22.

Engel, Mylan. 1992a. Personal and Doxastic Justification. *Philosophical Studies* 67: 133–51.

1992b. Is Epistemic Luck Compatible with Knowledge? *Southern Journal of Philosophy* 30: 59–75.

Fantl, Jeremy and Matt McGrath. 2009. *Knowledge in an Uncertain World*. Oxford University Press.

Feldman, Richard. 1974. An Alleged Defect in Gettier Counter-Examples. *Australasian Journal of Philosophy* 52: 68–92.

1988a. Subjective and Objective Justification in Ethics and Epistemology. *The Monist* 71: 405–19.

1988b. Epistemic Obligations. *Philosophical Perspectives* 2: 235–56.

2000. The Ethics of Belief. *Philosophy and Phenomenological Research* 60: 667–95.

2004. Foundational Beliefs and Empirical Possibilities. *Philosophical Issues* 14: 132–48.

Field, Hartry. 1998. Epistemological Nonfactualism and the Apriority of Logic. *Philosophical Studies* 92: 1–24.

Firth, Roderick. 1981. Epistemic Merit, Intrinsic and Instrumental. *Proceedings and Addresses of the American Philosophical Association* 55: 5–23.

Fitelson, Branden. In press. Evidence of Evidence Is Not (Necessarily) Evidence. *Analysis.*

Fogelin, Robert. 1994. *Pyrrhonian Reflections on Knowledge and Justification.* Oxford University Press.

Foley, Richard. 1987. *The Theory of Epistemic Rationality.* Harvard University Press.

2001. The Foundational Role of Epistemology in a General Theory of Rationality. In A. Fairweather and L. Zagzebski (eds.), *Virtue Epistemology: Essays on Epistemic Virtue and Responsibility.* Oxford University Press, pp. 214–31.

Foot, Philippa. 1972. Morality as a System of Hypothetical Imperatives. *Philosophical Review* 81: 305–16.

1985. Utilitarianism and the Virtues. *Mind* 94: 196–209.

Fumerton, Richard. 1995. *Metaepistemology and Skepticism.* Rowman and Littlefield.

Gardner, John. 2005. Wrongs and Faults. *Review of Metaphysics* 59: 95–132.

2007. *Offenses and Defenses.* Oxford University Press.

Gemes, Ken. 2009. A Refutation of Global Scepticism. *Analysis* 69: 218–19.

Gettier, Edmund. 1963. Is Justified True Belief Knowledge? *Analysis* 23: 121–3.

Gibbons, John. 2001. Knowledge in Action. *Philosophy and Phenomenological Research* 62: 579–600.

2006. Access Externalism. *Mind* 115: 19–39.

2009. You Gotta Do What You Gotta Do. *Noûs* 43: 157–77.

2010. Things That Make Things Reasonable. *Philosophy and Phenomenological Research* 81: 335–61.

Ginet, Carl. 1975. *Knowledge, Perception, and Memory.* Reidel.

1990. Justification: It Need Not Cause but It Must Be Accessible. *Journal of Philosophical Research* 15: 93–107.

Ginsborg, Hannah. 2006. Reasons for Belief. *Philosophy and Phenomenological Research* 72: 286–318.

Goldman, Alvin. 1976. Discrimination and Perceptual Knowledge. *Journal of Philosophy* 73: 771–91.

1979. What Is Justified Belief? In G. Pappas (ed.), *Justification and Knowledge.* Reidel, pp. 1–23.

1980. The Internalist Conception of Justification. *Midwest Studies in Philosophy* 5: 27–52.

1986. *Epistemology and Cognition.* Harvard University Press.
1988. Strong and Weak Justification. *Philosophical Perspectives* 2: 51–69.
1993. Epistemic Folkways and Scientific Epistemology. *Philosophical Issues* 3: 271–85.
1999a. Internalism Exposed. *Journal of Philosophy* 96: 271–93.
1999b. *Knowledge in a Social World.* Oxford University Press.
2002. *Pathways to Knowledge: Private and Public.* Oxford University Press.
2009a. Internalism, Externalism, and the Architecture of Justification. *Journal of Philosophy* 106: 309–38.
2009b. Williamson on Knowledge and Evidence. In P. Greenough and D. Pritchard (eds.), *Williamson on Knowledge.* Oxford University Press, pp. 73–92.
Goldman, Alvin and Erik Olsson. 2009. Reliabilism and the Value of Knowledge. In A. Haddock, A. Millar, and D. Pritchard (eds.), *Epistemic Value.* Oxford University Press, pp. 19–42.
Graham, Peter. 2010. Theorizing Justification. In J. Campbell, M. O'Rourke, and H. Silverstein (eds.), *Knowledge and Skepticism.* MIT Press, pp. 45–71.
Greco, John. 2000. *Putting Skeptics in Their Place.* Cambridge University Press.
2005. Justification Is Not Internal. In E. Sosa and M. Steup (eds.), *Contemporary Debates in Epistemology.* Blackwell, pp. 257–70.
2010. *Achieving Knowledge: A Virtue-Theoretic Account of Epistemic Normativity.* Cambridge University Press.
Haddock, Adrian. 2010. Knowledge and Action. In A. Haddock, A. Millar, and D. Pritchard, *The Nature and Value of Knowledge: Three Investigations.* Oxford University Press, pp. 191–259.
Harman, Gilbert. 1973. *Thought.* Princeton University Press.
Hawthorne, John. 2004. *Knowledge and Lotteries.* Oxford University Press.
Hawthorne, John and Jason Stanley. 2008. Knowledge and Action. *Journal of Philosophy* 105: 571–90.
Herman, Barbara. 1993. *The Practice of Moral Judgment.* Harvard University Press.
Hieronymi, Pamela. 2005. The Wrong Kind of Reasons. *Journal of Philosophy* 102: 37–57.
2008. Responsibility for Believing. *Synthese* 16: 357–73.
Hooker, Brad. 2000. *Ideal Code, Real World.* Oxford University Press.
Horder, Jeremy. 2004. *Excusing Crime.* Oxford University Press.
Hornsby, Jennifer. 2007. Knowledge in Action. In A. Leist (ed.), *Action in Context.* De Gruyter, pp. 285–302.
Huemer, Michael. 2001. *Skepticism and the Veil of Perception.* Rowman and Littlefield.
2006. Phenomenal Conservatism and the Internalist Intuition. *American Philosophical Quarterly* 43: 147–58.
2007a. Compassionate Phenomenal Conservatism. *Philosophy and Phenomenological Research* 74: 30–55.

2007b. Moore's Paradox and the Norm of Belief. In S. Nuccetelli and G. Seay (eds.), *Themes from G. E. Moore*. Oxford University Press, pp. 142–58.

Hursthouse, Rosalind. 1991. Arational Actions. *Journal of Philosophy* 88: 57–68.

Husak, Doug. 1999. Conflicts of Justification. *Law and Philosophy* 18: 41–68.

Hyman, John. 1999. How Knowledge Works. *Philosophical Quarterly* 49: 433–51.

2006. Knowledge and Evidence. *Mind* 115: 891–916.

Jackson, Frank. 1991. Decision-Theoretic Consequentialism and the Nearest and Dearest Objection. *Ethics* 10: 461–82.

Jacobson, Stephen. 1997. Externalism and Action-Guiding Epistemic Norms. *Synthese* 110: 381–97.

Kelly, Thomas. 2008. Evidence: Fundamental Concepts and the Phenomenal Conception. *Philosophy Compass* 3: 933–55.

Kolodny, Nico. 2005. Why Be Rational? *Mind* 114: 509–63.

Korcz, Keith. 2000. The Causal-Doxastic Theory of the Basing Relation. *Canadian Journal of Philosophy* 30: 525–50.

Kornblith, Hilary. 2001. *Epistemology: Internalism and Externalism*. Blackwell.

Kvanvig, Jonathan. 2003. *The Value of Knowledge and the Pursuit of Understanding*. Cambridge University Press.

2007. Propositionalism and the Metaphysics of Experience. *Philosophical Issues* 17: 165–78.

2009. Assertion, Knowledge, and Lotteries. In P. Greenough and D. Pritchard (eds.), *Williamson on Knowledge*. Oxford University Press, pp. 140–61.

Kvanvig, Jonathan and Christopher Menzel. 1990. The Basic Notion of Justification. *Philosophical Studies* 59: 235–61.

Lackey, Jennifer. 2007. Norms of Assertion. *Noûs* 41: 594–626.

Langsam, Harold. 2002. Consciousness, Experience, and Justification. *Canadian Journal of Philosophy* 31: 1–28.

2008. Rationality, Justification, and the Internalism/Externalism Debate. *Erkenntnis* 68: 79–101.

Lemos, Noah. 2007. *An Introduction to the Theory of Knowledge*. Cambridge University Press.

Lemos, Ramon. 1980. Duty and Ignorance. *Southern Journal of Philosophy* 18: 301–12.

Leplin, Jarret. 2009. *A Theory of Epistemic Justification*. Springer.

Lewis, David. 1973. *Counterfactuals*. Blackwell.

Littlejohn, Clayton. 2008. From E = K to Scepticism? *Philosophical Quarterly* 58: 679–84.

2009. On Treating Something as a Reason for Action. *Journal of Ethics and Social Philosophy*, www.jesp.org/articles/download/DiscussionNoteClayton Littlejohn.pdf, accessed January 4, 2012.

In press. Concessive Knowledge Attributions and Fallibilism. *Philosophy and Phenomenological Research*.

Lord, Errol. 2008. Dancy on Acting for the Right Reason. *Journal of Ethics and Social Philosophy*, www.jesp.org/articles/download/ErrolLordDiscussion.pdf, accessed January 4, 2012.

Lowy, Catherine. 1978. Gettier's Notion of Justification. *Mind* 87: 105–8.
Lyons, David. 1965. *Forms and Limits of Consequentialism*. Oxford University Press.
McDowell, John. 1978. Are Moral Requirements Hypothetical Imperatives? *Proceedings of the Aristotelian Society, Supplementary Volumes* 52: 13–29.
  1995. Knowledge and the Internal. *Philosophy and Phenomenological Research* 55: 877–93.
  1997. *Mind and World*. Harvard University Press.
  1998. Criteria, Defeasibility, and Knowledge. In *Meaning, Knowledge, and Reality*. Harvard University Press, pp. 369–95.
  2008. The Disjunctive Conception of Experience as Material for a Transcendental Argument. In A. Haddock and F. Macpherson (eds.), *Disjunctivism: Perception, Action, and Knowledge*. Oxford University Press, pp. 376–90.
McGlynn, Aidan. In press. Believing Things Unknown. *Noûs*.
McHugh, Conor. In press. Epistemic Deontology and Voluntariness. *Erkenntnis*.
McKinsey, Michael. 1991. Anti-Individualism and Privileged Access. *Analysis* 51: 9–16.
McNaughton, David. 1996. An Unconnected Heap of Duties? *Philosophical Quarterly* 46: 433–47.
Madison, Brent. 2010. Is Justification Knowledge? *Journal of Philosophical Research* 35: 173–91.
Maher, Patrick. 1996. Subjective and Objective Confirmation. *Philosophy of Science* 63: 149–74.
Maitzen, Stephen. 1995. Our Errant Epistemic Aim. *Philosophy and Phenomenological Research* 55: 869–76.
Majors, Brad and Sarah Sawyer. 2005. The Epistemological Argument for Content Externalism. *Philosophical Perspectives* 19: 257–80.
Matheson, Jonathan and Jason Rogers. 2011. Bergmann's Dilemma: Exit Strategies for Internalists. *Philosophical Studies* 152: 55–80
Mele, Al and Paul Moser. 1994. Intentional Action. *Noûs* 28: 39–68.
Mellor, D. H. 1988. *The Facts of Causation*. Routledge.
Menzies, Peter. 1989. A Unified Account of Causal Relata. *Australasian Journal of Philosophy* 67: 59–83.
Millar, Alan. 1991. *Reasons and Experience*. Oxford University Press.
  2000. The Scope of Perceptual Knowledge. *Philosophy* 75: 73–88.
  2009. What Is It That Cognitive Abilities Are Abilities to Do? *Acta Analytica* 24: 223–36.
  2010. Knowledge and Recognition. In A. Haddock, A. Millar, and D. Pritchard, *The Nature and Value of Knowledge: Three Investigations*. Oxford University Press, pp. 91–190.
Miller, Christian. 2008. Motivation in Agents. *Noûs* 42: 222–66.
Moore, G. E. 1993. *Principia Ethica*. Cambridge University Press.
Moore, Michael. 1997. *Placing Blame*. Oxford University Press.
Moser, Paul. 1991. *Knowledge and Evidence*. Cambridge University Press.

Müller, O. L. 2003. *Wirklichkeit ohne Illusionen*, vol. 1. Mentis.

Nelkin, Dana. 2000. The Lottery Paradox, Knowledge, and Rationality. *Philosophical Review* 109: 373–409.

Nelson, Mark. 2002. What Justification Could Not Be. *International Journal of Philosophical Studies* 10: 265–81.

2010. We Have No Positive Epistemic Duties. *Mind* 119: 83–102.

Neta, Ram. 2008. What Evidence Do You Have? *British Journal for the Philosophy of Science* 59: 89–119.

2009. Treating Something as a Reason for Action. *Noûs* 43: 684–99.

Neta, Ram and Duncan Pritchard. 2007. McDowell and the New Evil Genius. *Philosophy and Phenomenological Research* 74: 381–96.

Neta, Ram and Guy Rohrbaugh. 2004. Luminosity and the Safety of Knowledge. *Pacific Philosophical Quarterly* 85: 396–406.

Nozick, Robert. 1981. *Philosophical Explanations*. Harvard University Press.

Owens, David. 2000. *Reason without Freedom*. Routledge.

Parfit, Derek. 1997. Reasons and Motivation. *Proceedings of the Aristotelian Society, Supplementary Volumes* 71: 99–130.

Peacocke, Christopher. 2004. *The Realm of Reason*. Oxford University Press.

Plantinga, Alvin. 1993. *Warrant: The Current Debate*. Oxford University Press.

Pollock, John. 1974. *Knowledge and Justification*. Princeton University Press.

1987. Epistemic Norms. *Synthese* 71: 61–95.

Pollock, John and Joseph Cruz. 1999. *Contemporary Theories of Knowledge*. Rowman and Littlefield.

Pollock, John and Anthony Gillies. 2000. Belief Revision and Epistemology. *Synthese* 122: 69–92.

Pritchard, Duncan. 2005. *Epistemic Luck*. Oxford University Press.

2007. Recent Work on Epistemic Value. *American Philosophical Quarterly* 44: 85–110.

2008. Greco on Knowledge: Virtues, Contexts, Achievements. *Philosophical Quarterly* 58: 437–47.

2010. Knowledge and Understanding. In A. Haddock, A. Millar, and D. Pritchard, *The Nature and Value of Knowledge: Three Investigations*. Oxford University Press, pp. 3–90.

Pryor, James. 2000. The Skeptic and the Dogmatist. *Noûs* 34: 517–49.

Rawls, John. 1955. Two Concepts of Rules. *Philosophical Review* 64: 3–32.

1971. *A Theory of Justice*. Harvard University Press.

Raz, Joseph 1990. *Practical Reason and Norms*. Oxford University Press.

1999. *Engaging Reason*. Oxford University Press.

Reynolds, Stephen. 2002. Testimony, Knowledge, and Epistemic Goals. *Philosophical Studies* 110: 139–61.

Riggs, Wayne. 2008. The Value Turn in Epistemology. In V. Hendricks and D. Pritchard (eds.), *New Waves in Epistemology*. Palgrave MacMillan, pp. 300–24.

Rizzieri, Aaron. 2011. Evidence Does Not Equal Knowledge. *Philosophical Studies* 153: 235–42.

Robinson, Paul. 1996. Competing Theories of Justification: Deeds v. Reasons. In A. Simester and A. Smith (eds.), *Harm and Culpability*. Oxford University Press, pp. 45–70.

Rödl, Sebastian. 2007. *Self-Consciousness*. Harvard University Press.

Ross, W. D. 1930. *The Right and the Good*. Oxford University Press.

Ruben, David-Hillel. 1990. *Explaining Explanation*. Routledge.

Ryan, Sharon. 2003. Doxastic Compatibilism and the Ethics of Belief. *Philosophical Studies* 114: 47–79.

Sadock, Jerrold. 1978. On Testing Conversational Implicature. In P. Cole (ed.), *Syntax and Semantics*, vol. ix, *Pragmatics*. New York: Academic Press, pp. 281–97.

Schaffer, Jonathan. 2006. The Irrelevance of the Subject: Against Subject-Sensitive Invariantism. *Philosophical Studies* 127: 87–107.

Schiffer, Stephen. 2009. Evidence = Knowledge: Williamson's Solution to Skepticism. In P. Greenough and D. Pritchard (eds.), *Williamson on Knowledge*. Oxford University Press, pp. 183–203.

Schroeder, Mark. 2008. Having Reasons. *Philosophical Studies* 139: 57–71.

Shah, Nishi. 2006. A New Argument for Evidentialism. *Philosophical Quarterly* 56: 481–98.

Shoemaker, Sydney. 1996. *The First-Person Perspective and Other Essays*. Cambridge University Press.

Silins, Nico. 2005. Deception and Evidence. *Philosophical Perspectives* 19: 375–404.

Slote, Michael. 1979. Assertion and Belief. In J. Dancy (ed.), *Papers on Language and Logic*. Keele University Library, pp. 177–90.

Smith, Michael. 1987. The Humean Theory of Motivation. *Mind* 96: 36–61.

Smithies, Declan. In press. The Normative Role of Knowledge. *Noûs*.

Sorensen, Roy. 1988. *Blindspots*. New York: Oxford University Press.

　　1995. Unknowable Obligations. *Utilitas* 7: 247–71.

Sosa, Ernest. 1991. *Knowledge in Perspective*. Cambridge University Press.

　　2003. Beyond Internal Foundations to External Virtues. In L. BonJour and E. Sosa (eds.), *Epistemic Justification: Internalism vs. Externalism, Foundations vs. Virtues*. Blackwell, pp. 99–170.

　　2007. *A Virtue Epistemology: Apt Belief and Reflective Knowledge*, vol. i. Oxford University Press.

　　2010. *Knowing Full Well*. Princeton University Press.

Stanley, Jason. 2005. *Knowledge and Practical Interests*. Oxford University Press.

　　2008. Knowledge and Certainty. *Philosophical Issues* 18: 33–55.

Steup, Matthias. 1999. A Defense of Internalism. In L. Pojman (ed.), *The Theory of Knowledge: Classical and Contemporary Readings*, 2nd edn. Wadsworth Publishing, pp. 373–84.

　　2001. Epistemic Duty, Evidence, and Internality. In M. Steup (ed.), *Knowledge, Truth, and Duty: Essays on Epistemic Justification, Responsibility, and Virtue*. Oxford University Press, pp. 134–51.

　　2008. Doxastic Freedom. *Synthese* 161: 375–92.

Steward, Helen. 1997. *The Ontology of Mind*. Oxford University Press.

Stocker, Michael. 1973. Act and Agent Evaluations. *Review of Metaphysics* 27: 42–61.

1990. *Plural and Conflicting Values*. Oxford University Press.

Strawson, P. F. 1962. Freedom and Resentment. *Proceedings of the British Academy* 48: 1–25.

Sutton, Jonathan. 2007. *Without Justification*. MIT Press.

Sverdlik, Steven. 2011. *Motive and Rightness*. Oxford University Press.

Swain, Marshall. 1979. Justification and the Basis of Belief. In G. Pappas (ed.), *Justification and Knowledge*. Reidel, pp. 25–51.

1981. *Reasons and Knowledge*. Cornell University Press.

Swanton, Christine. 2003. *Virtue Ethics: A Pluralistic View*. Oxford University Press.

Thalberg, Irving. 1969. In Defense of Justified True Belief. *Journal of Philosophy* 66: 794–803.

Thomson, Judith. 1991. Self-Defense. *Philosophy and Public Affairs* 20: 283–310.

2001. *Goodness and Advice*. Princeton University Press.

2008. *Normativity*. Open Court.

Turri, John. 2009. The Ontology of Epistemic Reasons. *Noûs* 43: 490–512.

2011. Believing for a Reason. *Erkenntnis* 74: 383–97.

In press. Reasons, Answers and Goals. *Journal of Moral Philosophy*.

Unger, Peter. 1968. An Analysis of Factual Knowledge. *Journal of Philosophy* 65: 157–70.

1975. *Ignorance*. Oxford University Press.

Vahid, Hamid. 2006. Aiming at Truth: Doxastic vs. Epistemic Goals. *Philosophical Studies* 131: 303–35.

Van Cleve, James. 2004. Externalism and Disjunctivism. In R. Schantz (ed.), *The Externalist Challenge*. De Gruyter, pp. 481–95.

Velleman, David. 2000. *The Possibility of Practical Reason*. Oxford University Press.

Von Fintel, Kai and Anthony Gillies. 2007. An Opinionated Guide to Epistemic Modality. In T. Gendler and J. Hawthorne (eds.), *Oxford Studies in Epistemology*, vol. II. Oxford University Press, pp. 32–62.

Way, Jonathan. 2009. Two Accounts of the Normativity of Rationality. Journal of Ethics and Social Philosophy, www.jesp.org/articles/download/ TwoAccountsOfTheNormativityOfRationality.pdf, accessed January 4, 2012.

Weatherson, Brian. 2005. Can We Do without Pragmatic Encroachment? *Philosophical Perspectives* 19: 417–43.

2008. Deontology and Descartes's Demon. *Journal of Philosophy* 150: 540–69.

Wedgwood, Ralph. 2002a. Internalism Explained. *Philosophy and Phenomenological Research* 65: 349–69.

2002b. The Aim of Belief. *Philosophical Perspectives* 16: 267–97.

Weiner, Matthew. 2005. Must We Know What We Say? *Philosophical Review* 114: 227–51.

Whiting, Daniel. 2010. Should I Believe the Truth? *Dialectica* 64: 213–24.

Williams, Bernard. 1965. Ethical Consistency. *Proceedings of the Aristotelian Society, Supplementary Volumes* 39: 103–38.

  1973. *Problems of the Self.* Cambridge University Press.

  1981. *Moral Luck.* Cambridge University Press.

Williams, John. 1994. Moorean Absurdity and the Intentional 'Structure' of Assertion. *Analysis* 54: 160–6.

Williamson, Timothy. 1990. *Identity and Discrimination.* Blackwell.

  2000a. *Knowledge and Its Limits.* Oxford University Press.

  2000b. Skepticism and Evidence. *Philosophy and Phenomenological Research* 60: 613–28.

  2007. On Being Justified in One's Head. In J. Greco, A. Mele, and M. Timmons (eds.), *Rationality and the Good: Critical Essays on the Ethics and Epistemology of Robert Audi.* Oxford University Press, pp. 106–23.

  2009. Replies to Critics. In P. Greenough and D. Pritchard (eds.), *Williamson on Knowledge.* Oxford University Press, pp. 279–385.

Wright, Crispin. 1991. Scepticism and Dreaming: Imploding the Demon. *Mind* 397: 87–115.

Zagzebski, Linda. 1996. *Virtues of the Mind: An Inquiry into the Nature of Virtue and the Ethical Foundations of Knowledge.* Cambridge University Press.

  2003. The Search for the Source of Epistemic Good. *Metaphilosophy* 34: 12–28.

Zimmerman, Michael. 1996. *The Concept of Moral Obligation.* Cambridge University Press.

  2002. Taking Luck Seriously. *Journal of Philosophy* 99: 553–76.

  2008. *Living with Uncertainty.* Cambridge University Press.

Index